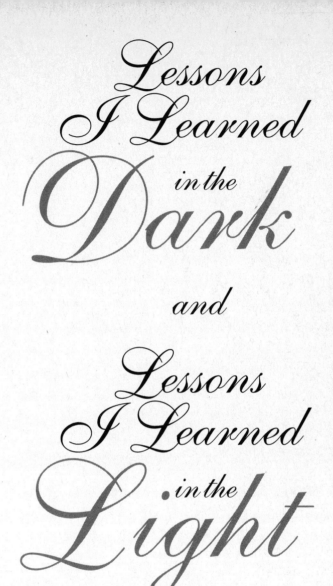

Lessons
I Learned
in the
Dark

and

Lessons
I Learned
in the
Light

JENNIFER ROTHSCHILD

Multnomah® Publishers, *Sisters, Oregon*

Lessons I Learned in the Dark

Jennifer Rothschild

Multnomah®Publishers *Sisters, Oregon*

LESSONS I LEARNED IN THE DARK
published by Multnomah Publishers, Inc.

© 2002 by Jennifer Rothschild

Cover design by Koechel Peterson and Associates

Unless otherwise indicated, Scripture quotations are from:
The Holy Bible, New International Version © 1973, 1984 by International Bible
Society, used by permission of Zondervan Publishing House

Other Scripture quotations:
New American Standard Bible (NASB) © 1960, 1977 by the Lockman Foundation
The Holy Bible, New King James Version (NKJV) © 1984 by Thomas Nelson, Inc.
The Holy Bible, King James Version (KJV)
Holy Bible, New Living Translation (NLT) © 1996. Used by permission of
Tyndale House Publishers, Inc. All rights reserved.
The Holy Bible, New Century Version (NCV) © 1987, 1988, 1991
by Word Publishing. Used by permission.
New Revised Standard Version Bible (NRSV) © 1989 by the Division of Christian
Education of the National Council of the Churches of Christ
in the United States of America
Holy Bible, American Standard Version (ASV) © 1901 by Thomas Nelson & Sons

Multnomah is a trademark of Multnomah Publishers, Inc.,
and is registered in the U.S. Patent and Trademark Office.
The colophon is a trademark of Multnomah Publishers, Inc.

Printed in the United States of America

For information:
MULTNOMAH PUBLISHERS, INC.•POST OFFICE BOX 1720•SISTERS, OREGON 97759

ISBN: 978-0-7394-7159-3

"Jennifer may be blind, but she is leading people who are in the dark to really see God and to act on His empowering love."

STEPHEN ARTERBURN, CREATOR OF WOMEN OF FAITH CONFERENCES AND AUTHOR OF *FINDING MR. RIGHT*

"After reading *Lessons I Learned in the Dark,* I began to ask some soul-searching questions: Am I looking at those around me with my heart or with my eyes? What about my relationships with family and friends and my personal relationship with Jesus Christ? Jennifer challenges me with the statement, 'Unless we trade our fear for fight, we may never find the treasures that are hidden in the dark.' This book has prompted me to see God's treasures with a different set of eyes."

YVETTE MAHER, VICE PRESIDENT OF RENEWING THE HEART WOMEN'S MINISTRIES AT FOCUS ON THE FAMILY

"Your story is a living witness to what God can do if given the chance! Your steadfast faith, Christian principles, and integrity will serve as a witness to many...my heart was touched!"

ROBERT H. SCHULLER, SENIOR MINISTER, CRYSTAL CATHEDRAL, GARDEN GROVE, CALIFORNIA

"Jennifer Rothschild allows us the privilege of learning the valuable lessons she's learned "in the dark" by shining light on her past and inviting us to follow in her footsteps. This journey is a page-turning, heart-shaping, eye-opening view into the life of a talented woman walking alongside the Light of the World."

LISA WHELCHEL, ACTOR AND AUTHOR OF *THE FACTS OF LIFE AND OTHER LESSONS MY FATHER TAUGHT ME*

"Jennifer Rothschild is a vibrant reflection of the grace and faithfulness of God. I have been touched and challenged by her tender, surrendered heart and her powerful ministry."

NANCY LEIGH DEMOSS, SPEAKER, AUTHOR OF *LIES WOMEN BELIEVE* AND *THE TRUTH THAT SETS THEM FREE* AND HOST OF *REVIVE OUR HEARTS*, A DAILY RADIO MINISTRY FOR WOMEN

"With great depth, wisdom, and a light, joy-filled heart, Jennifer Rothschild shares treasures she learned in the dark so those of us who have the privilege of reading her book could continue our spiritual journey with more clarity, focus, and light. I highly recommend it!"

CHERI FULLER, SPEAKER AND AUTHOR OF *WHEN MOTHERS PRAY*, THE NEW RELEASE *WHEN TEENS PRAY*, AND FOUNDER OF FAMILIES PRAY USA

"What a treasure you hold in your hand, written from the heart of a godly woman. You will not only feel you are sitting in Jennifer's presence; you will certainly feel you are sitting in God's presence, learning to walk in faith."

ESTHER BURROUGHS, CONFERENCE SPEAKER AND AUTHOR OF *SPLASH THE LIVING WATER* AND *TREASURES OF A GRANDMOTHER'S HEART*

"For years audiences have been awed, inspired, and uplifted by Jennifer Rothschild's stories and songs. As I read this book and experienced again Jennifer's godly heart, I knew that God was truly directing her pen."

PEG CARMACK SHORT, EDITOR-IN-CHIEF, *BECOMING FAMILY* AND AUTHOR OF *A COUNTRY SAMPLER OF SIMPLE BLESSINGS*

Dedication

I lovingly dedicate this book
to my first and greatest teachers, my parents,
Lawson and Judy Jolly.

Because of their faith, wisdom, and example,
I learned to see God.

TABLE *of* CONTENTS

With Heartfelt Thanks

To Judith St. Pierre, editor extraordinaire. Thank you for your skill and craftsmanship. I am most grateful for your love of God's Word and your effort to promote and protect the message of this book.

To Bill Jensen. Thank you for your guidance and enthusiasm. You've been both coach and cheerleader, and I will be forever grateful.

To Cheri Fuller, Karen True, and Peg Short. God used you in more ways than I can list to help me along the way. Thank you for your faithfulness to Him and for your friendship.

To Chris Hagen, my wonderful writing assistant. I am indebted to you for your tireless dedication and your extraordinary patience. May you never have to read this book out loud again!

To Phil, my husband. Who I am today is a reflection of your faithfulness to God and your unwavering commitment to me. I am honored to be your wife, and I will never outlive my love for you.

To Clayton and Connor, our precious boys. Of all the things in my life, you are what I'm proudest of and most thankful for.

To Beth Moore. Thank you for setting such a high standard for me. You have meant more to me than you will ever know.

To Don Jacobson and the entire Multnomah staff. Thank you for what you do for the kingdom. May God multiply your ministry.

To Jesus, my Lord and Savior. Your grace truly is sufficient for me. Thank You that, whatever my lot, You make it well with my soul.

Foreword

I remember the first time I saw Jennifer Rothschild. She was warming up on the keyboard in preparation for praise and worship preceding the message I had been asked to give at the event. I always look forward to meeting and interacting with the vocalist or worship leader where I speak because we are undoubtedly partners in ministry for that measure of time. I recall doing an immediate double take when I first saw Jennifer. I was oblivious to any challenges because I did not know her story and in no way could have guessed in a simple glance.

I have never tried to articulate what I found so unique about Jennifer until preparing to write this foreword. At the time I first saw Jennifer, I simply would have told you that something was wonderfully different about her. Now as I write in retrospect and with the aid of a few more years and a bit more experience, I can identify more clearly what I saw. She was so young, so fresh and beautiful, yet she had a knowing in her eyes that seemed unusual for one her age.

After I heard Jennifer's testimony, I had an "aha" moment and knew why her maturity exceeded her years. Not only did her eyes reveal a knowing; there was something indefinably *chosen* about her. From this vantage point I now know that I was seeing Jennifer not so differently from how

Jennifer sees most all the time—*with eyes of the Spirit.* I saw the invisible hand of God upon her. And I've never failed to see it since.

Years ago, when I was in my midtwenties, I attended a training seminar taught by Florence Littauer for prospective Christian speakers and communicators. I have laughed many times about receiving the seminar brochure in the mail because I wasn't on a mailing list and had little familiarity with Florence at that time. I'm convinced I received the application because I was pitiful and, in view of what God called me to do, He knew I needed emergency speaking assistance. I'm pretty sure He addressed the brochure Himself. I am definitely on *His* mailing list— even when I've tried to move. I learned a principle at the seminar that I still use as a plumb line for every message I prepare to speak or write. According to Florence each person must ask herself two critical questions before addressing any group:

"Do I have anything to say?"

"Does anyone need to hear it?"

Beloved, Jennifer Rothschild has something to say.

And all of us need to hear it.

Since the first time I saw Jennifer she has become a mother of two, a seasoned communicator, and a singer who can practically sing glory down on your head. Yet she still has that same freshness and graceful beauty that struck such a deep chord in my soul years ago. To my delight, Jennifer and her husband are also tremendous fun. I have an affinity for believers who don't view *godliness* and *good humor* as exclusive terms.

That's why I knew I was safe to make a spontaneous phone call to her home after seeing a photo spread of her and her family in a Christian magazine last year. The message I left on her voice mail went something like this, "Okay, young lady, I'm not about to leave it to your husband to tell you how you look in that layout. Men don't tell nearly enough details. Let me just tell you that you are stunning!" I then proceeded to tell her how sassy and cute her hair, makeup, and outfits were. It was strictly a girl moment, but I had a feeling she'd get a kick out of it. Then I read the article. And cried. Somehow Jennifer possesses that rare, God-given combination of lightness and depth. Grace and truth. Just like the One who called her.

Lessons I Learned in the Dark is gripping. I don't know the person to whom it has nothing to say. Jennifer Rothschild is the real thing. She knows what she's talking about. She does not have the luxury of telling and retelling a testimony from years past of challenges long since resolved. She lives in present tense, making daily choices to step over a plethora of seen and unseen obstacles. Jennifer is a living, breathing testimony still actively being written by the hand of God. I have a feeling this book won't be the last we hear from her. I am honored to recommend Jennifer Rothschild and her stirring new book to you. May God grant us all the gift of eyes that truly see.

Beth Moore

The
GREATEST
LESSON

~

L ife is a fascinating school. Tucked in the corners of its dailiness are countless lessons, large and small. Some I've learned as a matter of course, almost unconsciously. Others have frustrated all my attempts to comprehend. I've raised my hand time and again in life's classroom, longing for answers. I've scrutinized the pages of its textbook, yearning to understand. I've walked its hallways and climbed its stairs, searching for its meaning.

We learn many of life's lessons when times are good and circumstances easy. Others, we learn only in seasons of hardship, loss, and great darkness. Although suffering can be the harshest of headmasters, its curriculum may open the door to freedom beyond our loftiest expectations. *Sometimes it's only in the adversity we dread that we begin to discover the kind of life we've only dreamed of.*

That was the lesson God began to teach me in 1979....

I began my sophomore year of high school experiencing all of the usual teenage changes.

But there had also been one very unusual one.

Near the end of junior high school, I began to realize that my eyesight was deteriorating.

As I picked my way carefully through the packed hallways of Glades Junior High, I was amazed at how my classmates streamed through the crowd with such ease—even in dark stairwells. How could they do that without bumping into schoolmates or lockers? When we played softball in P.E., I couldn't understand how my teammates could catch the ball so easily. I would stand out in right field, glove in hand, and stare intently at the ground, trying to see the shadow of the approaching ball. Then I'd listen to where it landed and hope I could find it.

My math grades were beginning to drop because, even though I didn't know it at the time, I couldn't see the difference between a 3 and an 8. My friends could see the numbers on the telephone pad, while I hadn't been able to see the numbers on my locker for months.

Difficult as it was to admit...I began to realize that it wasn't normal for me not to be able to see a softball in the air, the stairs in a stairwell, or the numbers written on a blackboard. As a result, I began to feel more awkward and self-conscious. At last I became so concerned that I told my mother, who (as you might imagine) immediately took me to an ophthalmologist.

The eye doctor tried to remedy my failing sight with prescriptions for stronger glasses, but they didn't help. Eventually, he referred me to an eye hospital.

After several days of testing, the doctors at the Bascom Palmer Eye Institute met with my folks and me in a conference room. They told us that I had retinitis pigmentosa, a degenerative disease that slowly eats away the retina of the eye.

There was no cure, and no way to correct damage already done.

The doctors said I had lost so much vision that, at fifteen, I was already legally blind. And they told us that my retinas would continue to deteriorate until I was totally blind.

Blind...totally blind.

The words sounded so final. So certain. So cold. I felt a chill inside that I'd never felt before. Maybe that's what finality feels like. It was almost surreal.

Nothing else was said. Silence fell upon that conference room like shadows fall just before night, and it shrouded us as we left the hospital, walked across the parking lot, got in the car, and journeyed home.

I have often thought that it was probably much harder for my parents that day than it was for me. Yes, my eyes were being robbed of sight, but their hearts were being crushed. Can you imagine their heartache? Can you hear the sound of that door slamming in their souls? Surely one of life's greatest sorrows must be to watch your child suffer…and to feel helpless to prevent it.

My dad gripped the steering wheel tightly as he piloted us home through the spidery Miami streets. I could only imagine the prayers he must have been praying. He had always been my source of wisdom, my counselor, my comforter, my rescuer, and the one man I trusted completely. And even though he had also been my pastor, not even more than twenty years of ministry could have prepared him for this moment. I wonder if he was thinking, *Dear Lord, how can I fix this?*

Yet on the ride home he was silent.

My mother sat next to him in the front seat. I could feel her broken heart. A mother's heart is so tender. I don't know any mother who wouldn't willingly trade her own comfort to ease the suffering of her child. I wonder what her prayers were like on that day. My mom was my standard, my cheerleader, my encourager, my mentor, and my friend. I think she must have been wondering, *Will she be safe?*

Yet on the ride home, she too was silent.

I had always been strong willed, trusting, sensitive, and talkative. Yet sitting in the backseat on the ride home that day, I also kept silent. I remember the reasons for my silence as if it were yesterday. My heart was swelling with emotion, and my mind was racing with questions and thoughts. *How will I finish high school? Will I ever go away to college? How will I know what I look like? Will I ever get a date or a boyfriend? Will I ever get married?* I remember feeling my fingertips and wondering how in the world people read Braille.

And then it hit me.

I would never be able to drive a car.

Like most teenagers, I thought that having wheels was just like having wings. I couldn't wait to drive! That was a step toward independence to which nothing else compared. But now it was a rite of passage I would never experience, and I was crushed.

After forty-five long minutes, we arrived home. Once inside, I went immediately to the living room and sat down at our piano. It was old and stately and had a warm, comforting sound. For me it was a place of refuge.

By then I had been playing the piano for several years. In fact, I'd had almost five years of lessons. The funny thing about my lessons, though, was that I'd managed to stretch them out over an eight-year period. I was one of those kids who would *beg* my mother to let me take piano lessons— and then after about six months *beg* her to let me quit! Three or four months later we'd start the whole routine over again.

I barely muddled through my lessons with many piano

teachers, and I'm sure it wasn't pleasant for the listener to hear me practice what I'd learned. Let's just say that I was a little short on natural talent! I did, however, practice diligently every night after dinner. That's because if I did, I was excused from clearing the table and washing the dishes.

But this time was different.

I wasn't seeking refuge from chores, and I didn't play just the few songs I'd memorized. Instead, I began to play by ear, and the melody that filled the living room that afternoon belonged to a song I'd never played before. My fingers followed a pattern along the keyboard that was new to me, yet…somehow familiar.

The song I played was "It Is Well with My Soul."

I think God guided my heart and hands to play that hymn. Some people have told me it was a miracle that I could sit down at the piano that day and begin to play by ear for the first time. Perhaps it was. Who knows? But to me, there was a bigger miracle that day, that dark day of shock, loss, and quiet sorrow.

The real miracle was not that I played "It Is Well with My Soul," but that it actually *was* well with my soul.

On that day more than twenty years ago—in the hospital, on the ride home, and at the piano—even as I mourned my loss, I looked into the heart of my Teacher. I knew His Word and His character, and they were what allowed me to say, "Whatever my lot…it is well with my soul."

Today I still sit at the piano and play by ear. I listen to books on tape. I walk with a cane and rely on others to drive me places. I know well the trappings of blindness. I understand the isolation and hardships it can bring. Yes, blindness can be painful—all life's heartaches are—but through it, God has taught me the greatest lesson to be learned in the school of suffering: *Even when it is not well with our circumstances, it can be well with our souls.*

That is the first and greatest lesson I learned in the dark, and the foundation for all the lessons that have followed.

When peace like a river attendeth my way
When sorrows like sea billows roll
Whatever my lot, Thou hast taught me to say
It is well, it is well with my soul

Not by Sight

Though my eyes may see darkness
    and the lamps be dimly lit
I can see beyond this earthly shell
For the faith that brought me so far
    gives me hope to carry on
For my eyes will behold Him someday

We walk by faith not by sight
Looking through His eyes
I can see the light
The Morning Star shines so bright
    until our faith becomes sight

Earthly dreams and shadowed pictures
Of the one I used to be
*   were left to become the one I am*
And though my mind may not understand
*   with my eyes I'll look to You*
For You are the substance of my faith

We walk by faith not by sight
Looking through His eyes
I can see the light
The Morning Star shines so bright
*   until our faith becomes sight*

WORDS AND MUSIC BY JENNIFER ROTHSCHILD © 1980 ROTHSCHILD MUSIC (ASCAP)

One

TAKE *the* FIRST STEP

My friend and I stood in the hallway of my new home exchanging decorating ideas. When I commented on how much I loved the wallpaper in my hall bath, there was an awkward pause.

"But Jennifer…how do you *know* you love the wallpaper if you can't see it?"

It was a fair question.

I told her that my mother had described the Jacobean print to me in vivid detail, and that with every word I heard, I fell more in love with it. In my mind's eye I could see the honey mustard, cranberry, and forest green colors twining through the vines and leaves on the wallpaper.

It's funny: Even though I couldn't see, I could see it.

That's how I like to explain faith sometimes. The dictionary says that faith is a firm belief in something for which there is no proof—a belief that does not have to rest on visible evidence. Just because my eyes can't see the design of the wallpaper doesn't mean it's not there. I *know* it's there, so my eyes don't have to confirm what I know is real. In fact, it's so real that even though I can't see it, I can still enjoy and delight in it.

I think that's what the writer of Hebrews had in mind when he wrote, "Faith is the substance of things hoped for, the evidence of things not seen" (Hebrews 11:1, NKJV). If we understand that this is what faith is, we can exercise it in the confidence the apostle Paul talked about when he said, "We walk by faith, not by sight" (2 Corinthians 5:7, NASB). Walking by faith is acting upon a reality not yet seen.

Relying on sight in our faith walk never allows us to accomplish God's best. What's more, it never reveals the hidden treasures that only the eyes of faith can see. But most of us never learn to walk by faith…until we learn to walk in the dark. We don't lean on God until fear makes us feel shaky and weak.

SHAKY STEPS

On a warm summer afternoon in 1982, my mother and I sat down on the soft grass under the silk oak tree in our front yard for our final heart-to-heart talk of the summer. It was August 14, and the next day I would leave my home in

Miami for Palm Beach Atlantic College.

In the three months since I'd graduated from high school, we'd spent every day preparing me to go. Mom and I had shopped for a new wardrobe for me and bought furnishings for my dorm room, including a much-coveted rainbow comforter.

During that long, lingering summer, I'd also spent several weeks in "mobility training"—that is, learning to walk with a cane. The Lighthouse for the Blind assigned me an instructor named Mike, who diligently taught me how to use my new cane so that I would be as self-sufficient as possible in my new setting. Mike taught me all the techniques I'd need to know as I learned to walk in the dark.

By mid-August the U-Haul was loaded, my suitcases were packed, and I knew how to walk with my cane. I was ready for college and rarin' to go. Then on August 14, my confident expectation suddenly turned to dread. The frightening reality of leaving home squelched all the excitement of preparing to be an independent college student.

I was leaving behind my sense of security.

I was leaving behind the comfort of familiar surroundings.

I was leaving behind all that was well-known and safe, trading it in for a new kind of darkness that was unfamiliar and scary. When I began to weigh the new clothes, the new dorm furnishings, and the new cane against the security of my old friends and my old room, my heart froze with fear.

As my mother and I leaned against the tree that after-noon, I suddenly cried, "I *can't* go to college, Mom! Who's going to check my makeup for me? Who's going to make sure my clothes aren't wrinkled or stained? Who's going to tell me what food is on my plate? How will I really know if there are no cars coming when I'm trying to cross the street?"

My tears soon drowned out my questions. "Please don't make me go, Mom," I begged.

My mother gently consoled me. Then she said, "You have to go to college, honey. We've prepared you to go, you've chosen to go, and deep down you want to go to college. But...," she continued, wiping away her own tears, "you only have to go for two weeks. If you really can't handle it, your dad and I will come get you. And you can even keep your new rainbow comforter!"

So when the sun rose on August 15, Dad got behind the wheel of the U-Haul, Mom and I loaded my suitcases and our heavy hearts into our Ford Fairmont, and we drove north to West Palm Beach. After we arrived and unloaded, we hugged good-bye, and they got back in the car and headed south.

Now I was alone with my fear, and suddenly I felt blinder than ever. It was the emptiest feeling I'd ever had. Walking in the dark was scary enough, but walking *alone* in the dark was terrifying.

But I believe that where there is fear, there is fight! My

terror fueled my tenacity, and for two weeks I held on doggedly. I was determined to make it until I could legitimately call home and say, "I'm sorry. I tried. It's not working. Please come get me!"

During that time, I used my cane to navigate the campus just the way Mike had taught me, and it helped me feel a little less scared. Then one day I tapped my cane into the cafeteria, and there I found an unexpected treasure.

It was a guy.

Not just any guy, mind you. This guy was the handsomest and most charming and intelligent guy I'd ever stumbled upon. His name was Philip Rothschild, and we quickly began to spend time together. Let's just say that I barely noticed when the two weeks had passed. But I did call my mom just to say, "Please don't ever make me come home from college!"

Here's the lesson I learned: *Unless we trade our fear for fight, we may never find the treasures that are hidden in the dark.*

I found my future husband when I chose to risk walking in the dark. It's the same with our spiritual walk. It's often scary. Most of the time, God doesn't reveal what's next—and we can't begin to anticipate what the future holds. But most of us never learn to walk by faith until we first walk in the dark.

As a loving Father, God says, "You must take a step. I've prepared you to go, and deep down you want to walk by faith." When we do step out, like the heroes of the faith in Hebrews 11, we'll find the treasures that God has reserved for those who lean completely on Him.

A STEADY PACE

I believe that one of the ways God wants us to learn to walk by faith is by following the examples set for us in the Bible. In fact, Paul writes, "Brethren, join in following my example, and observe those who walk according to the pattern you have in us " (Philippians 3:17, NASB). We need to observe those who walk well and follow in their footsteps.

All the amazing folks in the Hall of Faith in Hebrews 11 knew how to exercise "spiritual mobility"—they knew how to walk by faith, not by sight.

And all of them learned how by walking in the dark.

They didn't understand God's plan when they began to carry it out, and they didn't know what was coming next when they took that first step. Their faith became realized only as they *exercised* it—as they began to put one foot in front of the other. They chose to rely on something greater than what they could see or understand.

They chose to walk by faith.

And they can teach us how to walk with them on that path.

Noah teaches us how to go against common sense when we sense God in an uncommon way. Imagine if he had relied on sight rather than faith. Instead of building an ark, he might have opened a petting zoo!

Abraham teaches us how to willingly obey even when we don't understand. If he had been relying on sight as he trudged up Mount Moriah, he might have been scanning the bushes for a lamb instead of obeying God.

Sarah teaches us that it's possible to believe the impossible. Surely it was not "sight" that prompted her to knit tiny blue baby blankets at her age!

Moses teaches us how to value God's reward more than man's riches. If he had been walking by sight, he probably would have milked his position as Pharaoh's grandson for all its royal worth.

You get the idea. It was faith that prompted Noah, Abraham, Sarah, Moses, and the other heroes of Hebrews 11 to step out the way they did. Faith always propels us to action.

But walking by faith isn't always easy. I'm sure that each one of those Hebrews 11 heroes went through some wrenching internal agony along that walk of faith.

Noah experienced it, pounding one more nail into a ship in the middle of the desert. Sarah felt it with a baby's tiny kick in her once sterile womb. Abraham knew it when he lifted that gleaming blade heavenward, ready to plunge it into the chest of his beloved son. (Who can imagine the agony and terror of that moment?)

And let's not forget Moses. He felt so out of his league that he begged God to send his brother Aaron to plead with

Pharaoh. I can just hear him: "God, I stutter like M-M-Mel Tillis, but Aaron—he sings like M-M-Mel Tormé!" All of us feel the ground shaking beneath us when we step out in faith. But even if we feel insecure, walking by faith requires us to take a risk. To take a step.

A CONFIDENT STRIDE

When I was learning to walk in the dark, what made it easier to risk walking with a cane was knowing that Mike was right next to me. If I felt wobbly, I knew I could hold on to him. If I reached out or cried out, he was right there. On our walks, he would quickly extend his arm when I'd lose my footing or become disoriented.

In the same way, when we feel shaky in our faith walk, we can hold on to God. Leviticus 26:12 reminds us that God Himself walks among us because we are His people. His strong arm is always there to help us. We can reach out for Him in the dark, and He will be there every time. And just as Mike patiently listened to me when I told him my fears, God will patiently listen to ours.

Learning to walk by faith is very much like learning to walk in the dark. The mobility techniques Mike taught me gave me security in my stride, and they're the very ones we need to apply to walk by faith. Check out the following tips for spiritual mobility and ask God to show you if you need a little instruction from Him in your faith walk.

Remain centered

As I learned to maneuver with my cane, Mike stressed the importance of remaining centered. He showed me how to hold my cane in the center of my body. Then with a steady arm, I would move my wrist from left to right. I did this in order to walk in a straight line and stay oriented. It allowed me to tap the sidewalk with the tip of my cane just before my next step, helping me anticipate any changes in my path.

It's also essential to remain centered as we learn to walk by faith. Losing your center will lead you astray. "Let your eyes look directly ahead and let your gaze be fixed straight in front of you," Solomon advises. "Watch the path of your feet and all your ways will be established. Do not turn to the right nor to the left; turn your foot from evil" (Proverbs 4:25–27, NASB). Being centered keeps you on your intended path.

When we stay on God's path and allow Him to be the center of our lives, we won't get disoriented when life falls under a deep shadow. When every step is steady, we won't slip, even when the ground buckles beneath us. "My steps have held fast to your paths," says the psalmist. "My feet have not slipped"(Psalm 17:5, NASB).

What is the center of your life? Have you lost your orientation?

Follow a mental map

I also learned that it was essential to know exactly where I **was** going. No aimless strolling when you are blind! Mike told me to think through my path before I took the first step and to always have a map locked in my mind. Knowing where I was going made every step purposeful and prevented missteps and mishaps. The map for a Christian is God's Word, and when "the law of his God is in his heart[,] his steps do not slip" (Psalm 37:31, NASB).

When we know God's precepts, they guide us. "The steps of a good man are ordered by the LORD" (Psalm 37:23, NKJV). But they also protect us. Paul says that the sword of the Spirit is the Word of God, a part of the armor of light that protects us against the dark powers of the world (see Ephesians 6:12, 17 and Romans 13:12). This world is a dark and shadowed place at times. If we naively step out unprotected, we'll be susceptible to the evil influences of the darkness around us. But if we wisely follow the map God has given us in His Word (no aimless wandering!), it will guide and protect us, making each step of our walk intentional. Then we can say with Paul, "I run straight to the goal with purpose in every step" (1 Corinthians 9:26, NLT).

What guides your steps? Do you follow the Master's map?

Listen to the Teacher

As I learned to use my cane, I felt my senses awakening in a whole new dimension. I became aware of the smell of diesel fuel from the buses that roared down the main street of my neighborhood. And as Mike encouraged me to tune in to the music of the motor, I learned to hear the difference between the sound of an engine when a car was in full motion and when it was idling at a red light. Learning to recognize what was coming (and how fast) helped me know when it was safe to go—or when I'd better stop and wait.

To walk by faith, we need to tune in to the voice of our Teacher. Isaiah 53:6 reminds us that we are all like sheep who have gone astray. And like sheep, we need a shepherd. But in order to hear the voice of our Shepherd above the din of all the other voices in our lives, we must be tuned in. We must *learn* to recognize His still, small voice.

Jesus said, "My sheep listen to my voice; I know them, and they follow me" (John 10:27). His sheep hear and follow Him because they are familiar with His voice. When we learn to discern the Holy Spirit's voice, we'll know when to go and when to stop.

As the prophet Isaiah wrote:

Although the Lord gives you the bread of adversity and the water of affliction, your teachers will be hidden no more; with your own eyes you will see them. Whether you turn to the right or to the left, your ears will hear a voice behind you, saying, "This is the way; walk in it." (Isaiah 30:20–21)

Are you tuned in to the voice of the Master? Do you recognize His voice as it resonates through your soul?

Jesus said, "God is spirit, and his worshipers must worship in spirit and in truth" (John 4:24). Walking by faith means that we allow the Holy Spirit to illuminate our eyes so that we can see beyond the here and now. Eyes of faith see every problem as solvable because they see every problem as spiritual in nature. What is merely physical is confined by the laws of nature, but what is spiritual has no confines except those our supernatural, sovereign God chooses.

This means that as we walk by faith, the Holy Spirit will help us fix our eyes on the source of our help, not on the sting of our problems. He will whisper in our ears the gentle reminder that "now we see in a mirror dimly, but then face to face" (1 Corinthians 13:12, NASB). Someday the faith by which we walk will become sight, or as St. Augustine put it, the reward of our faith will be to *see what we believe*. Can you see how important it is to walk by faith? Look where it will eventually lead us—face to face with God Himself!

> *"I am the light of the world.*
> *Whoever follows me will never walk in darkness,*
> *but will have the light of life."*

JOHN 8:12

Never Alone

Never alone
In my darkest hour I am never alone
Not far from home and I can feel You near me
For I am never alone

In the midst of trials there is a triumph that I know
While trusting in the One who never changes
And though my heart grows weary in the struggle of it all
I have such assurance that You hear me when I call

Never alone
In my darkest hour I am never alone
Not far from home and I can feel You near me
For I am never alone

WORDS AND MUSIC BY JENNIFER ROTHSCHILD © 1990 ROTHSCHILD MUSIC (ASCAP)

Two

GIVE YOUR GUIDE *a* TASTE TEST

I've had many guides since the onset of blindness. In fact, there are very few places I can go without one. Over the years my guides have included an entire cast of characters. I've held on to the arms of strangers in airports and the hand of my ninety-five-year-old grandpa. I've had tall, staid men and short, squirmy boys guide me. A few women who've walked with me have said very confidently, "We're going left here," as they very conspicuously turned to the right. (Sorry, girls, but there are some among us who are directionally challenged!) In college, I had a guide named Karen and, more recently, one named Stephanie. Both these friends are in wheelchairs, so I hold the handles, they push go…and we're off! My guides walk or roll. I trust.

You know what qualifies someone to be my guide?

Sight!

Let's face it, though. Just because people can see better than I can doesn't mean they're worthy of my trust. Trust is a choice I make. Trust is a risk I take. Why? Because otherwise I'd never go anywhere! The journey is worth the risk.

The members of my family were my first guides. My brothers were in elementary and middle school at the time, and they learned the basic techniques right away. I would loosely grip the elbow of one of them and walk next to him. This meant, of course, that we had to touch. How painful for them! How agonizing for me! Cooties may be invisible, but believe me, they exist. We all had to swallow our pride.

We were taught that when we came to narrow halls or doorways, my guide was to gently pull his arm behind his back. That was the signal for me to get behind instead of beside. It worked well. My brothers learned to quickly count steps, bark commands like *left!* or *right!* (they loved that part), and describe our path using a clock: "Branches at two o'clock...*duck!*" They learned to guide, and I learned to trust them as my guides.

It was pretty easy to trust my family to guide me. We already had a relationship, so it didn't seem like much of a risk. I *knew* I could trust them. Nevertheless, I still had to *choose* to trust them.

The apostle Paul reminds us that our heavenly Father has grafted us into His family through our faith in Jesus Christ, and that Jesus Himself pursued relationship with us so we could come to know and trust Him (see Galatians 4:5–6 and 1 Peter 3:18).

Still, it's not always natural or easy to trust God. Perhaps our relationship with Him is new or untested and we don't yet have a photo album of family life we can flip through to remind us of His guiding presence in our life.

That's why trust is a risk. We never learn whether someone is worthy of our trust unless we risk walking with him. And that's exactly what God invites us to do: "Oh, taste and see that the LORD is good," David says, "blessed is the man who trusts in Him!" (Psalm 34:8, NKJV). God wants us to give Him a taste test.

A TRUSTWORTHY GUIDE WILL PASS THE TASTE TEST

In 1993 I learned that a taste test is a good way to find out if a guide is trustworthy. That's the year I flexed my trust muscle with a new kind of guide—you know, one of the canine variety—a Seeing Eye dog!

I was very naive when the process began. I assumed that I'd get a dog that would be smarter than most humans I know. I figured that he'd be so well trained that we'd go to the mall; I'd say, "Forward! Fifty-percent-off rack"; and he'd take me there. What I didn't realize was that I was going to be trained as much as the dog, if not more so.

I went to Southeastern Guide Dog Training School and

stayed for a month. On the first day there, I met Jim, the trainer, who told me that he tried to match each dog with just the right person. Using the harness that would eventually sit on the back of my guide dog, Jim took me on what he called a "Juno walk." He held on to one end of the harness and I held on to the other, and as we walked around the school campus, he tested the pace of my walk and the strength of my pull.

Jim also asked me lots of questions. He wanted to know about my family, my temperament, my schedule, my activities. When I told him that I traveled frequently to speak and sing, he took special note. I mentioned that I needed a dog with exceptional bladder control because I spend a lot of time in airports—which usually don't have portable puppy potties. He asked for a copy of one of my CDs, and later he took it to the kennel and played it for the dogs. I guess he wanted to make sure that none of them howled at the sound of my voice!

By the next day, Jim had chosen our dogs. He led a boisterous line of canines into the large room where we all waited. "Okay," he said, "I'm going to call your name, and then your dog's name. Then you call your dog."

I felt a thrill of anticipation. This dog represented a new form of freedom and mobility for me. He or she would be my constant companion and trusted guide. I figured that after the walk and all the questions, this would be a match made in heaven. I've had girlfriends who didn't go to that much trouble in choosing a husband!

Roll call began.

"Elizabeth," Jim said, "call your dog. His name is London." *What a classy name,* I thought. *Sounds sleek and sophisticated.*

"Deborah, call your dog. His name is Shoney." *What a cute name! Shoney must be bouncy and energetic.*

"Jeremy, call your dog. His name is Recon." *Now that's a studly name if I ever heard one!*

Jim called out ten more names. Each was creative and fun. Not a Fido in the bunch!

At last it was my turn. "Jennifer," Jim said, "call your dog. His name is [drum roll, please]…William." *William? What kind of name is that for a dog? A great name for a senator, maybe. But for a guide dog?*

Well, now I had a guide dog: William Rothschild. I only wish his behavior had been as dignified as his name. But it wasn't. He was loyal, but he had a problem—a besetting sin, you might say. William had a food distraction. In dogspeak that means the people who raised him fed him people food. Having tasted the finer things of life, whenever William was around people food, he wanted it so badly that he became totally distracted. Instead of focusing on me and my commands, he fixed his attention on the forbidden fodder just beyond his paws.

Let's just make sure you understand the scenario: Guide dogs go where people go. So in William's case, restaurants, food courts at malls, and hotel banquet rooms were all settings for potential disaster.

I realized that a food distraction was a pretty serious deal one afternoon when William and I joined the class on a field trip to McDonald's. Proudly, the members of the class entered the restaurant one at a time with their dogs. When it was our turn, William and I stood in the doorway, and I gave him the command: "Forward." He hesitated. I'd been taught that when a guide dog hesitates, I should check in front of us for an obstruction. There might be a table or a stair in front of me. Since William could recognize potentially hazardous outcomes like falling down stairs or banging into tables, he had been taught to simply stop when he sensed danger. This is called "intelligent disobedience," and it's one of the amazing features of guide dogs.

I checked in front of us. No table, no step, no obstruction—no reason for disobedience. So I issued another command. This time when I said "Forward, William," I added an arm gesture, which he recognized as "Move it, buddy!" Finally, he moved. But unfortunately, he did not move forward. Carrying me along with him, he bounded toward the left side of the restaurant, where he landed in a booth with his paws on the table. Then, looking like a happy, furry human, he proceeded to scarf down the french fries of the lady pinned next to him in the booth.

Listening to the screams of the terrified woman, I stood there in disbelief, still strapped to that food-obsessed canine with french fries hanging out of his mouth. When I managed to regain my composure, I used all my strength to pull William down from the table. Then I commanded him to sit, cupped his ketchup-smeared muzzle in my hand, and made him look me straight in the eye.

Those of you who follow the political scene will understand this next part. Early in the Clinton administration, there was extensive media coverage of the president's affection for fast food. So I looked in William's eyes and said, "From this day on, I call you Bill." Then I whistled "Hail to the Chief" as we marched off.

You've probably guessed that Bill and I had a little more training after that. When Jim realized just how serious the food distraction was, he suggested that we do morning doughnut walks. Sounds like a stroll through paradise, doesn't it? Well, believe me, it wasn't!

Every morning at 7:00 A.M., Bill and I would begin the doughnut drill. After I placed a special correction collar around his neck, we would proceed to walk. To our left, the sidewalk was dotted with small white powdered doughnuts, and the air was fragrant with the smell of the proscribed treat.

If Bill so much as looked at those doughnuts, I would immediately pull up on his leash…and *zing!* His correction collar would remind him to focus on me instead of on the doughnuts. We walked back and forth every day for a week, and it worked. Bill's behavior was definitely modified.

Pavlov would have been proud! It was so effective that I still can't eat a doughnut without getting a little bit uncomfortable around my collar.

As I risked walking with William and we forged a relationship, I learned what makes a guide trustworthy. After some more time and testing, he eventually proved to me that he had my best interest and safety at heart, and I came to trust him.

It could have been different. William could have failed the test and stayed focused on those doughnuts. Our God, however, always passes the taste test. "The LORD is good, a refuge in times of trouble. He cares for those who trust in him" (Nahum 1:7). With everything that's going on in the universe, He still remains focused on us. Everything He has done through the ages reflects that.

In the Garden, He pursued us.

In the ark, He protected us.

In the wilderness, He provided for us.

And on the cross, He proved to us that He alone is worthy of ultimate trust.

FEELINGS AREN'T TRUSTWORTHY GUIDES

Because God is trustworthy, what He says is also trustworthy. "In the beginning was the Word," says John, "and the Word was with God, and the Word was God" (John 1:1). It is impossible to separate who God is from what He says.

The psalmist says that God's Word is "a lamp to my feet

and a light for my path" (Psalm 119:105). There will be times when your path will be dark, times when you'll desperately need a light to guide you. When life's shadows hide Him from your view, you'll need the light of His promise that He will "never leave you nor forsake you" (Joshua 1:5). When life's circumstances rob you of your sense of security, you'll need the beacon of His assurance that He "knows what you need before you ask him" (Matthew 6:8). We can trust what God says to guide us when life is dark because He can see better than we can. "A man's ways are in full view of the LORD, and he examines all his paths" (Proverbs 5:21).

So why *don't* we allow His Word to guide us?

Why *don't* we trust the promises in the Bible?

I think it's because we trust our feelings more than we trust what God tells us.

Feelings are tough obstacles to overcome, aren't they? They seem so immediate and real. But we can learn to trust in spite of them. How? By looking at Someone who had it figured out and imitating Him.

Jesus knew what it was like to feel human because although He was fully God, He was also fully man. When He came to earth for us, He clothed Himself in humanity:

Being in very nature God, [He] did not consider equality with God something to be grasped, but made himself nothing, taking the very nature of a servant, being made in human likeness. And being found in appearance as a man, he humbled himself and became obedient to death—even death on a cross! (Philippians 2:6–8)

Does this mean that Jesus struggled with His feelings just as you and I do?

Yes, He did.

Emotions accompany all the events of our lives. If you have a broken relationship, chances are you'll feel sad or rejected. If your spouse dies, you'll likely feel lonely. If you're unjustly accused, you'll probably feel angry. The more importance you assign to the event, the more intensely you'll feel the emotion. So when Christ approached the most important event in His life, He did so with an intense emotion.

The Bible calls it *shame.*

"For the joy set before Him [He] endured the cross, despising the shame, and has sat down at the right hand of the throne of God" (Hebrews 12:2, NASB).

What really strikes me in this passage is a word that appears before *shame.* It is a word that graphically describes how Jesus dealt with His strong emotion. The word is translated several different ways, depending on the version. One says that Christ *scorned* the shame; another that He *despised* the shame. But in the original Greek, the word is *kataphroneo.* (Now, indulge me here! These are five foreign syllables that will help build your trust muscle!) *Kataphroneo* means "to consider with disregard" or "to esteem lowly."

What an awesome example Jesus gave us! He had feelings of shame, but He held them in low esteem.

What we hold in high esteem will eventually govern us, but what we hold in low esteem, *we* will govern. Yes, we need to acknowledge our feelings, but we should never regard them more highly than God's Word. Don't ever bow to your feelings because you hold them in such high regard. Instead, make them bow to your God.

Often we can't choose the feelings we experience. But we can always choose our *response* to them. We don't have to allow our feelings to dictate our choices. It may seem risky at the time, but if we don't esteem God's eternal Word more highly than we do our fleeting human feelings, we'll miss the blessings that wait on the other side of choosing to trust. Paul tells us what happened when Jesus esteemed God's Word more than His feelings and, in obedience to it, went to the cross:

> Therefore God exalted him to the highest place and gave him the name that is above every name, that at the name of Jesus every knee should bow, in heaven and on earth and under the earth, and every tongue confess that Jesus Christ is Lord, to the glory of God the Father. (Philippians 2:9–11)

Recently a lady at a conference told me that even though her friend Susan had wanted to attend, she wouldn't come with her. Susan has the same handicap I do. "Her husband is her eyes," her friend said. "She won't go anywhere without him." Since Susan thought her husband would feel out of place at a conference for women, she chose to stay home.

Why wouldn't Susan let her friend be her eyes for the day? A lack of trust? What keeps us from truly trusting? When I think about what keeps me from trusting, I realize that it's a feeling of fear that makes me unwilling to risk. But why did Jesus risk everything at the cross? *For the joy that was set before Him.* And what was His reward? *To sit down at the right hand of the throne of God.* The bigger the risk, the bigger the blessing! Who knows what blessings Susan missed because she was afraid to trust her friend?

A lot of us are that way and don't even realize it. When we say that we trust Him yet never risk acting upon His Word, we really don't trust Him at all. Trust shows itself when it leaves the tip of our tongue and lands on our tennis shoes. We begin to walk our faith, not just talk it.

Yes, of course we all feel afraid at times. It comes with the territory in our fallen human nature. But we can risk the frightening discomfort in order to find that we really can trust God. To trust Him fully means that we believe Him and act upon what He says. And when we do, His Word really does illuminate our path.

Fear Is a Feeling; Trust Is a Choice

Feeling fearful is a natural reaction to many of life's circumstances, but trust is always a supernatural choice.

The terrorist attacks on September 11, 2001, left all Americans reeling. In the aftermath, threats to airlines were a daily reality, and I struggled with the same feelings of fear as everyone else. My calendar, however, had been booked for a year, and I was scheduled to fly every weekend after September 11. A traveling companion who was scheduled to accompany me on several trips suddenly had to cancel when her husband was called to military duty.

That meant that I had to make several trips in a row by myself.

And I must admit that I was fearful.

The atmosphere in airports and airplanes was tense, and I was not looking forward to being alone. At least a companion could help me know what was happening and what to do if there was a problem.

I remember getting on my knees before God and telling Him that I was afraid. Immediately, this verse came to my mind: "When I am afraid, I will trust in you" (Psalm 56:3).

God knows that sometimes fear and trust share the same heartbeat. As I meditated on the verse, I suddenly realized that *I am afraid* describes a condition and that *I will trust* describes a volition. The verse is definitive: My volition can change my condition. For example, if *I am down,* but *I will get up,* my choice will change my situation. So if *I am afraid,* yet *I will trust,* my choice to trust God will inevitably change my feeling of fear.

When I resolved to trust God and fly, I flew without fear. Then I could quote with confidence what Paul told Timothy: "God has not given us a spirit of fear" (2 Timothy 1:7, NKJV).

It's true—He hasn't. So what has He given us?

The verse goes on to say that He has given us a spirit "of power and of love and of a sound mind." It is *God's* power in us—not our own—that gives us the ability to triumph over fear. The Bible also tells us that "perfect love drives out fear" (1 John 4:18) and that having a sound mind—taking captive every thought to make it obedient to Christ—can "demolish arguments and every pretension that sets itself up against the knowledge of God" (2 Corinthians 10:5). That includes fear.

Choosing to trust God gives us the resources we need to cast out fear. Yet ironically, fear can also help us trust God. How? By making us wise.

Through the years I've heard people talk about how much courage I must have. I'm amused by their comments. There's a line in a popular song to the effect that underneath a warrior's armor, you'll find a child. Isn't that a tender picture of someone fearlessly pursuing a life of trusting our Father? Well, here's another picture for you: Underneath this warrior's armor, you'll find a chicken. That's right! A grade-A, yellow-bellied, lily-livered chicken! It's scary walking through life in the dark.

Still, I would rather use fear wisely than foolishly waste it. So I'm learning to keep my feelings in check and exercise the kind of fear that will fuel my faith. The Bible says, "The fear of the LORD is the beginning of wisdom" (Psalm 111:10). Having a healthy reverence for God allows us to view our fears from the perspective of His mighty throne, and the wisdom that's born out of a genuine respect for Him gives us the discernment to gauge what is truly worth fearing.

Wisdom wears the garment of trust and walks without fear. Solomon said, "Wisdom is more precious than rubies, and nothing you desire can compare with her" (Proverbs 8:11). And God is willing to give us wisdom just for the asking!

When I was thirteen, I memorized James 1:5: "If any of you lacks wisdom, he should ask God, who gives generously to all without finding fault, and it will be given to him." I trusted God enough to ask. So when anyone marvels at my apparent "courage," I attribute it to my trusting prayer for wisdom. God has taught me to lovingly fear Him, and as a result, little else is really worth fearing. When we fear God most of all, trusting Him will be our wisest choice.

Even when life gets dark and scary.

Who among you fears the LORD and
obeys the word of his servant?
Let him who walks in the dark, who has no light,
trust in the name of the LORD and rely on his God.

ISAIAH 50:10

Be Thou My Vision

Be Thou my Vision, O Lord of my heart
Naught be all else to me, save that Thou art
Thou my best thought, by day or by night
Waking or sleeping, Thy presence my light

Riches I heed not, nor man's empty praise
Thou mine Inheritance, now and always
Thou and Thou only, first in my heart
High King of heaven, my Treasure Thou art

High King of heaven, my victory won
May I reach heaven's joys, O bright heaven's Sun!
Heart of my own heart, whatever befall
Still be my Vision, O Ruler of all

EIGHTH-CENTURY IRISH POEM TRANSLATED BY MARY BYRNE VERSIFIED BY ELEANOR HULL

Three

REMEMBER *What* MATTERS

Here's a question for you: What do these ten things have in common?

1. a ballpoint pen
2. a bicycle
3. a snowman
4. a Volkswagen bug
5. a five-dollar bill
6. a monkey's tail
7. a golf club
8. a pair of glasses
9. a submarine periscope
10. ten little Indians

On the surface they don't seem to have much of anything in common—but you might be surprised! Each item on the list contains a symbol, and each symbol represents a number. Assigning a symbol and a number to things is the way I memorize grocery and to-do lists.

I learned how to do this when I was a junior in college. One day my psychology professor asked each of the forty students in our class to name any item he or she chose. After the fortieth person added something, I listened in astonishment as the professor began to tick off everything on the list—in perfect order. Next he challenged us to call out numbers at random, and he then proceeded to connect each one with the correct item. It was amazing!

Inspired by that demonstration, I vowed to learn to remember just like he did. To remember the items on this list, for example, I would imagine number 1 with a ballpoint stuck in it, number 2 riding on the seat of a bike, or a monkey swinging by his tail from number 6. That's pretty much the technique. I mastered it, and now if you ask me to remember a list, almost all of the time I can.

For me, memory is more reliable than sight. One of the oddities of living with failing sight is that the changes are often sudden, yet subtle. Many times I've operated on the mistaken notion that I could see where I was going, only to realize—when I walked into a wall—that my sight had worsened. If I had made it a point to remember where the doorway was, I would have made it safely down the hall.

In a spiritual sense, that's true for all of us. As we're learning to trust God and walk by faith, we also need to learn to remember His Word. That's because knowing what God tells us in the Bible helps us to act upon what we *know* is true, rather than merely reacting to what we see.

Life presents us with many optical illusions. Have you ever been in the desert and seen that tantalizing shoreline of water shimmering on the horizon? You could chase it all your life and never wet so much as your big toe. It isn't really there! And that's often true with what we think we're seeing so clearly. The information provided by our eyes may simply be unreliable. There are also times when we can't see at all. So we must memorize the truth and make sure we remember what matters.

SOMETHING TO KEEP IN MIND

One cold January afternoon, our family had just returned to Springfield, Missouri, after a long, tiring drive. Before going home, we had to stop at the store, and as we pulled into the parking lot, it was all I could do to wait for the car to stop before I opened the door. The heat in our van had abandoned us about three hours from home, and I was cold! As soon as Phil shut off the engine, I swung the door open and held on as it pulled me swiftly out of the van. By the time Phil and our oldest son, Clayton, had opened their doors, I was headed to the middle of the parking lot.

"Stop, Mom," Clayton yelled. "There's a car coming!"

Phil ran over to me. "Why are you in such a hurry?" he asked.

Before I could answer, Clayton said, "Mom, you could have been hit by a car. That would've been awful!"

I was pleased with his concern and ashamed of my impetuousness. "You're right," I said. "That would have been awful."

"Yeah," Clayton said. "Because if you died, Dad and I would *never* be able to find anything!"

Well, that was about the most accurate statement I'd ever heard!

My guys are fully sighted, but I'm still their eyes. They're constantly asking me, "Where's my...?" and "Have you seen my...?" Since they don't pay any attention to where they put things, it's easier for them to ask me than it is to search. Clayton feared that if I died, he and his dad would never find anything because they rely heavily on my memory to find their stuff for them.

My world is pretty dark, so I must depend on my memory. If something is out of its place, I can't access it, and it's as though it doesn't exist. I have to diligently maintain my closet, my pantry, and my refrigerator because I can't rely on others to find the chocolate chips when my hormones are screaming, "Feed me! Feed me!" And that's only the beginning. There are so many things I have to order and organize in my life—knowing that I can't always rely on someone being there to check it out for me visually. Do my socks match when I leave the house in the morning? They do if I've put them in the right place! I must rely completely on remembering where things are and maintaining good habits to keep them in the places I've memorized.

Relying on sight is okay…as long as we can see. But what if the electricity goes out? Let's face it: We all have times when life gets dark, times when we just can't see. To shed light on our path, we have to know God's Word. The psalmist put it this way: "I will delight in your principles and not forget your word" (Psalm 119:16, NLT).

None of us can be certain that we'll have access to a Bible just when we need it, and we can't rely solely on others, like our pastor or Bible-study teacher, to find the exact Scripture we need. If we don't discipline ourselves to memorize the truth, it won't be accessible when we reach for it. That means we must sear the Word into our gray matter. We must learn to remember the Scripture that will guide us when we can't see.

Suppose one day a job layoff, a car accident, or a serious illness shakes your tranquil world. Life suddenly seems mercilessly dark. But if you have memorized the truth that God will keep in perfect peace those whose minds are stayed on Him (Isaiah 26:3), you will react peacefully based on what you know to be true.

Is there a darkness threatening you? Try to identify it, and then memorize what God says about your situation.

Here are some examples from the New Century Version of the Bible:

- Is it fear? Remember Matthew 10:29–31: "Two sparrows cost only a penny, but not even one of them can die without your Father's knowing it.... So don't be afraid. You are worth much more than many sparrows."
- Is it loneliness? Remember Hebrews 13:5: "God has said, 'I will never leave you; I will never forget you.'"
- Is it guilt? Remember 2 Corinthians 5:17: "If anyone belongs to Christ, there is a new creation. The old things have gone; everything is made new!"
- Is it worry? Remember 1 Peter 5:7: "Give all your worries to [God], because he cares about you."
- Is it getting older? Remember Isaiah 46:4: "Even when you are old, I will be the same. Even when your hair has turned gray, I will take care of you."
- Is it disappointment? Remember Matthew 5:4: "Those who are sad now are happy, because God will comfort them."

Memorizing the truth will allow the Light of the World to illuminate even your darkest places with the radiance of His Word. If you remember what matters, a good memory will see you through.

Memories That Matter

When I was a little girl, long before my eyes grew dim, I used to lie upon the grass in my front yard and gaze at the sky. The sun always fell softly on my skin on those warm Florida afternoons. As I stretched out under the silk oak tree and gazed at the billows of white in the clear blue sky, the clouds would become images in my imagination. I could see hammers and elves. Trucks and teapots. Once I raced into the house to proudly announce that I had seen Snow White and all seven dwarfs.

At times I still gaze heavenward into that vast blue canvas stretched out overhead, but now, even on the most brilliant days, all my eyes see is gray. Sometimes that makes me feel sad—until I remember the clouds. They still dance through my imagination to the music only my memory can hear. Then I smile, for I have a treasure hidden in my memory that no eye disease can ever touch. I can stretch out in the front yard with my two sons and enjoy the pictures the clouds draw for them.

Memory will sustain you even when sight won't serve you. That's why it's essential to remember what really matters. It's important to remember the clouds.

The Bible says that when the children of Israel were in the wilderness, God "guided them with the cloud by day and with light from the fire all night" (Psalm 78:14). I bet the nation of Israel remembered the cloud that led them. But I also bet that when they remembered the cloud, they couldn't help but recall the difficulties of their journey through the wilderness. The desert was a place of longing and need, a place that required them to depend totally upon God.

Why did God allow His covenant people to wander in the desert for so long? The Old Testament suggests that it was because the harsh conditions of the wilderness revealed the true nature of the sojourners. Early in the book of Exodus we begin to read accounts of grumbling and complaints on the part of the Israelites. Their faith grew faint, and they often lost their perspective. Later, Moses reminded them about that: "Remember how the LORD your God led you through the wilderness for forty years, humbling you and testing you to prove your character, and to find out whether or not you would really obey his commands" (Deuteronomy 8:2, NLT).

I believe that God allows all of us to wander through deserts at times in order to test us. The wilderness shows who we really are and whom we really trust. Sometimes God lets us be hungry just so He can feed us, and sometimes He lets us wander just so we'll look for Him in the cloud.

So when you think of your desert, remember the cloud. In the Old Testament it always represents God's presence. When the Israelites' journey through the wilderness was over, they still faced an uncertain future across the Jordan, and they were afraid. But even though the cloud was no longer there to guide them, God was still there. "The LORD himself goes before you and will be with you," Moses reminded them; "he will never leave you nor forsake you. Do not be afraid; do not be discouraged" (Deuteronomy 31:8).

Even when clouds darken our world, if we look closely, we'll see that He is with us, and His presence will always lead us to our promised land.

Remember what matters.

If you do, you'll never forget in the dark what you knew was true in the light, and you'll be able to smile even when you see nothing but gloomy shadows. Remembering what really matters, however, takes some memory maintenance.

That Reminds Me

Okay. I'm sure you've already asked yourself—especially the ladies—*How in the world does she put on makeup?* Someday—in the middle of a massive power blackout—that might become an issue of paramount importance for you. So I'll let you in on my secret.

I do it through concentration and reinforcement.

My mother taught me the system years ago, and over time I've adjusted it slightly to accommodate style and fashion. It all involves counting. I know just how many times to brush my blush brush against my blush palette (I dare you to read that out loud three times fast!) and exactly where and how many times to swish that brush along my cheekbone. The system works the same for eyeliner, mascara, lipliner, and eye shadow. It's very reliable as long as I concentrate and don't lose count. In fact, it's more reliable than looking in a mirror. If you make it a habit, you can apply your makeup during a full solar eclipse!

But here's the catch: My system for putting on makeup is only as reliable as my ability to *reinforce* what I have memorized. Sure, I know just how many strokes and swishes it takes to make myself over, but if I didn't habitually practice what I've memorized, I'd soon forget. And the result wouldn't be pretty!

Well, guess what? The result of allowing truths we've memorized to be forgotten due to mental laziness isn't pretty either. The psalmist says, "Your Word I have treasured in my heart, that I may not sin against You" (Psalm 119:11, NASB).

Still, the truths we find in God's Word are far more than precepts that help us not to sin; in and of themselves they are treasures worth preserving. All throughout Psalm 119, the writer says "I will remember" and "I do not forget."

And guess what he's referring to?

God's Word.

He knew the value of remembering it. Look at some of the things that are ours when we hide it in our heart:

- God's Word is our counselor. (v. 24)
- God's Word strengthens us. (v. 28)
- God's Word is our delight. (v. 35)

⌒ God's Word comforts us in our affliction. (v. 52)

⌒ God's Word makes us wiser than our enemies. (v. 98)

⌒ God's Word gives us more insight than our teachers. (v. 99)

⌒ God's Word is sweet to our mouths. (v. 103)

⌒ God's Word gives us understanding. (v. 104)

⌒ God's Word renews our lives. (v. 156)

⌒ God's Word gives us peace. (v. 165)

See what a precious treasure you have in God's Word? Treat it like the treasure it is and hide it in your heart. Write it upon the tablet of your memory, and to maintain it frequently, review what you've memorized.

There are a number of ways to reinforce your memory. One of the things I do to help me not forget and keep my Scripture memory agile is to take my cues from the clock. Here's what I mean. If I'm sitting down to hot tea and sugar cookies in the afternoon, I press my talking watch. If it says 3:23, I immediately think of a verse with that address. Ah, Romans 3:23, "For all have sinned and fall short of the glory of God." Or perhaps Colossians 3:23, "Whatever you do, work at it with all your heart, as working for the Lord, not for men."

If I can't quote the verse, I get out my Bible on tape, look it up, and work on reciting it. If I can't think of any address that corresponds with the time, I try to find one. Our family also uses Scripture cards at the dinner table. We read one each night and take turns practicing reciting it.

These are just two ways to maintain what we've memorized. We can memorize anything if we concentrate on it and reinforce it. Then it becomes near to us, and we act upon what we have memorized. "The word is very near you, in your mouth and in your heart, that you may do it" (Deuteronomy 30:14, NKJV). If we can do it with cosmetics, we can certainly do it with the Word!

Now that I've told you my secret of applying makeup, I want to let you in on a Rothschild family secret for applying Scripture.

It's our personal family code. It consists of two numbers, and it contains all we need to have a power-packed day. The two numbers are 4 and 13.

When Clayton leaves for school in the morning, I'll call out, "4:13."

When I'm feeling overwhelmed, Clayton will respectfully say, "4:13 it, Mom."

When Phil has a major project due at work, I'll remind him, "4:13, honey."

When Connor has a toddler meltdown in the candy aisle at the grocery store, I...*pay four dollars and thirteen cents to the cashier just to get him to be quiet!*

Just kidding!

You may have already guessed that 4:13 stands for the well-known and much beloved Scripture in Philippians, "I can do all things through Christ who strengthens me" (NKJV). For us, that verse is an awesome reminder that with the power and presence of Christ in our lives, nothing, but nothing, is too big, too hard, too puzzling, or too overwhelming to warrant an "I can't" attitude.

Corrie ten Boom's family had a secret, too. When they were arrested by Hitler's regime, the family members whispered to one another, "What do you have in your shoe, Corrie?" "What do you have in your shoe, Daddy?" "What do you have in your shoe, Betsy?"

What was in their shoes? Romans 8, Ephesians 1, and 2 Corinthians 4. According to Corrie, they had torn pages of Scripture from their Bibles and placed them in the soles of their shoes. Talk about *standing* on the promises! Even while they were confined to a concentration camp and enduring harsh conditions of hunger and abuse, they knew they were walking with the Word.

When we have memorized God's Word, it becomes real to us—it becomes what we speak and what we stand on—and it empowers us to do all things through Christ, regardless of our circumstance. So learn to remember His Word. Speak it to yourself and to those around you. Stand firmly upon it. May it be written on your soles and penetrate your soul.

You shall put these words of mine in your heart and soul, and you shall bind them as a sign on your hand,

and fix them as an emblem on your forehead. Teach them to your children, talking about them when you are at home and when you are away, when you lie down and when you rise. (Deuteronomy 11:18–19, NRSV)

Never forget that the important things sealed in your memory are never lost. So spend time memorizing what matters, and maintain what you have memorized. When it's dark and you can't see, God will become your vision if His truths are hidden in your heart.

Most of all, remember the Lord, for He never forgets you. You are always on His mind and in His thoughts. He remembers what matters—you! So by day or by night, make Him your best thought, and make sure you always remember to thank Him for His Word and His goodness to you.

Remember His wonders which He has done,
His marvels and the judgments uttered by His mouth.

PSALM 105:5, NASB

Matchless Grace

Just when I need You most, You hear me
Just when I least deserve, You rescue me
All of the times I've failed You
Just show Your promises to be true

Matchless grace, oh how kind
That in Your heart You would find
Matchless grace to forgive
And to lend the strength to live
By matchless grace

All of my earthly strength is weakness
My soul depends on You for completeness
It's by Your grace that I am
And by Your grace that I will stand

Matchless grace, oh how kind
That in Your heart You would find
Matchless grace to forgive
And to lend the strength to live
By matchless grace

WORDS AND MUSIC BY JENNIFER ROTHSCHILD © 1990 ROTHSCHILD MUSIC (ASCAP)

Four

RECEIVE GOD'S GIFTS *with* THANKS

D o you remember the robot in the 1970s TV show *Lost in Space?* Most of the time when he showed up, his arms waved and his lights flashed a warning: "Danger! Danger!" That's what I often feel like—as though my blindness somehow sends a silent signal that says "Warning: Danger!"

Most women can call a friend and say, "Let's go shopping." It's simple and straightforward. But if I call a friend to make the same suggestion, I fear that what she really hears is "Will you come pick me up, lead me around the store, pick out clothes, read the labels to me, and then be my mirror? After that, will you place my pen on the line so I can sign for my purchase, and then will you drive me home and walk me into the house?"

It's kind of like having to get a toddler in and out of a car seat while you run errands. It's not that you don't love the child's company; it's just that it's so much easier to go alone. That's how I feel in a lot of my friendships—loved and enjoyed, yet a complicating factor in someone's otherwise uncomplicated world. That feeling makes me stare at my blindness and decide if I'm going to gratefully receive it as a gift from God and become a better person, or despise it and become a bitter one.

The only difference between becoming *bitter* and becoming *better* is the letter *I*. Approaching our difficulties from the standpoint of what *I* want, what *I* have lost, or what *I* think is fair will embitter us. Bitter eyes can perceive only the injustice and the sorrow in our situation. Grateful eyes, however, will always see the grace of God, regardless of how difficult our circumstances might be. Grateful eyes allow us to see "the goodness of the LORD in the land of the living" (Psalm 27:13).

Even though blindness has been a difficult gift to receive, I now can accept it with thanks. As I've learned to view my circumstances from God's perspective, I've learned to gratefully receive.

DIFFICULT GIFTS

One reason many people struggle with bitterness and ungratefulness is that they've never learned to receive difficult gifts. Blindness is just one of many such gifts. Illness, broken relationships, wayward children, and financial strain can be very hard to receive, much less be thankful for. But the interesting thing is that God expects us to be thankful anyway. "Give thanks in all circumstances," the apostle Paul reminds us, "for this is God's will for you in Christ Jesus" (1 Thessalonians 5:18).

I vividly remember the night before Christmas when I was nine years old. One of our family traditions was that each child got to open one gift on Christmas Eve. My brothers and I spent most of the month deciding which gift that would be. We began our research in early December, and as each gift appeared beneath the tree, we carefully examined it, checking the weight and shape of each box, looking for clues to what was inside. As you can well imagine, by Christmas Eve the gift we had chosen to open had become the most coveted one under the tree.

That year my brother Lawson and I both chose a gift from Aunt Patti. (Our brother David was a baby and still too young to care.) Aunt Patti was young and hip. She knew what kinds of presents kids liked, and now she joined my parents on the couch to watch the events unfold.

Lawson went first. He carefully removed the wrappings—and there was a brand-new GI Joe action figure. It had been on his list, so, boy, was he excited! I was excited, too, because it confirmed my hopeful suspicion that my gift from Aunt Patti was the number one thing on my wish list—a Barbie doll.

My gift was in a rectangular-shaped box. It wasn't the traditional box that a Barbie doll came in, but it was *shaped* like one, and I was convinced that Aunt Patti was just trying to fool me. I pulled off the narrow rectangular top, peeled back the tissue paper—and there were seven pairs of neatly rolled underwear.

Underwear! I wanted a Barbie doll, not underwear. I didn't even care if I wore underwear. My mother obviously noticed my disappointment because without hesitation, she said, "Jennifer, what do you say to Aunt Patti?"

"Thank you," I said.

Now, why did I say thank you for a gift that I hadn't asked for and obviously didn't want? Because from as early as I could remember, my mother had taught me that I was always to receive whatever anyone gave me and say thank you for it. She had instilled in me how important it is to always honor the giver by gratefully receiving the gift. So one reason for saying thank you was to honor Aunt Patti. Another was that it was my mother's will—and I knew that I would be a lot happier if I obeyed her!

Being thankful in all circumstances shows that we're acting in accordance with the will of God—who always gives us what is best for us. Often we struggle with an attitude of ungratefulness because our eyes are fixed so fiercely on the gift. Some things that God allows to come into our lives are genuinely hard to be thankful for. But if we fix our eyes on God, we can see beyond the difficulty of the gift into the heart of the Giver. Regardless of whether we asked for it or want it, it's a gift of God's grace, and our response should always be to receive it with thanks.

Is your response to a difficult gift based on your feelings about the gift itself or on your desire to honor the Giver and do His will? Is your closed fist extended in anger, or is your open hand lifted to Him? Only an open hand receives the blessings that accompany difficult gifts, and sometimes it's only in a package wrapped in heartache that we receive the fullness of God's grace.

Faith is the most essential ingredient for gratefully receiving whatever God lovingly allows, and it can be the greatest source of blessing in our lives when we learn to see what it sees. But to do that, we have to look at our lives from the right perspective.

THE RIGHT PERSPECTIVE

Connor had a new balloon and insisted on taking it to the backyard.

"Connor," I told him, "if we take the balloon out in the backyard it will probably get popped."

But he would not relent, so out we went. He swept the brightly colored balloon up into the air, and it slowly glided downward. He caught it and repeated the motion several times. Up, down; up, down. Eventually, the balloon lifted and dropped earthward for its final descent. He didn't catch it. *Pop!* Bits of wrinkly red rubber dotted the grass. With stunning composure, Connor gathered the tattered pieces in his chubby hands and ran toward me.

"Mommy," he said, "fix it!"

Why didn't that little guy fall apart over the demise of his beloved balloon? Because of his perspective. Although the reality was that the balloon couldn't be fixed, little Connor's perspective on life was still *Mommy can fix anything*. His confident response to the situation was based less on reality itself than on the way he perceived it.

Sometimes you and I find ourselves on the brink of a spiritual meltdown when the reality we face is hard. But I believe that our perspective on our adversity can often be more powerful than the hardship itself. If beauty is in the eye of the beholder, so is pain and heartache.

I remember a creative writing class I took years ago. "I want everyone to stare at this chalkboard and imagine that it's a window," the professor announced, "and then write an essay about what you see through it." Pens began to dance on crisp, white paper, and after forty-five minutes the teacher called for volunteers to read what they had written.

One not-so-deep thinker gave mind-numbing details of the Bills versus Dolphins game he was watching through the window of his luxurious skybox. Another more imaginative writer saw through delicate snowflakes sticking to the glass to the ice-capped mountains on the other side of the window. Yet another saw the dark, mysterious cemetery that beckoned him to his father's grave.

Keep in mind that all we *really* saw was a plain old unat-
tractive chalkboard. And sometimes it seems as though that's
all life offers, doesn't it? Uninviting situations with no inherent beauty or appeal—just dusty gray slate. Hard stuff. But
if seeing is a physical function of the eye, it's also a spiritual
function of the soul, and what we see through the window
of hardship depends on the perspective we choose. Like
those creative writers, we need to choose how we will perceive it.

Shifting our gaze can help us. If we look around, we'll see
bigger problems than our own. In moments when my blindness makes me feel frustrated and discouraged, I think of a
man I know who lives and performs in Branson, Missouri.
He is a gifted singer and plays the guitar masterfully—with
his feet, for he was born without arms. I think about what
his life must be like. Yes, he can drive a car, read a book, and
see his surroundings. But he can't embrace his wife or hold
his children. When I think about that, I begin to genuinely
thank God for what I do have, because it's so much greater
than what I've lost.

I'm not saying that we should dismiss our heartache as
trivial because "someone else has it worse." The bottom line
is that someone else will *always* have it worse, and we will
always have heartache. I'm simply suggesting that shifting
our gaze to a bigger problem will put our own situation in
perspective—and prompt an attitude of gratefulness that
will release us from the shackles of bitterness.

Sometimes, though, it's hard to look around for a bigger problem, because the one we're dealing with seems awfully big to us.

That's why we also need to look up.

As we shift our gaze heavenward, it becomes focused on God and His promises. "The LORD God is a sun and shield," writes the psalmist; "the LORD will give grace and glory: no good thing will he withhold from them that walk uprightly" (Psalm 84:11, KJV). When we choose to view our life from that perspective, our grateful eyes will see God's goodness all around us.

GRATEFUL EYES SEE GRACE AND GLORY

Before I lost my sight, my career goal was to be a commercial artist. I loved to draw! I had several years of lessons, and cartooning and lettering were my forte. I inherited my talent from my mother, who is quite the artist.

Mom had a special knack for training her children to perceive the subtle nuances of every color of the spectrum. It was rare for her to use less than five adjectives to describe a color.

I knew what red looked like when it was warm and orangey on the skin of a tomato. I knew what it was to see the beautiful blue undertones just beneath the red paint of a fire engine. I loved the color yellow, whether it was splashed upon an ear of corn or lying gently upon a buttercup. Even though my eyes no longer see color, every one I ever saw is still fresh and vibrant in my mind's eye. There I can still see all the hues of all the colors I saw when I was growing up.

How special it was for me, then, when one day Clayton came home from preschool and showed the same eye for color as his grandmother. He held a crumpled piece of paper toward me and said, "Mommy, look at this beautiful flower."

By the time he was three, Clayton had learned that in order for his mommy to see, he needed to use words. So he began to describe the picture of his beautiful flower. "Mommy," he said, "the flower is pink. And the leaves are not just green, they are a yellowish green."

I remember sitting on our front porch, holding the picture in my hand. I could have felt it stab me as a painful reminder that I would never draw again and never have the opportunity to enjoy art with my son. Instead, I felt amazed that Clayton's little eyes could perceive the difference between a bluish and a yellowish green.

That day it was as if God illustrated for me a beautiful picture of His goodness. It was as if I could see a shade of His grace I'd never seen before. And I think that I wouldn't have seen the beauty in that picture if God had not already taught me to have grateful eyes.

Grateful eyes see God's glory as well as His grace, and the glory of God is what turns all the pictures in our lives into beautiful works of art. Thumbing through the photo album of my life, I see many snapshots in my mind's eye, including one that at first glance doesn't seem very delightful to behold. But when I take a closer look through grateful eyes, I see it bathed in the radiance of God's glory.

One spring evening I arrived at a hotel in Destin, Florida, where I was to speak at a women's conference the following day. I didn't feel well at bedtime, but I assumed that I just needed a good night's sleep and that I'd be fine in the morning.

Boy, was I wrong! The next morning I was in severe pain. If I'd been pregnant, I would have assumed I was in labor. But I wasn't—and this was worse than labor! I ended up in the emergency room of the local hospital, where I quickly learned what kidney stones are.

Surgery took the place of my speaking engagement that night, and when I came out of the anesthetic, I was very discouraged. *Had I flown across the country just to be stuck in a hospital?* It was hard to be grateful for such a strange turn of events.

But then the words of Peter began running through my mind: "Dear friends, do not be surprised at the painful trial you are suffering, as though something strange were happening to you. But rejoice that you participate in the sufferings of Christ, so that you may be overjoyed when his glory is revealed" (1 Peter 4:12–13).

It was the very verse I was to have spoken on that night, and it encouraged me to go ahead and rejoice.

So I did.

Instead of thinking about the strange thing that had happened to me, I chose to be grateful and to settle into what God had allowed. I knew from Matthew 24:27 that someday Jesus would burst like lightning through the eastern sky and I'd see His glory. *And then,* I thought, *I'll be more than joyful—I'll be overjoyed.* What I didn't expect was that right then His glory was about to burst into my hospital room.

As I lay there, I heard a soft knock, quickly followed by the sound of a door opening.

"Jennifer," a female voice said, "you don't know me, but I work here, and I saw your name come up on my computer screen. You spoke several years ago at a conference I attended when I was battling breast cancer. God used you to help me, and—I had to come to say thank you. By the way, my name is Gloria."

Gloria.

And just like that, God's glory began to fill that hospital room. It was as though God shone a huge spotlight on that strange, painful *incident* in my life and turned it into a beautiful picture for the album of my life. I didn't have to wait until "someday" to see His glory revealed; His glory had walked right into my hospital room. As Gloria spoke words of encouragement and purpose, God's glory washed over my discouragement, allowing me to see His goodness.

I was overjoyed, not by the difficult circumstance, but by how God *used* it.

Do you see the distinction? It's so critical to let this truth seep into the roots of your heart. I'm convinced that God often wraps difficult gifts with His grace—and then uses them to display His glory. For that reason, we are the ones who truly benefit when we choose to gratefully receive them.

THE LONE LEPER

Often we assume that it would be easy to be grateful if God would simply *remove* the difficult gifts from our lives. Right? Nothing could be easier for Him. Then we would just naturally well up with feelings of gratitude that would overflow in praise to God. But believe me, the chances of that happening are slim. I struggled with statistics in college, but looking at Luke 17, even I can see that the odds are against us.

In fact, they're just one in ten.

Jesus was on His way to Jerusalem when ten lepers called out to Him to have pity on them. To put it mildly, those lepers had it very hard. The disease had ravaged and disfigured their bodies, and made them outcasts in a society that considered them unclean. So they cried out for Jesus to show them mercy, and He did. Then He told them to go show themselves to the priests.

One of the lepers, when he realized he had been healed, immediately came back to find Jesus. In verse 16, Luke says that the leper "threw himself at Jesus' feet and thanked him." Jesus asked the grateful man about the other nine. Where were they?

I wonder about them, too. Why didn't they return? Why didn't sheer gratitude catapult them back to Jesus? I wonder…until I look in the mirror and realize that centuries later I scurry through my busy life just like one of the nine. When I was eight years old, I received an unspeakable gift: the redemption of my soul. It came to me through a hand of mercy in the rugged wrappings of the Cross, and it has given me light in the darkness, water in the desert, and hope amid sorrow.

Yet sometimes I forget to return to say thank you. Like the nine heedless, forgetful ones, I hurry on my way, savoring the gift but forgetting all about the One who gave.

May we all be like the one, rather than the nine.

May we all be like the leper who exhibited his faith by choosing to give thanks.

We often think that faith is a recipe for getting what we want from God. If that were true, it would mean that if I could just muster enough faith, I would no longer be blind. But faith is not meant to offer an escape from life's difficulties; its purpose is to give us strength to endure them. God allows hardship because of His great mercy and love for us, and He often removes it for the same reason. However, we should not thank Him more fervently on the day our difficult gift is removed than we do on the days we carry it. It takes just as much faith to bear a burden as it does to believe that it can be removed.

Your faith shows itself in a response of thankfulness in all circumstances. Bitterness never kneels at God's throne; it just shakes an angry fist. Gratitude, however, like the lone leper, throws itself before Christ. When you smash the last brick of your wall of bitterness with the hammer of gratitude, you will hear the echo of the words Jesus spoke to the leper: "Your faith has made you well" (Luke 17:19).

Have you come back, thrown yourself at His feet, and thanked Him? Until you do, you'll never experience the wellness that your faith can provide.

To be reminded of God's great gift of salvation makes all other gifts pale in comparison. All of us who have received it need to come back to Jesus and throw ourselves before Him, praising and thanking Him loudly. When we learn to be truly grateful for His greatest gift, we'll learn to gratefully receive any other gift He may allow.

"You are worthy, our Lord and God,
to receive glory and honor and power, for you created all things,
and by your will they were created and have their being."

REVELATION 4:11

Rejoice in You

I will rejoice in You
God of my salvation
You always see me through
I will rejoice in You

Out of the darkness, into the light
Healed from blindness, given new sight
Walking in victory, power, and might
I am triumphant over the fight

When I rejoice in You
God of my salvation
You always see me through
I will rejoice in You

A song of deliverance now I can sing
Your love has conquered; death has no sting
New every morning mercies you bring
I shout it boldly, You are the King!

When I rejoice in You
God of my salvation
You always see me through
I will rejoice in You

Five

REJOICE— MATTER WHAT!

We had just moved into our new home in Springfield. Our things were barely out of the boxes—and I was almost out of my mind!

That's no big surprise. Moving has been on the short list of top stressors since at least the 1960s. But it's especially stressful if you're blind.

Part of what makes life easier for a blind person is having an orderly world. Everything has a place, and everything must be in its place. But moving is the antithesis of an orderly world. At any given moment, chaos threatens to reign! Nothing has a place, and even if it did, it probably wouldn't be in it.

In order for me to know where everything is, I have to

unpack all the boxes, touch each item, and literally put it in its place. When I'm done, my kids can use me as their own personal tracking device. Why waste your energy searching the house for something when Mama's brain is equipped with GPS?

Finally, I was almost finished unpacking. Phil had helped me mark all the appliances with raised dots and tactile markings, and the kitchen was serviceable, so we graduated from delivered pizza to homemade lasagna. After I got it ready, I preheated the oven to 350 degrees and opened the door to put it in. First attempt…*ouch!* Second attempt… *ouch!* Third attempt…a very loud and unladylike *ouch!* I fought to get that lasagna in the oven, and I have the battle scars to prove it! (Yes, I should have learned the inside of the oven *before* it reached 350 degrees.)

As I nursed my wounds, I longed for my world to become orderly again. My stinging arms were a painful reminder of how difficult change can be. I didn't like having to adjust; I was tired of tripping over boxes and feeling my way around my new domain. "I'm tired of making adjustments, Lord," I cried. "I'm tired of having to unpack each box by hand just so I know where everything is. And I'm tired of all the bumps, bruises, and burns!"

No one heard me except God. *Whew!* It's a good thing, because I was already beginning to hear that violin tuning up to play dirges for my pity party. I don't think anyone else would have had much fun.

Sometimes it's good to let it all out…and I did. God is a patient listener. But there's a fine line between inviting God into our heartache and gearing up to send invitations for the "poor me" event of the year. In fact, nowhere does God tell us to throw pity parties. Instead, the Bible says: "Consider it pure joy, my brothers, whenever you face trials of many kinds" (James 1:2). If we think of a trial as joy, our response will be to rejoice.

James doesn't say to consider it joy *if* hardships come; he says to consider it joy *when* they come. They will come— that's just reality—and that means we'll certainly have oppor- tunities to rejoice. All throughout the New Testament, we are told to rejoice in our trials. *Well, that's tough,* I thought, *learning to rejoice when our world heats up and life stings!*

That got me to thinking about what joy really is. One of the Hebrew words in the Old Testament that is translated as our English word *joy* means "a special goodness in the widest sense." When I realized that's what God intended this trial to be, I no longer wanted to whine and wither. I wanted to rejoice!

God's Word tells us not only what joy is, but also what happens when we learn to rejoice in our trials. Now there's a reason to strike up the band and throw a party!

A DISCIPLINE THAT STRENGTHENS

When we rejoice in hardship, we acknowledge that God permits it for a purpose—to discipline us. I've got to tell you: *Discipline* is one of my least favorite words. I think the reason is because in the past I have misunderstood it. Parenting, however, has taught me that the true nature of discipline is not punishment but training.

I think that's God's view of discipline, too. His discipline is not to punish us, but to change us, and He allows suffering to be the hurdles we jump to strengthen us. He uses suffering to make us strong.

My friend Katharyn willingly subjects herself to the torture of running marathons. I don't know why. Personally, I enjoy running my mouth, running the dishwasher, and running to the mall. But running 26.2 miles? *Yikes!* Katharyn applies a lot of discipline and training in order to succeed in a marathon. Months in advance she wakes up before sunrise and starts to run. As the days progress, her route lengthens. Even though it's never easy, her training pays off. By the time of the marathon, she is lean, strong, and ready to race.

You should see her at the end of the race! She looks like someone ran her skinny body through the washing machine, bleached the color out of it, and then wrung it relentlessly until all that remained was wet, wrinkly, and worn.

But Katharyn really doesn't care what she looks like when she crosses the finish line at the end of the race. Her goal is to finish, and it's worth all the training just to cross that finish line.

Training and discipline are also the very things that

enable us to finish the race. Paul said, "I buffet my body" (1 Corinthians 9:27, ASV). In the American Standard Version of the Bible, you could easily mistake the verb in this verse for *buffet*—you know, like the midnight smorgasbord on a Carnival cruise. But no one can run well if they spend too much time doing that kind of "buffeting," so it's a good thing that's not what it means.

In the original Greek the word *buffet* actually means *to discipline by hardships.* A runner will discipline himself and endure arduous training in order to be fit for the race.

It's not easy. We can become weathered and weary. And even though discipline is intended to produce deep-seated character change, it can cause us pain, as the writer of Hebrews reminds us: "God disciplines us for our good, that we may share in his holiness. No discipline seems pleasant at the time, but painful. Later on, however, it produces a harvest of righteousness and peace for those who have been trained by it" (Hebrews 12:10–11).

God chooses to allow suffering to discipline us, yet it is our choice to discipline ourselves to respond with rejoicing. Both forms of discipline will strengthen us. I'm not convinced that suffering in and of itself creates strength. It's our *response* to the suffering that does that. The discipline of rejoicing in suffering is a response that bears fruit. We can rejoice even in suffering because of the harvest of peace and righteousness we will certainly enjoy when the training is complete.

Right after James gives us reason to rejoice, he reminds us what the result will be: "You know that these troubles test your faith, and this will give you patience" (James 1:3, NCV). We all can use a good dose of patience—and most of us could use it right now! But interestingly enough, the original Greek word means far more than passive endurance. It refers to the kind of perseverance that actively overcomes the trials of life.

A great example of this kind of patience was the brilliant composer Ludwig van Beethoven. When he realized that he would be deaf—a musician's greatest nightmare—he said, "I will take life by the throat." That's the kind of tenacity James is talking about.

Perseverance is one fruit of rejoicing in sufferings. Paul tells us what else God has promised: "We also rejoice in our sufferings, because we know that suffering produces perseverance; perseverance, character; and character, hope. And hope does not disappoint us, because God has poured out his love into our hearts by the Holy Spirit, whom he has given us" (Romans 5:3–5).

God's loving purpose is to conform us to the image of His Son, and Peter reminds us that persevering in trials is how we become more like Him: "In this you greatly rejoice, though now for a little while you may have had to suffer grief in all kinds of trials. These have come so that your faith—of greater worth than gold, which perishes even though refined by fire—may be **proved genuine and may** result in praise, glory and honor when Jesus Christ is revealed" (1 Peter 1:6–7).

The character produced by rejoicing in hardship is Christlike character—His glory revealed in us—and that character produces hope.

In the New Living Translation, Romans 5:3–5 reads this way:

> We can rejoice, too, when we run into problems and trials, for we know that they are good for us—they help us learn to endure. And endurance develops strength of character in us, and character strengthens our *confident expectation* of salvation. And this expectation will not disappoint us. For we know how dearly God loves us, because he has given us the Holy Spirit to fill our hearts with his love. (emphasis added)

Hope is the *confident expectation* that God will use our painful circumstances for good. It's what turns a hardship into "a special goodness in the widest sense." Hope is not a wishful "what if." The hope that emerges from Christlike character is certain and confident—sure that "He who has begun a good work in you will complete it" (Philippians 1:6, NKJV). This kind of hope is generated and confirmed in us by the Holy Spirit, who fills our hearts with God's love. It's what allows us to choose to rejoice amid hardships and to say to God, "I will rejoice in *You!*"

A DECISION THAT DELIVERS

One night when our son Clayton was eight months old, Phil and I returned home from an evening out and were greeted by the babysitter, who had frightening news. When she collapsed the stroller, Clayton had fallen headfirst onto the sidewalk. We were very concerned, and Phil checked Clayton for a concussion. He seemed fine.

Over the next three days, however, Clayton grew increasingly uncomfortable and fussy. Eventually he became listless. We were in and out of doctors' offices and hospital emergency rooms. He didn't have the symptoms of a concussion, so doctors were baffled. I didn't know medicine, but I knew my son—and I knew that something was dreadfully wrong. When Clayton began vomiting, we took him to the doctor's office again.

The doctor did another exam, and this one revealed blood in Clayton's diaper—so much blood that we were whisked away to the hospital where a surgeon waited. Clayton's large intestine was turning itself inside out—a condition called "intussusception"—and the damage was so severe that the surgery took several hours.

Friends quickly arrived to give blood and offer prayers. We were on our knees in that waiting room asking God to help our baby when our surgeon interrupted our prayers with the news that the operation had been successful.

"I know you have prayed to your God," he told us, "because your baby should not have survived. It's a miracle that he didn't have to have a colostomy." It was indeed a miracle, and we knelt in humble adoration of our Great Physician.

When we learned that Clayton had to remain in the hospital for at least a week, Phil and I decided to take turns staying with him. Phil would do the night shift, so I went home alone that night. When I entered the empty apartment, powerful feelings bubbled to the surface. I couldn't help but think about how close we came to never having Clayton there with us again. To drown out the silence and hush the myriad emotions of the day, I sat down at the piano and began to play. And as I did, a song began to form in my heart and move beneath my fingers:

> I will rejoice in You
> God of my salvation
> You always see me through
> And I will rejoice in You!

All that remains of that dark July day in 1990 is a physical scar. Over the years, as Clayton has grown larger, his scar has become smaller. When he got old enough to ask me about it, I told him that it meant "God takes care of us."

Perhaps you too have a scar.

You may have trouble rejoicing in it.

But Nehemiah 8:10 tells us that "the joy of the LORD is our strength," so if you think of your scar as a showcase of

God's power to take care of you, you can rejoice in the Savior who strengthens you. And when you do, God will use your joy to minister to others.

A MOURNING THAT MINISTERS

My friend Joni had been married for five years when her husband learned that he had cancer. This was certainly not what she had envisioned when she and Vance stood at the altar to exchange marriage vows just five years earlier. And it was definitely not what she had anticipated when she held their baby girl in the delivery room two years later. Yet as Vance persevered through hospitalizations and treatments, he and Joni prayed and believed for God's healing, even when the living room furniture was removed and a hospital bed was put in its place.

One afternoon while their three-year-old daughter was visiting a friend, Joni left Vance's bedside to answer the phone. When she returned, she realized that her prayers and belief for healing had been answered. God had lovingly and ultimately healed Vance by gently ushering him into heaven.

I met Joni shortly after Vance died. She was early in the mourning process, and there were days when just taking a shower was a paramount achievement for her. There were days when she would begin a sentence with a laugh and end it with tears. And there were days when she couldn't find any words at all.

The way Joni mourned ministered to me. Her sorrow

was a showcase for the joy of the Lord, which became her strength. As I watched her walk boldly through her heartbreak with the kind of perseverance James talks about, our friendship was forged. The joy of the Lord strengthened her even on the darkest days—and it became contagious.

I remember shopping with Joni a couple of years after Vance died. It was near Memorial Day, and she wanted to buy flowers for his grave. We found ourselves in one of those "super centers"—you know, a place where you can purchase a garden hose, pantyhose, and fresh tomatoes all at once! We began to look through the flower arrangements. Evidently we were a little late, because what was left looked pretty bad.

Joni systematically picked up each arrangement.

"These all look awful," she said.

"This one's ugly."

"This one's wilted."

"This one's turning brown."

Finally, in frustration, she laid the last flowers down and said, "These are so ugly that if I put them on Vance's grave, he'd just die!"

We giggled awkwardly—and then roared with laughter!

Often it's hard to rejoice in our circumstances. The difficulty of change, the sickness of a loved one, the pain of loss—these seem to give us little reason for rejoicing. But if you choose to rejoice anyway, your suffering will strengthen you in your faith walk, your joy will showcase the power of God, and your mourning will minister to others. You have

God's word that "He will give beauty for ashes, joy instead of mourning, praise instead of despair" (Isaiah 61:3, NLT). So if life presents you with a burn, a scar, or wilted grave flowers…rejoice!

> *Rejoice in the Lord always.*
> *I will say it again: Rejoice!*
>
> PHILIPPIANS 4:4

Pure Gold

Sitting with this man of God
Looking at his life
A young man sent to a foreign land
With his children and his wife

For years he was found faithful
And if the truth be told
He came out pure gold

I've seen her age in beauty
I've seen God's truth unfold
For years she served Him fervently
Even when her call felt old

I've seen her in the fire
I've seen her stand so bold
And she came out pure gold

So hang on dear believer
He rewards those who endure
When you feel refining fire
You will know you'll become pure

For there's such a cloud of witnesses
Who applaud you when you hold
You'll come out pure gold

I have searched for inspiration
In the pages of my mind
And it's those who stood adversity
That encouraged me to find
Pure gold

You'll come out pure gold
Stay with the fight
And earn the right
For God's riches to unfold
You'll see many a trial
You'll be tried by the fire
And you'll come out pure gold

WORDS AND MUSIC BY JENNIFER ROTHSCHILD © 1993 ROTHSCHILD MUSIC (ASCAP)

Six

RUN *with* ENDURANCE

For several summers when I was a teenager, I attended a Christian camp in Black Mountain, North Carolina. One summer early in my blindness, I arrived at camp without my cane. It hadn't yet become an extension of my right arm, and I was still at a point where I didn't want it to be obvious that I couldn't see. So I muddled through without it by just going places I was familiar with.

One night, however, a group of us girls decided to t.p. the car of the cutest guy in camp. The plan was to pull the prank after dark, and there was no way I was going to miss out on the fun. I was as thrilled as the others as we carried out our covert operation. Our egos swelled with pride—until we heard the sound of a car coming toward us.

"It's camp security!" someone cried.

We immediately began to run. As we fled into the darkness, I instinctively grabbed a fellow escapee's arm. In our frenzied flight I lost my grip, lost the group, and lost my footing. I did, however, find a tree.

Smack!

I ended up in a ditch, totally disoriented and pretty sore. One of the girls quickly returned to help me, and we ran for home.

The apostle Paul tells us to "run with endurance the race that is set before us" (Hebrews 12:1, NASB). Believe me, I learned the hard way that we can never run with endurance when we're running where we're not supposed to be. If I'd resisted the temptation of that forbidden flirtation, I would have been safe in camp.

But sometimes we *are* in the right place. We're running the race God has marked out for us, and we're trying to run with endurance. So why is it that we sometimes still threaten to hit the wall?

It's because often there are unanticipated hurdles in our path that we can clear only by stripping away anything that could weigh us down or trip us up as we run. That's why in the same verse, Paul also tells us to "lay aside every encumbrance and the sin which so easily entangles us." Sin will get us off track and leave us disoriented, and before we know it, we can find ourselves in a ditch.

STAY ON TRACK

In 1991, Phil and I moved to Tallahassee, Florida, so he could pursue his Ph.D. This meant that he traded in his job and salary for the financial status of a graduate student. If you're unfamiliar with that status, I can sum it up for you in two words: *no dinero*. No, that isn't Spanish for *no dinner*—although it could have meant that on Phil's wages as a teaching assistant. It means "no money," which was a pretty accurate description of our finances—and the reason we had to call a family budget meeting.

Red pen in hand, Phil prepared to excise the expense of anything not essential to our new lifestyle. One of the first things cut from the list was fabric softener. We figured that as long as the clothes were clean, it really didn't matter if they were stiff or full of static.

I'll admit I was a bit disappointed. Because I can't see, I really don't care if my laundry is stained or discolored after I wash it. I just want it to smell good, and I'd grown accustomed to the fragrance of Bounce on my freshly laundered clothes. But it was a small sacrifice, and I got over my initial disappointment.

Or so I thought.

After a week in our new apartment, I grabbed a basketful of dirty clothes and headed for the laundry room. When I arrived, the room was empty except for me, my dirty laundry…and one big temptation. Someone had left behind an industrial size box of Bounce. It was so huge that even I could see it. It beckoned me. *Come, smell, partake....*

I dropped the basket in front of the washer and reached out to grab the box. *God knows how faithful I've been to keep our new budget!* I thought. *And He's left this here for me!* I was already drafting a letter for financial guru Larry Burkett to read on the air when a voice interrupted my thoughts.

That is not your fabric softener.

I didn't have to look around for the source of the voice— I knew!

You're right, Lord; that's not my fabric softener. I sighed and began to load the washer.

After I shoved in the last dirty dish towel and lowered the lid, I thought, *If this box of Bounce is still here when I come back to fill the dryer, I'll just assume that it was left here for me. After all, my God owns the cattle on a thousand hills. He even owns the hills! Surely He provided this Bounce for me!*

But as I walked back to my apartment, I heard the voice again. *That is not your fabric softener.* I gave a spiritual shrug and (reluctantly) agreed.

While I waited for the wash cycle to finish, I tidied up my kitchen, and as I swept the floor, I began to list my justifications. Finally I announced out loud the top five reasons I should take the fabric softener.

1. I want it!
2. If I take it, no one will ever know.
3. If it wasn't meant to be mine, why was it left there?

4. Blind people need good smelling laundry.
5. The Bounce would be a blessing to me.

(Note: when attempting to justify sin, be sure to use spiritual words like *blessing*.)

I put away the broom and headed back to the "integrity torture chamber." The Bounce was still there, demanding a response. I stared it down as I put the wet, crumpled laundry in the dryer. But before I shut the door, I turned back to that box and lifted the lid. *One sheet*, I told myself, *just one itty-bitty sheet.*

As my guilty fingers clutched it, I once again heard the voice. *That is not your fabric softener.* It was as if I'd been arm wrestling with God and finally my arm went limp.

You're right, Lord. It's not my fabric softener—not even one little sheet of it. I went back to my apartment without the fabric softener, but with a new sense of how sin can sneak in and trip me up.

Now don't miss the point. In the grand scheme of things it doesn't seem that taking a sheet of fabric softener is a big deal. After all, it's not like robbing a bank or stealing someone's husband! But every day we are challenged in the laundry rooms of life with issues of integrity and purity, and private thoughts that aren't submitted to the still, small voice of the Holy Spirit will eventually lead to public failures. We are to resist *all* sin, and Paul reminds us that God never asks us to do something that He doesn't empower us to do:

No temptation has overtaken you but such as is common to man; and God is faithful, who will not allow you to be tempted beyond what you are able, but with the temptation will provide the way of escape also, so that you will be able to endure it. (1 Corinthians 10:13, NASB)

We must learn to confront temptation and sin head-on by obeying God. Otherwise, what may seem to be molehills will become mountains in our path, making it impossible for us to run with endurance.

Running with endurance means not only resisting and repenting of sin, but also giving up things that can hinder our ability to run. Sometimes that means giving up a good thing, for even a good thing can become a weight if isn't the best thing.

SHED SOME WEIGHT

One Sunday morning after I'd had William the guide dog for several months, he and I were sitting attentively in our Bible-study group. Well, actually, I was trying to be attentive to the teacher, but it was awfully hard because William's attention was riveted on a grasshopper that had made its way into our room via an open door. William was determined to catch that critter—even if he had to knock over a stack of Bibles and three Baptists in the process! He slapped his paws forward and jerked his head in pursuit. I, of course, was holding him on a leash and could feel his every move. With each muscle twitch, I pulled the leash a little more firmly.

Well, the tension in the room and the tension in the leash gave all at once as William defied gravity and all seventy pounds of him pounced on the grasshopper. The Bible teacher recoiled as William surged forward. Phil quickly subdued the mischievous mutt, and everyone laughed.

Everyone, but me, that is.

My friend Lori, who was sitting next to me, knew exactly why I wasn't laughing, and she instinctively rose with me. We excused ourselves, leaving William with the class in the hope that he would "get some religion."

In the months after William and I arrived home from the dog school, things hadn't gone as well as I had hoped. One day he bolted up onto the platform at my church while I was singing. And once when we were at the mall, he relieved his bladder right in front of Petite Sophisticates. It was a mess! I didn't even know it was happening until some man graphically described it to me. Then I had to somehow manage to maintain my dignity while I cleaned up the mess. Believe me, at that moment this petite did not look or feel very sophisticated!

Many incidents like these over the previous months had made me feel like giving up trying to use a guide dog, and it all came to a head that Sunday. As soon as Lori and I entered the ladies' room, I burst into tears. "It's just not working," I cried. "This is more of a liability than an asset. I've never wanted to quit so badly before, but—I don't know if I should."

As she almost always does, Lori responded judiciously.

"Jennifer," she said, "if you were deaf, you'd want to wear hearing aids that fit your ears. It would be discreet and practical. I don't think you'd function as well with big ol' Mickey Mouse ears hanging on either side of your head." I giggled with relief at Lori's homespun Southern wisdom. "Giving the guide dog back doesn't mean you're giving up or giving in just because it's hard," she said.

Endurance isn't a virtue if you persevere just to prove you're not a quitter. The point of running with endurance is to run well and finish the race—to do God's will as we follow the course until we reach the finish line. This means that once in a while we have to assess our lives to see if there's anything we need to get rid of. Serious runners in a race don't carry ice chests and portable tape players. They don't carry a change of clothes just in case there's a change in the weather, and they definitely don't have a Happy Meal in hand. Tape players, Happy Meals, and extra clothes are all good things, but none of them are the best things to carry while running a race.

A guide dog is a good thing. I could trust William to get me safely where I wanted to go. But for me he wasn't the best thing, because instead of enhancing my ability to run, he hindered it. Any good thing can weigh us down if we substitute it for what is really best.

In order to run well, we must listen to God. He has great plans for us and knows the best way for us to succeed. "'For I know the plans that I have for you,' declares the LORD, 'plans for welfare and not for calamity to give you a future and a hope'" (Jeremiah 29:11, NASB). God is our Coach. He's run this way before, and He can guide us through the choices and help us over the hurdles.

RUN TO GOD

In the Gospels we see many needy people running to Jesus. Mark tells us about a rich young man who had a need and knew that Jesus could tell him how to meet it.

"As Jesus started on his way," Mark writes, "a man ran up to him and fell on his knees before him. 'Good teacher,' he asked, 'what must I do to inherit eternal life?'" (Mark 10:17). When Jesus answered by reminding him of the commandments that any upstanding Jewish citizen would obey, the man said, "Teacher…all these I have kept since I was a boy" (v. 20). Mark says that when the rich young man said this, "Jesus looked at him and loved him" (v. 21).

The man had led a decent, respectable life. But inheriting eternal life involves much more than respectability; it requires complete commitment to Christ. And because Jesus loved the man, He told him what he really needed.

"One thing you lack," He said. "Go, sell everything you have and give to the poor, and you will have treasure in heaven. Then come, follow me." Mark says that "at this the man's face fell. He went away sad, because he had great wealth" (vv. 20–22). This was not what the rich man had expected to hear, and he was not willing to strip down for the race.

Just like the rich man, we often run to Jesus and fall down before Him because we have needs that only He can meet. And Jesus looks at us and loves us. We feel His penetrating gaze and His enveloping love. But then we hear His words, and sometimes our faces fall and we go away sad because He doesn't tell us what we want to hear. What He tells us to do seems like too great a sacrifice.

But whatever that sacrifice might be, it's small compared to the prize we receive in His presence. So don't run to Him with preconceived notions or an agenda.

Just run to Him to be with Him.

Run to Him with abandon.

Fall before Him, and cling to Him alone.

He knows what you truly need, and you'll never be disappointed. In fact, you will be amazed and overwhelmed, just like the folks in Mark 9:15: "As soon as all the people saw Jesus, they were overwhelmed with wonder and ran to greet him." They saw something in Jesus that the rich man missed—something that was worth everything. When was the last time you caught a true glimpse of Jesus? If you truly see Him, you too will be overwhelmed with wonder, and you will run to Him.

Always remember that after you've run for a while, the race begins to feel long. As you pound the pavement, winded and weary, you can easily get discouraged and feel like dropping out before you reach the finish line. Charles Spurgeon, the great preacher, felt that way so often that he tried to resign thirty-two times! To keep in the race, I bet he had to remind himself of Hebrews 10:36: "Patient endurance is what you need now, so you will continue to do God's will. Then you will receive all that he has promised" (NLT).

Staying in the race takes something more substantial than not wanting to quit. It takes something more important than wishing our needs were met. It even takes something more gratifying than yearning to reach the goal. It takes a deep desire for God. David knew what it was to desire God and to run to Him. "My soul followeth hard after thee," he said (Psalm 63:8, KJV). Another psalmist described his longing for God this way: "As the deer pants for the water brooks, so pants my soul for You, O God" (Psalm 42:1, NKJV).

Do you remember what it felt like in P.E. class when you had to run laps around the perimeter of the basketball courts? I do! I know what it felt like to pant after running so hard. But what I really want to know is what it feels like for my soul to pant after God with the kind of intensity the psalmist describes. When we run to Him with that level of desire, we'll be breathless, and He will become the air we breathe.

Do you run after God with that intensity? Does your soul follow hard after God? Running after God will always be strengthening and motivating. When our souls follow hard after Him, He upholds us with His right hand (Psalm 63:8). I believe that running with endurance is easy when we run to God out of complete desire to know Him and to be with Him.

When I was eight years old, I ran to Jesus in my heart, and He saw me and loved me. He saw my greatest need, and He saved me. Now the path to Him is familiar and well-worn. I run to Him on it daily because I desire to know Him. Every day we have the opportunity to run with urgent desire to show Him that we love Him and want to serve Him. And even though we don't deserve it, when God sees us quicken our pace toward Him, He Himself runs to meet us.

GO FOR THE GOLD

During the 1992 Olympics in Barcelona, a young runner from Great Britain crouched in the block at the starting line, ready for the run of his life. Derek Redmond's lifelong dream was to win a gold medal in the four-hundred-meter run, and now he had made it to the semifinal heat. The gun sounded and Derek ran with all his might. He was running well...until a pulled hamstring sent him sprawling facedown on the track.

Determined to finish the race, Derek somehow got to his feet and began to hop toward the finish line. As he struggled, an older man made his way down from the stands. Showing the same kind of determination as the injured runner, he made his way through the crowds, pushing aside security guards. When he reached Derek, a great crowd of spectators watched Jim Redmond throw his large arms around his son. Jim stayed in his son's lane, supporting Derek the entire time, and when they crossed the finish line together, the onlookers were on their feet, weeping and cheering.

Derek Redmond didn't win the gold medal that day, but he walked away from the race knowing that he had a father who loved him too much to stay in the stands watching him suffer.

That's the kind of Father we have.

You know that, don't you?

He's a Father who loves us too much to stand back and watch us struggle and suffer. He comes down from the stands and joins us as we run.[1]

In Luke 15, Jesus draws a word picture of how God responds to us when we come to Him. He tells a story of a father with two sons. The younger of the two insisted that his father give him his inheritance early. Then he left home and squandered the money on reckless living. When the money ran out, so did his dignity, and he stooped to feeding swine so he wouldn't starve.

At last the son resolved to return home. "So he got up and went to his father," Luke tells us. "But while he was still

a long way off, his father saw him and was filled with compassion for him; he ran to his son, threw his arms around
him and kissed him" (Luke 15:20).

When our Father sees us making strides toward home,
He runs to meet us.

If the race seems too long and you begin to lose heart,
run to God, and He will run to you. "Come near to God,"
writes James, "and he will come near to you" (James 4:8).
He will strengthen you and help you finish the race.

In Hebrews 12:1, Paul says that you are surrounded by a
great cloud of witnesses, the great heroes of the faith who
have run that way before you. They are cheering you on,
because they know that the reward of running with
endurance is sure. When you cross that finish line, you'll not
only get the prize—you'll come out pure gold.

*I guide you in the way of wisdom and
lead you along straight paths.
When you walk, your steps will not be hampered;
when you run, you will not stumble.*

PROVERBS 4:11–12

To Be like You

Sometimes I feel just like a stranger
The things I think put me in danger
And I want so much to be
Constrained by purity
Oh, Lord, will I ever be like You?

Inside my mind there is an image
Of what the world expects to see
But regardless of my call
I still so often fall
Oh, Lord, will I ever be like You?

To be like You
In the quiet of my heart
To be like You
In the deepest private part
To struggle with my humanity
Yet to cling to purity
Is to be, to be like You

Sometimes I feel weakness defines me
Yet still I pray weakness refines me
But no matter what the case
I am desperate for Your grace
Oh, Lord, will I ever be like You?

To be like You
In the quiet of my heart
To be like You
In the deepest private part
To struggle with my humanity
Yet to cling to purity
Is to be, to be like You

Seven

FALL *Down*...
GET UP

M y shining moment as a communication major at Palm Beach Atlantic College occurred in Professor McGee's "Fundamentals of Acting" class in the fall of my junior year. By then I had already muddled through the basics of blocking, character development, and improvisation, and there was one thing I knew for sure—Katharine Hepburn I was not!

But one day Professor McGee announced that he was going to teach us the art of skillful falling, and suddenly I felt confident. *Yes!* I thought. *Finally, something I'm good at!* When you're blind, falling comes with the territory, and by then I'd had lots of experience at it.

I'd fallen up stairs.

I'd fallen into holes.

I'd fallen down hills.

I'd fallen just about everywhere.

Now I was ready to show my stuff!

After Professor McGee taught us to fall convincingly but safely, he set the scene for us. We were a group of townspeople all busily doing our jobs. Unbeknownst to us, there was a murderer among us, and when he caught our eye, he would wink, meaning *Bang! You're dead!* Then we were to fall to our demise as we'd been taught. Because I couldn't see, Professor McGee said that instead of winking, the murderer would tap my back.

The professor gave each of us a prop to use in our improvisation. Mine was a broom, so when he yelled "Action," I began to sweep. All around me my classmates busied themselves with their tasks. Suddenly one of them fell. Within minutes, another one went down. Professor McGee threaded his way through our band of thespians, monitoring falls and carefully stepping over fallen students.

I heard a young man fall to my right and felt his feather duster land on my foot. Then I heard Professor McGee moving toward me, and soon I felt the pat of death. The moment to display my falling prowess was at hand, and as luck would have it, the professor was right in front of me. He would have a front-row view of my acting talent. Without hesitation, I folded my knees and collapsed my shoulders—and down I went, all in one relaxed, fluid, flawless fall.

But Professor McGee didn't get to witness my glorious moment. Yes, he was standing right in front of me—but not for long. When I let go of the broom, it landed on his...I mean between his...well, let's just say he doubled over in pain and then staggered off to his office trying to catch his breath.

While my classmates convulsed in laughter, I lay there for a moment not quite sure what had happened. I only knew that right after class I was going to the registrar's office to change my major to psychology. Oh, it was so embarrassing!

When we fall in our faith walk, we can also end up surprised, confused, and embarrassed. Falling isn't anything we plan. It just happens. Something trips us up, and down we go. And sadly, falling is not a one-time deal. We're all going to encounter lots of spiritual stumbling blocks. Some of these may just cause us to stagger, but others might result in a nose-first face plant on the ground. When that happens, it hurts. And unfortunately, our fall can hurt others, too. (Just ask Mr. McGee!)

To avoid falling, we need to learn more about why it happens. Since I'm a card-carrying frequent faller (in the physical sense), I've learned a bit about it. Perhaps what I've learned can help you.

What Makes Us Fall?

It was the end of spring semester, time to say good-bye to my college buddies for the summer. Soon my dad would arrive to transport me home, so I began packing all my worldly goods. I placed my B. J. Thomas and Amy Grant cassettes neatly in boxes. I carefully rolled up my rainbow posters and placed them in cylinders. I meticulously arranged my twenty-two pairs of shoes in their individual boxes and stacked them up. (Oh, was I prissy)! At last everything was ready for Dad and the U-Haul.

When Dad arrived, he surveyed my stuff and then issued marching orders. He told me which items to take and in what order. We must have made thirty treks up and down those familiar dormitory stairs. Finally only my hanging clothes were left. They were my passion—my very identity!—and with so much at stake, I took charge. I told Dad which clothes to take first and how he should carry them.

I saved the best for last—my nicest suits, dresses, and pantsuits. I was certain that I was the only one who could carry them correctly and put them in just the right place. I folded the generous stack over my arm and headed down the stairs.

"Wait, I'll come get those," my dad called out.

"Oh no, Dad, I'm fine," I replied. Confidently, I continued speeding downward.

"Be careful," he called again. "You're going too fast."

"Really, Dad. I've got them. I'm fine." And I thought I was! I practically pranced down those stairs with my treasures. I was in charge, in a hurry, and invincible. I was also just three steps from the bottom when I lost my footing and began to tumble.

In the few seconds it took to complete my descent, all I could think about were my beloved clothes. Soaring through the air, I imagined the damage about to be inflicted on my wardrobe, and instead of dropping the clothes so I would have a soft landing field, I held them high to keep them out of harm's way. The Olympic runner falling across the finish line with torch held high—that was me! (Liz Claiborne should have personally thanked me for my selflessness.)

Mentally and physically unbalanced, I collapsed under the weight of freshly dry-cleaned rayon. The real casualty was a broken ankle. But I think what hurt most was my shattered pride. I'd always heard that "pride goes before a fall," but before that day, I had assumed that it was just a figurative expression.

When I thought back on that incident, I could see a number of reasons why I fell, and it occurred to me that they are the very things that can cause us to fall in our spiritual walk as well. Learning to recognize these stumbling blocks can help keep us upright.

Stumbling Block #1: Pride

I did not take the stairs seriously enough, and I took myself much too seriously. Sometimes when we're familiar with life's routine, we don't consider the potential pitfalls in our path. Pride can seep in and convince us that we are in charge, sufficient, and independent. Proverbs 18:12 reminds us that "before his downfall a man's heart is proud, but humility comes before honor." That also goes for the heart of a female obsessed with fashion! Clothing ourselves in humility protects us from falling, and a little humility is far less painful than a lot of humiliation.

Are you prancing with pride, or are you walking humbly with your God?

Stumbling Block #2: Priorities

I protected the wrong thing. Yes, my life's savings were tied up in that mangled mess of material that landed on top of me at the bottom of the stairs. But was it really worth a broken ankle? I suspect that if my priority had been safety instead of vanity, the result of the fall would have been different, or perhaps I wouldn't have fallen at all. "Be careful how you walk," the apostle Paul warns us, "not as unwise men but as wise" (Ephesians 5:15, NASB). We'll be secure in our spiritual walk when we recognize what is *truly* important and allow Him to direct us.

Do the right priorities direct your steps, or do misplaced ones cause you to stumble?

Stumbling Block #3: Preoccupation

I was in a hurry. In my rush to complete my task, I failed to follow the disciplines that allow me to navigate safely, like counting the stairs and holding on to the rails. Sometimes schedules and the pressing demands of life set us up for a fall. Being busy, even with good things, can distract us from the best.

When God commands us to "be still" (Psalm 46:10), it's so we'll take time to learn about Him. When we do this, the frenzied pace of life is less likely to lead to a fall. If we learn to schedule stillness into our lives, we'll find rest in the rat race as we lean into Him.

Is your discipline in your calendar, or in your heart?

Stumbling Block #4: Pressure

I carried too much stuff. I'd obviously forgotten how the limitations of my blindness affected my ability to walk with an unusually heavy load. It's easier to keep our balance when we monitor the weight of our cargo.

We all need to measure how much we can carry in view of our life situations. Stress inevitably depletes us and leaves us vulnerable to a fall, while keeping a sense of balance not only reduces our chance of falling, but also speeds us on our way. The psalmist said, "I run in the path of your commands, for you have set my heart free"(Psalm 119:32). When we are unencumbered by the stresses of life, we too are free to run.

Are you weighed down with the load you carry, or is liberty your lifestyle?

Once we recognize and learn to avoid these stumbling blocks, it's easier to keep from falling. But unexpected potholes in life can sometimes still trip us up, so it's important to learn how to get back up again when we falter. Why do some people quickly recover from their falls and move on, while others remain prostrate and immobilized after hitting a bump in the road of life?

I'm glad you asked.

Understanding how to get up is as important as learning why we fall. The two go together.

How Can We Get Up?

If the bad news is that sin can trip us up, the good news is that we can get up again. Proverbs 24:16 tells us that "though a righteous man falls seven times, he rises again." When I let pride take over, I stumbled and fell. But I learned from that fall. I was able to look back on it, see what caused the tumble, and ask God to help me avoid it in the future. Once I'd repented, I was able to move forward with renewed confidence.

I'm reminded of a couple of familiar people in the Bible, both of them kings—David and Saul. Here's the JAV version (that's Jennifer's Abridged Version) of their stories.

King Saul failed to destroy the Amalekites as God had commanded. Then, when the prophet Samuel confronted him, he was unwilling to admit his sin and repent of it. Instead, he made excuses and placed blame on others. God was so grieved by his willful disobedience that He withdrew His blessing from Saul's reign. In other words, Saul's sin caused him to fall, but his refusal to acknowledge it and repent kept him lying flat on the ground.

Read the rest of Saul's story in 1 Samuel 15, and then compare it to the story of David in 2 Samuel 11. King David not only failed to lead his people in battle as God had commanded, but he compounded that sin by committing adultery with the wife of Uriah, one of his officers. If that wasn't bad enough, he then attempted to cover up his sin by having Uriah killed.

Unlike Saul, however, David's sin broke his heart. His prayer of repentance clearly reveals why he recovered from his fall: "I know my transgressions, and my sin is always before me. Against you, you only, have I sinned" (Psalm 51:3–4). David bounced back after his fall because he humbled himself and repented.

Both Saul and David had pretty nasty falls, but it was their heart's response to the sin that determined whether they would get up. The Bible tells us that David was a man after God's own heart (1 Samuel 13:14). If a man like David felt it necessary to ask God to create in him a pure heart, how much more do we need to ask for the same thing? We need cleansed hearts to keep us choosing the right path. Our feet will tread the paths our hearts pursue.

WHERE ARE WE WALKING?

If you're walking through a flowerbed and you fall, you can pretty much assume that you'll end up smelling like a rose. But if you're strolling through the city dump and you trip over an old tire, all the Tide in the supermarket won't be able to remove the stench.

When I was in the ninth grade, my family visited my grandparents. My granddaddy had several stout hunting dogs. While my brothers played, I tiptoed over to the dog pen. I opened the gate and, once inside, closed it quickly behind me. Then the party began. Were those dogs happy to see me! It was canine chaos. Vying for my attention, those big hounds began to jump up on me to lick my face, and almost immediately, they knocked me to the ground. As I lay there, I noticed a peculiar aroma filling the air. Actually, it would have been hard not to notice, since I was lying in its source. The happy dogs were prancing all over me, leaving behind their smelly reminder that I had fallen in the *wrong* place.

As I discovered in the dog pen, we need to be careful where we walk. We must choose our paths wisely on our faith walk as well. Sometimes a path may appear harmless, but if you stumble there, you might end up in quicksand. "There is a way that seems right to a man," says Proverbs 14:12, "but in the end it leads to death."

I have a friend who used to enjoy Internet chat rooms. They seemed innocent enough—until she become emotionally involved with a fellow chatter and found herself drowning in the quicksand of adultery.

I'm not saying that we can't chat on the Internet; we just must be mindful of our individual weaknesses. A path that is harmless for one may be deadly for another. You can't become a chocoholic if you never plant a Hershey's kiss on your lips, and it's impossible to get into credit card debt if you don't own those persuasive little pieces of plastic.

"In the way of righteousness there is life; along that path is immortality," says Proverbs 12:28. Where do you walk? Does each step lead you toward life, or does it lead you toward death? If you stumble there, will you fall on the Rock, or will you end up sinking like one? We need to choose wisely where we walk.

Who Is Walking with Us?

Okay, by now it's obvious: I'm into falling! Although most of my falls haven't been intentional, there have been times when I have chosen to fall.

One time was when Philip and I had been married for about six years. We were on a vacation in Pigeon Forge, Tennessee, where a seven-story bungee-jumping platform caught my husband's eye. This triggered him to challenge me. I believe his exact words were: "You would *never* bungee jump!"

"Would so," I shot back.

"Would not!"

"Would so!"

"Would not." Then we began to exchange chicken sounds—you know: *pok, pok, pok!*

We may have been married for six years, but we were acting like six-year-olds. As a result of our childish banter, I ended up buckled in a safety harness and tied to a bungee cord. There I was—seven stories above common sense! And when the platform attendant said "Jump," I did! At first the falling was euphoric. I felt free, yet secure; weightless, yet strangely grounded. I actually liked it until the bungee stretched to its full extension and jerked me back into the inescapable reality that I had just broken the law of gravity and was now falling *up*.

In many ways life is like bungee jumping. We fall down. We get up. What makes the difference is what we are tied to. The reason I felt secure in my seven-story fall was that I knew I was tied to something immovable. As believers, our security is found in the law of spiritual gravity. Never heard of spiritual gravity? That's okay, neither had Isaac Newton, but boy, did he need it. We all do.

When Christ found us, we had already fallen, just as if we had jumped off a seven-story platform—tied to nothing. We were doomed, with no hope of recovery. Then His forgiveness became our bungee cord. When He redeemed us, He fastened us to Himself, wrapping us safely in the unbreakable cords of His great salvation. As the writer of Hebrews tells us, "We have this hope as an anchor for the soul, firm and secure" (Hebrews 6:19).

Once we are fastened to Christ, our heavenly Father lovingly guides us as we learn to walk with Him. Jude assures us that He is a reliable companion, one we can hang on to as we travel life's journey: "To him who is able to keep you from falling and to present you before His glorious presence without fault and with great joy" (Jude 1:24).

My decision to bungee jump wasn't the only time I've chosen to fall. In fact, I deliberately fall on a regular basis. Let me explain.

I know that it's hard for fully sighted people to imagine what it must be like to walk in the dark every day. And I know that they wonder how a blind person can carry out daily routines, handle a career, or raise kids. I know, because I was once fully sighted. I understand both worlds.

I admit that some days the weight of blindness falls heavy upon me. Sometimes even a simple thing like wearing matching socks can seem like a monumental challenge. *How will I get to the grocery store?* I ask myself. *Who will read my mail to me and clip the baby's fingernails?* When those times come, blindness becomes an uninvited guest that stifles my dreams by turning ordinary routines into such extraordinary tasks that they leave me worn out and discouraged. On those mornings, when the list of questions is longer than the list of answers, my fatigue seems more powerful than my faith, and not even sheer grit seems enough to propel me out of bed to face the day.

So guess what I do?

Before I get up, I fall down.

Yes, you read that right: Before I get up, I fall down! The *ultimate* fall is the one that happens in my heart when, with complete abandon, I yield my entire self and fall before my Father. He finds me there in my weakness and lovingly lifts me, reminding me of what the prophet Isaiah wrote:

> "How can you say the LORD does not see your troubles?... Don't you know that the LORD is the everlasting God, the Creator of all the earth? He never grows faint or weary.... He gives power to those who are tired and worn out; he offers strength to the weak." (Isaiah 40: 27–29, NLT)

That's the really wonderful thing I've learned about falling: On days when I can't rise, He *carries* me. God's great love for us is there to sustain us even when we can't get up after we fall. If you make sure that your first fall every morning is the one in which you surrender yourself completely to Him, you will find strength for the journey.

> *Cast your cares on the LORD and he will sustain you;*
> *he will never let the righteous fall.*

PSALM 55:22

Unfailing Love

I will trust in Your unfailing love
My heart rejoices in Your salvation
I will sing unto the Lord
For He has been good to me

Your goodness like the rainfall
Washes over me
I dance beneath the starlight
As You're dancing over me
Joy is now my heartbeat
Freedom is my song
So I soar on the wings of Your love

I will trust in Your unfailing love
My heart rejoices in Your salvation
I will sing unto the Lord
For He has been good to me

WORDS AND MUSIC BY JENNIFER ROTHSCHILD © 1997 ROTHSCHILD MUSIC

Eight

DANCE *the* NIGHT AWAY

If Webster were to allow me to make one spelling change in the English language, it would be this: I would change the third *e* in *independence* to *a*, and then the word would read *independance*. I like it so much better that way, because when the last five letters spell *dance,* the word makes me think of a life that is joyful and free. But then two other words would also end in *dance: dependance* and *interdependance.*

See, it's all a dance!

It's just a matter of listening to the music and learning how to respond.

Phil and I celebrated our tenth anniversary aboard a cruise ship. After our trip through the dessert line at the first midnight buffet, we realized that we were going to have to do something to burn all those extra calories. So I donned sequins, and off we went to the dance floor. It didn't take us long to realize that we needed lessons, and along with several other couples, we met with the dance instructor in the ballroom. *This will be fun,* I thought. Even though Phil and I had never danced before, I was determined to take the risk and not be self-conscious.

The music began, the instructor described and demonstrated each step we were to take, and Phil clumsily imitated her. I held on to him and tried to match his movements.

There we were: Phil, uncoordinated. Me, blind. We stepped on each other's feet and bumped into other dancers—and we weren't even doing the two-step or the bump. We were quite a spectacle!

After a while, we relaxed and began to follow the rhythm of the music. Soon we were actually dancing. It would have been less embarrassing for me and much safer for the other dancers if I'd never fox-trotted onto the scene, but oh, what I would have missed! It was worth risking my composure and feeling clumsy, because dancing made me feel surprisingly free. Yes, I depended on Phil for my every move. But we knew each other so well that when we connected in the movements of the dance, it felt fabulous!

There's a lot to be said for depending on others and becoming interdependent. But there are some dance lessons I've had to learn the hard way.

CELEBRATING IN-DEPENDENCE DAY

Like any other eighteen-year-old, I saw going away to college as a major step on my road to independence—to making my way in the world just as others did. As a freshman at Palm Beach Atlantic College, my greatest desire was to blend in. I didn't want to be known as "the new blind girl." I just wanted to be known as the new girl.

So I loved the fact that, as often as not, it wasn't obvious that I couldn't see. It was as if I could hide the painful reality of my blindness behind a facade that made me feel "normal."

One afternoon near the end of freshman orientation, after being tossed from meeting to meeting all day, I felt educated, irritated, placated...and dilapidated! Worn out, I decided to spend a few moments alone in the chapel before the final orientation meeting.

The campus was located on the intercoastal waterway in West Palm Beach, and the chapel was in the waterside amphitheater. To get to it, I had to cross Flagler Drive, a busy four-lane thoroughfare. By then I was accustomed to listening for the ebb and flow of traffic, so I stood confidently on the edge of the curb, ready to cross. But I didn't extend my cane, because I really didn't want the drivers of the passing cars to know I was blind. I could just imagine what they would think: *What is she doing? How dangerous!*

So I waited until I heard a lull in the traffic, took a deep breath, prayed...and *ran!* One lane, two lanes.... *Whew!*

What I didn't know was that the cars in the third and fourth lanes were going the opposite direction. I was terrified. I couldn't tell what was coming from where. I almost ran into a car, and the driver slowed just long enough to yell some choice locker-room words at me. I was humiliated, but I made it safely across. I'm sure my secret service angels filed an official complaint: *You didn't tell us we'd signed up for hazardous duty!*

I staggered into the amphitheater and collapsed into a seat. No one else was there. Not even my common sense had joined me—I'd left that on the other side of Flagler Drive. As my adrenaline rush faded and I began to think about what I'd done, a wave of nausea swept over me. *What did I think I was doing? How dangerous! I'll never do that again, God, I promise!* And boy, did I mean it! That close call squelched my desire to look normal and be independent.

Sitting there all alone in the Chapel by the Lake, I realized that independence is not all it's cracked up to be. In our search for it, we often end up in isolation. The same is true when we act independently of God. But fortunately, the unintended consequences of our self-reliance can often reveal our need for a helper, someone to rescue us—a Savior.

After I repented and started to regroup, I suddenly realized that I had no way to get back to campus. My meeting was in twenty minutes, and I was stuck. Now I knew I'd really blown it. *Will I even make it back before curfew?* I wondered. Hoping that a fellow student would walk by, I decided to stay put. I continued to pray as I listened for pedestrians.

Five minutes passed. Silence.

Ten minutes. Silence.

Far from blending in, I was totally alone, and I imagined college staffers out looking for the new blind girl.

A deep voice behind me interrupted my thoughts: "Miss, do you need help?"

I spun around. *Is it that obvious?* I asked myself.

It was a police officer. "Well…actually…," I stammered. Then, swallowing my pride, I told him all about my mortifying misadventure. When I finished, the policeman was really excited.

Excited?

Well, as it turned out, he had a story to tell, too—and it was even better than mine! He told me that he was scheduled to work security for the six o'clock service at the chapel and that he'd been home watching a football game when suddenly he became very distracted and felt an urgency to leave for work— more than an hour early. He told me he was a Christian and said he knew that God had been nudging him to go. Now he knew why, and he could hardly contain his excitement.

I was stunned. A stubborn, self-absorbed eighteen-year-old girl sat by the water and prayed. A kind and merciful Father answered. An obedient and loving policeman came to my rescue.

I wish I knew that officer's name. But I do know his

heavenly Father's name. It's Jehovah-Jireh, the God on whom I depend. That day in the chapel was my in-depen-dence day—the day when the fact that I had lost my inde-pendence was seared upon my heart. But it also catapulted me into the arms of God, changing my longing for indepen-dence into a desire to be a dependent daughter.

"My God will meet all your needs according to his glori-ous riches in Christ Jesus," Paul assures us in Philippians 4:19. Because the Lord is who He says He is and does what He says He will do, I know that I can depend on Him to meet *all* my needs—including my need to feel normal and to blend in.

RISKING WHAT YOU CAN'T LOSE

We can depend fully on the name of the Lord because His name bears His character. But sometimes we are only mildly acquainted with His name—we *know of* Him. God, on the other hand, is intimately acquainted with us—He *knows* us. The psalmist reminds us of that:

> O LORD, you have searched me and you know me.
> You know when I sit and when I rise;
> you perceive my thoughts from afar.
> You discern my going out and my lying down;
> you are familiar with all my ways.
> Before a word is on my tongue you know it com-
> pletely, O LORD. (Psalm 139:1–4)

One of our most basic needs is to be known. Yet human companionship cannot provide the kind of complete knowing that our soul craves. God alone can do that because, as our Creator and our constant companion, He knows us completely. If we're truly honest, we have to admit that our desire to be known by Him is far greater than our desire to be independent.

Even though I have sometimes ended up isolating myself by choosing to be independent, I have more often felt isolated because independence has chosen me. Blindness may keep me in a state of physical dependence, but I feel the sting of independence most in the spiritual realm. Why? Because I have an overwhelming sense that blindness is a burden not to be shared.

Part of the isolation is a natural result of the fact that for most people blindness is an enigma, a mystery comprehensible on a cognitive level but baffling on an intuitive level. I find that pragmatists tend to casually dismiss it, while the tenderhearted are apt to enter into it with a degree of sympathy that prohibits real connection. Some even romanticize it, marveling at how "perceptive" I must be or how acute my other senses are. People like these think that every blind person longs to feel other people's faces.

Blindness, however, is just one of many things that can create islands within us. We all find ourselves in situations that make us feel isolated. Deep down they create a degree of separation from others because we feel that *no one else can truly understand our circumstances.*

As a result, a feeling of loneliness descends.

It's not an emotional loneliness produced by human feelings and urges, but a sort of soul-loneliness that makes me cry out to be connected by the cords of empathy to Someone who understands without words or explanation.

Sometimes I think that is why I can see God so clearly. Jesus is never fascinated by what I see or don't see. He doesn't marvel from a distance at how I've compensated.

He just knows.

He knows utterly. He knows intimately. To be understood by Him like that is to rest and revel in a place that never needs description. To wander endlessly through His secret place is a sort of freedom that I will never know in the physical realm.

If the isolation that accompanies blindness compels me to a deeper connection with God, I am the richer. All of us need to treasure anything within us that makes us feel just a little detached from the greater arena of human experience, for it may be the one thing that God mercifully gives us to tie us to Himself and fill our need to be known by Him.

A kind of unsought independence, soul-loneliness can teach us that we can depend fully upon the One who knows us so intimately. It should not only make us want to know God even as we are known by Him, but also compel us to risk becoming interdependent by allowing others to know us.

That's the life God designed us for. And since God

already knows us fully and we're eternally secure in Him, we're just risking something we can't lose anyway.

During college orientation, I'd learned that dependence isn't really so bad. A little later on in my freshman year, I learned that we would all be richer if we risked being interdependent. Early that fall, I called my mom with two important pieces of news.

"Mom," I announced excitedly, "I went out with this guy named Curtiss. And he wears an earring!"

I heard a gulp and then a faint sigh. I could tell that Mom was just as excited as I was—an earring, no less! His name wasn't even important; his earring was what mattered.

"And," I continued, "I got to drive Allison's car this morning!"

"You…*what!*" Mom's voice was no longer faint.

"It's true, Mom! We all piled in and went to the empty parking lot of a bank. It was so much fun!"

I wish I could remember my mom's exact words because I'll probably need a similar phrase to use on my kids when they do something foolish. However, I distinctly remember that she was not happy! The good thing was that after I told her about driving the car, dating the guy with an earring seemed completely harmless.

Well, I never did either again, but I did learn an interesting lesson from driving Allison's car. It was just another step in my dance lessons: Dependence is a good thing…and interdependence is even better!

Because Allison could see, I was totally dependent on her to tell me when to turn, when to brake, and how fast to go. And what did my dependence get me? An experience of a lifetime! It was fun—a kind of freedom I hadn't tasted yet—and I loved it! In the same way, we must depend fully on God for our direction in life. When we are willing to do what He tells us to do, we can park our pride at the curb, jump in for the ride of a lifetime, and find a fabulous freedom.

Yes, I had to depend on Allison to tell me how to drive, but she also had to depend on me to do what she said. Life is like that little car crammed with college students. We're all on the journey together, and our lives are filled with people who need us to be dependable. Our relationship with God inevitably affects our relationships with others, and they will find us fully reliable only when we depend fully on Him.

Of course, we all have times when we *aren't* completely reliable. When we don't depend on God for direction, we can fail others and ourselves. But no matter what is going on around us, when we've traded our independence for the freedom of fully depending on God and the fullness of depending on each other, we're ready to dance. We just have to listen for the music!

LISTENING FOR THE MUSIC

In 1996 we moved to Oklahoma. We had been there only a few weeks when the local TV station was all aflutter with warnings: The first tornado of the season was on its way. Our only TV was downstairs in the living room, so I trudged down the stairs, pillow and blanket in hand. I was going to watch the weather till the storm passed. By the time I settled in on the couch, the winds were howling, and the windows in our old town house were rattling with every gust. Just as the meteorologist had predicted, hail and lightning accompanied the wind, and the rain came in monsoonlike swells. It was enough to scare even this Florida girl!

As I cowered beneath the blanket, I began to notice another sound—one that Channel 9 news hadn't predicted. Between wind gusts and lightning crashes, I heard birds chirping. They sounded like newly hatched babies. Evidently, mama bird thought our chimney made a good home for her new arrivals. It was entertaining at first, but it quickly became annoying when Mama joined the chorus.

Mama bird was a full-throated whistler—and boy, was she loud! The soundtrack that evening was a dissonant mix of hail, thunder, wind, chirping, and whistling. Those birds never quit. Between swells, the storm grew silent, but not once did those birds stop singing.

Why aren't they scared? Don't they know there's a storm outside? This is not the time to sing!

But as the storm died down and I began to feel sleepy, it dawned on me. Those birds knew there was a storm, but they sang because they were birds. They responded to the life that was inside them, not the storm that was outside them.

Sometimes storms surround us, and the discordant sounds of our circumstances are so loud that they drown out the music. But deep inside us is a song that can rise from God's presence in our life. Even when the storm rages, our response can echo the melody of freedom within us.

So how can you dance when your independence has left you feeling lonely and isolated? How can you dance when you feel stuck in dependence? How can you dance when interdependence fails you and you find yourself in painful circumstances? Well, I figure we can all take dance lessons from Peter at this point.

You remember Peter. Jesus called him "the rock." Although that doesn't sound as though he was much of a dancer, I think the old fisherman could teach us all how to dance, because in the book of Matthew we see Peter learning to depend fully on the Lord of the dance.

Peter and the other disciples found themselves in the midst of a storm. The wind raged, tossing their boat and testing their courage. Suddenly, they saw someone walking on the surface of the water. After Jesus identified Himself, Peter immediately positioned himself for the dance.

"Lord, if it's you," he said, "tell me to come to you on the water."

"Come," Jesus said.

Jesus invites us to participate in the dance, too. No matter what storm rages around us, He beckons each one of us, just as He did Peter, to come, take a risk, and depend fully on Him.

You know the story. Peter stepped out of that boat into a perilous place that revealed his absolute need for God. Once there, he suddenly realized how hard it really is to dance. Especially over the waves. The Bible tells us that when he saw the raging wind, he became afraid and began to sink. Peter saw the storm raging because he took his eyes off the Lord of the dance. And when he did, the din of the chaos surrounding him drowned out the sound of the Lord's call to freedom.

Peter would have failed dance lessons at this point. He was ready to sink from the weight of his faithlessness. But he cried out three words—the same three words that will keep all of us in step with the rhythm of grace— *"Lord, save me!"* And immediately Jesus reached out and caught him (Matthew 14:28–31).

Sometimes our utter dependence makes us stumble awkwardly toward the arms of God. Sometimes we totter precariously as we learn to strike just the right balance in our interdependent relationships. God knows we are all weak and wobbly dancers, and He is always ready to extend His arm and reach out and catch us.

Lord, save me are my three favorite words in the book of Matthew. I spoke them as a frightened college student stranded at Chapel by the Lake. I whisper them quietly to my heavenly Father today as a wife and mother learning to walk by faith. They are the three most powerful words any of us can speak when we're learning how to dance, for they invite the Lord of the dance to teach us the real freedom that comes from full dependence on Him.

Don't wait for the storm to pass before you sing.

Don't wait for just the right situation in life before you let your spirit cut loose and dance.

You can dance in the dark or when the storm rages. Lean fully on the Lord of the dance. Listen closely, and you'll hear His music in your spirit. Rely on Him for your every step, and you'll experience the joy and freedom of dependence.

You turned my wailing into dancing;
you removed my sackcloth and clothed me with joy,
that my heart may sing to you and not be silent.
O LORD my God,
I will give you thanks forever.

PSALM 30:11–12

You Are Sufficient

When all that my eyes seem to see
Is the dark and the sadness in me
Deep in my heart I still know
That in everything I feel
Your strength serves to show
That You are sufficient for me
And You are the vision that I need in my eyes

When all I have come to count on slips away
My security's gone
Just as my lips start to pray
Emotions run so deep
That my heart can only say
That You are sufficient for me
And You are the vision that I need in my eyes

WORDS AND MUSIC BY JENNIFER ROTHSCHILD © 1990 ROTHSCHILD MUSIC (ASCAP)

Nine

FOLLOW *the* LEADER

One of the frustrations Phil and I experienced early in our married life was our inability to enjoy recreational activities together.

Phil loved sports! In fact, his claim to fame was that he once intercepted one of Doug Flutie's passes. I bet you didn't know I'd married such a jock! Oh, you know who Doug Flutie is! (Humor me.) He's been a popular pro quarterback. It's just that when Phil reminisces, he forgets to mention the fact that he caught the pass in 1977 during a Midget Might football game. Suffice it to say that the man is crazy about sports and wanted to find one we could enjoy together.

But what? Tennis? No, you both have to be able to see the ball. Golf? Maybe, but it's slow and expensive.

Canoeing? Ouch! Just the thought of it makes my wimpy arms ache. Jogging? Why? To run round and round in a vicious circle just to work up a sweat? I don't think so!

I guess it's becoming apparent that my lack of involvement in sports has little to do with my blindness. It has more to do with the fact that if I'm going to engage in something slow and expensive that makes me tired and sweaty, it's most likely to be shopping. Now that's healthy!

But Phil was determined, and one day he came home with something he was sure would remedy our (actually, his) frustration—a bicycle built for two. At first, I thought it was a great idea. I knew that I'd be on the backseat and that I could pretend to pedal and let him do all the work.

But then...I began to have second thoughts. Seated aft, I wouldn't be piloting the ship, and knowing that I would have no control on our maiden voyage made me feel a little uneasy. Even so, off we went!

TRAVELING IN TANDEM

I gripped my handlebars—and even began to pedal! It was a typical southern Florida late afternoon, breezy and warm. But as we rode down the intercoastal waterway in West Palm Beach, it was as hard for me to enjoy the trip as it was for Phil to hide his excitement. My uneasiness had given way to quiet panic.

My life is in his hands! I thought. *I don't have any control here!* Then it dawned on me: *I have to tell Phil how to maneuver this bike, or I'm a goner!* So I immediately began to bark commands from the backseat.

"Slow down!"

"I hear an in-line skater; veer left!"

"Move right. You're too close to the seawall!"

I went on and on! Oh yes, he could see perfectly; and oh yes, I was blind. But the woman in me knew my role: My job was to micromanage.

Suddenly, the bike came to an abrupt stop.

"Honey," a very tense, controlled voice said from the front seat, "Will you *please* stop telling me how to steer the bike?"

I said nothing. I wouldn't dignify that unreasonable request with an answer. How dare he? I know we hadn't been married all that long, but he still should have known that I was just doing my job. He had encroached on my turf, so I wielded the most effective weapon in the female arsenal—silent sulking. If my words couldn't put me in charge, my silence sure could!

Well, I was wrong on both counts, and when the ride ended, my analysis began. (The best part of having a degree in psychology is that I can analyze myself for free and no one else has to know how goofy I really am.) I admitted to myself that Phil was right and vowed that I'd try hard to relax and let him drive.

As we geared up for another ride the next night, I still felt uneasy. I didn't like feeling that I wasn't in control. But I was

determined—I was a changed woman! We took the same
path as the evening before, but this time I held on to the
handlebars a little more loosely and barely pedaled. (I liked
that part.) As we glided along, I began to notice the tang of
saltwater and feel the moist sea air as it caressed my cheeks. I
could smell the blooming gardenias and hear the majestic
palm fronds batting in the wind. The sound of children's
laughter and squeaky tricycles serenaded us.

I was pretty sure those gardenias hadn't bloomed
overnight. They had been just as fragrant yesterday. The
music of tricycles and palm fronds had been just as melodic
the night before. I simply hadn't noticed. On my first night
on the backseat of a bicycle built for two, I had been so consumed with being in control that I'd missed the essence of
the journey.

"Are you okay back there?" Phil asked after a while.
"You're so quiet."

"Oh yes," I sighed. This wasn't silent sulking; this was
wordless wonder.

Still, riding on the back of the bike is always just a little
unsettling. After all, it's a place where we aren't in charge,
and even when we trust the driver, we can still battle feelings
of wanting to be in control. Following the one on the front
seat is even more difficult when our journey takes us
through thorny places that make us feel particularly weak or
helpless.

The apostle Paul had some kind of affliction that made

him feel that way. In 2 Corinthians 12:7 he tells us that "there was given me a thorn in my flesh, a messenger of Satan, to torment me." Then he goes on to show us how to chart a course through thorns.

CHARTING A COURSE THROUGH THORNS

Scholars who have studied Paul's life have speculated that his thorn could have been a physical ailment like epilepsy or failing eyesight. Or perhaps it was his persecutors. Or maybe it was that he was single and lonely and longed for the companionship of a spouse.

We can't know for sure. I believe that the Bible doesn't tell us what it was because that information isn't necessary for us to understand what God wants us to know about thorns and how to manage them.

A thorn is anything that makes us feel that we are not in control of our lives. Paul had a thorn, I have a thorn, and you have a thorn. Thorns are a part of the fallen world in which we live. Unfortunately, we often don't deal with them very effectively. Here are a few examples of how we sometimes mismanage the weaknesses in our lives. Do any of these ladies look familiar?

First, there's the "matchless martyr." This helpless heroine wears her thorn as a badge of Christian martyrdom. She displays her thorn proudly for the benefit of all those "who have *no* idea what true suffering really is." She uses her thorn to create feelings of guilt and punish those whose lives are way too easy. She lifts up her thorn to God as her humble sacrifice, reminding Him and everybody else of her elite status in the kingdom.

Then there's the "perfect Pollyanna." This pristine princess disguises the scars her thorn has left. She plasters on a smile and hides her suffering behind a facade of religious rhetoric. Regardless of the pain her thorn might be causing, instead of crying, she emits a series of bouncy platitudes like "Praise the Lord" and "Isn't God good?"

And let's not forget the "determined denier." This militant mama has the lumpiest rug in town because she's constantly shoving her thorn under it—as if disowning it will make it go away. She's not into blaming or sugarcoating; she's into denying.

Of course, these are caricatures. But we can see ourselves and others in them because at times we can all go to theatrical lengths to disguise our weaknesses and feel in control.

Paul, however, shows us a better way to deal with our thorns. He didn't deny that he had a thorn, and he didn't pretend that he liked it. "Three times I pleaded with the Lord to take it away from me," he writes (2 Corinthians 12:8). I can understand that. I've felt that way before, and I bet that you have, too. Our thorns cause us pain and suffering, and like Paul, we need to lift them to God in prayer.

But like Paul, we should also be content with however God chooses to answer our prayer. The answer Paul received was the best answer God had to offer—but it wasn't to remove the thorn. God gave Paul something better. Even though Paul pleaded with God to take it away, God said to him, "My grace is sufficient for you, for my power is made perfect in weakness" (v. 9). Paul received the grace to deal with his weakness so God could show His strength through it.

A thorn should never be a platform for drawing attention to ourselves.

- If I used my blindness as a badge of martyrdom, I would be glorifying myself.
- If I sugarcoated the suffering associated with my sight loss, I would confuse people and distort the true message of God's grace. God *is* good, and He is worthy of our praise, but it is equally true that thorns hurt and it's okay to cry.
- Shoving my thorn under a rug would only trip me up. If I denied the frailty associated with my blindness, I would dismiss the strength of God that can abound in my weakness.

Only after I have admitted my insufficiency, yielded it to God, and received His grace do I have something to boast about. Paul continues:

Therefore I will boast all the more gladly about my weaknesses, so that Christ's power may rest on me.

That is why, for Christ's sake, I delight in weaknesses,
in insults, in hardships, in persecutions, in difficulties.
For when I am weak, then I am strong. (vv. 9–10)

Sometimes God delivers us *through* the thorns instead of
from the thorns. Why? So His grace can grow there. So His
strength can sustain us there. And so we can learn how to
travel in tandem with Him.

ABIDING BY PASSENGER PROTOCOL

Let's jump on the back of my bicycle built for two and see
how this works out in practice. On my second night of traveling tandem, I was able to trade in my desire for control for
the joy of following—but only because I had learned some
passenger protocol.

Let's take a look at what I learned.

Loosen your grip

On the first night I gripped the handles of the bike so
tightly that my knuckles turned white. In a frenzied, futile
attempt to stay in control, I grabbed what I thought I could
be in charge of and held it in a death grip. Don't we all do
this from time to time?

I used to do this with our closet. My husband and I
shared one, and let's just say that Phil never really understood the concept behind hangers. His side of the closet
looked like a group of men had been crammed in there

when the Rapture occurred. Just piles of shirts, belts, shoes, and crumpled pants—all left behind!

When I felt that I wasn't in control of my world, I aimed my sights at his closet. I grabbed on to that and nagged, fussed, and micromanaged until I was convinced that here, at least, was something I could control.

I thought that if only all his shirts were hung according to sleeve length and season, all would seem orderly in my world. I assumed that when all his pants were hung neatly in a row, I would breathe a little easier. But let's face it: I wasn't just trying to control his closet—I was trying to control him!

Well, that kind of control is a myth. It would be easier for me to get the toothpaste on my toothbrush back into the tube than it would be to control my husband or his messy closet. My behavior created only the *illusion* of control, and Phil became pretty *disillusioned* with me because of my controlling behavior. In the end, I still felt the insecurity of being out of control, and he felt the shackles of being overly controlled. I've since learned to grip the doorknob a little more loosely when I open the closet door.

Did you know that an unreasonable desire for control is just another form of greed? Jesus has a lot to say about greed. In the Gospel of Luke, He tells us of a rich man who had such abundance that he didn't have enough room to store it, so he tore down his old barns and built new ones— big as a half dozen Wal-Marts. When he was finished, the rich man said, "Soul, you have many goods laid up for many years; take your ease; eat, drink, and be merry" (Luke 12:19, NKJV).

This man fell for the illusion that he was in control of his world and that all was taken care of for years to come. He's called "the rich fool " because, unfortunately, he died that night and wasn't around to enjoy his bounty.

Greed, however, isn't reserved for material things. If we hold *anything* in our lives in a death grip, it's a manifestation of greed. It may make you feel as though you're in control, but it leads to death. A control freak never enjoys life—and people who share closets with control freaks don't enjoy life either! On the bicycle built for two, I was holding those handle bars in a death grip, and my knuckles turned white because it cut off the blood supply to my fingers.

We all need to be reminded not to choke the life out of things that aren't really important. Jesus said, "Do not worry about your life, what you will eat or drink; or about your body, what you will wear. Is not life more important than food, and the body more important than clothes?" (Matthew 6:25).

So hold things loosely and learn to rest.

Rest where you are

Paul's example of how to chart a course through thorns suggests that we rest in our weaknesses. Until we settle into the position where we've been placed by His grace, we'll never see His strength made perfect there. And we'll never experience the joy of the journey as we follow Him.

Yet instead of resting where God has placed us, lots of us resist. We do this by heaping guilt on others who don't seem to have it as bad, or perhaps by subjecting others to a litany of complaints.

Such behavior is a red flag signaling that we're resisting.

But part of learning to follow is flying the white flag of surrender. We surrender to the position in which God has placed us, and we surrender our behavior in that position.

When you stop to think about it, it takes an incredible amount of effort to gripe and micromanage. What an energy drain! Instead of creating burdens for ourselves by our negative behavior, we should unburden ourselves as we submit all to God and simply rest. Jesus said, "My yoke is easy and my burden is light" (Matthew 11:30).

If you feel that the weight of your circumstances is too heavy to bear, maybe it's because the burden is yours, not His.

On one of my travels, I sat next to a young woman on the airplane. It was her first time to fly, and I marveled at how remarkably calm she was. After a little small talk, I finally asked the question that had been on my mind since we met.

"Why aren't you nervous?" I asked. "Most people are scared, or at least uneasy, on their first flight."

Her answer struck me as very profound and a great example of what it really means to rest. "Well, I'm not a pilot," she said. "Even if something happened, I couldn't do anything about it. So I might as well just relax."

We could all learn a lot from that young college student. Many of us go through life resisting our circumstances because we operate under the mistaken notion that we are in charge. I once saw a bumper sticker that said "God is my co-pilot." That sounds spiritual, but it isn't true. The truth is that on our faith journey, God is the Pilot, and we must follow, not co-lead.

We are not in charge of the journey. We are called to restfully follow. Our Pilot is completely trustworthy. There's no need for us to fret, for He is capable of navigating us through all the turbulence of the journey. We can rest in the very situation where He has lovingly placed us. And when we do, we'll find the fabulous freedom of following.

Once I'd learned to rest on the backseat of the bike, riding in tandem was a pleasure. Instead of rigidly positioning myself for a life-threatening emergency, I decided to relax and enjoy the journey from where I was.

Follow the One in front

As a rookie rider on a tandem bike, I had to learn rather quickly that only one of us could be in front. I found that awfully frustrating because I love to be the one in charge.

For years my desire for complete control masqueraded as the socially acceptable trait of perfectionism. I once was a meticulous housekeeper, burning the midnight oil to make sure that even nonessentials like baseboards and blinds were immaculate. Much to the torment of my family and circle of friends, I insisted that everything in my home match perfectly. And when it came to my clothes, the standard was beyond perfection. I was a prototypical, type-A, firstborn perfectionist!

Well, I'm still a firstborn, but I'm recovering from my perfectionism, because it's really hard to be a blind perfectionist. Blindness has crucified the perfectionist in me, one nail at a time. To follow God, we need to die to our own desires, one nail at a time. "I have been crucified with Christ," Paul writes, "and I no longer live, but Christ lives in me. The life I live in the body, I live by faith in the Son of God, who loved me and gave himself for me" (Galatians 2:20). Our desire to be in complete control denies us the power to live a crucified life. God is the One in front, and living by faith means that God leads and we follow.

My problem on the backseat of a tandem bike wasn't my lack of control; it was my unwillingness to yield my desire for control. As we pedal along on our journey of faith, we struggle with the same tension. It's hard to let go of our desire to be in charge, but the life of faith requires us to trust in the Lord with all our heart and lean not on our own understanding (Proverbs 3:5). Learning to let go of control and willingly follow is essential for traveling the path God has chosen for us.

In the spiritual sense, the backseat of a tandem bicycle is a place of submission, where we yield control to the One who is trustworthy, capable, and knows exactly where we need to go. He alone can get us there by the best possible route. How silly it is for us who are shortsighted to bark commands at the One who sees all eternity.

Since God Himself goes before us and prepares the way, following His loving leadership is always the surest and safest way to travel.

"If anyone would come after me,
he must deny himself and take up his cross daily and follow me.
For whoever wants to save his life will lose it,
but whoever loses his life for me will save it."

LUKE 9:23–24

Satisfied

I'm satisfied with Jesus
I'm as happy as can be
I'm satisfied with Jesus
And Jesus is satisfied with me

I've heard it said a time or two
"I can't get no satisfaction"
And when I start to sing the blues
I have that same reaction
But in searching for significance
I've finally found the key
That Jesus is satisfied with the likes of me

I'm satisfied with Jesus
I'm as happy as can be
I'm satisfied with Jesus
And Jesus is satisfied with me

My soul is finally satisfied
For He is all I need
And that is why I testify
My spirit has been freed

Jesus has accepted me
My heart He's rearranged
No matter what the circumstance
My opinion doesn't change

I'm satisfied with Jesus
I'm as happy as can be
I'm satisfied with Jesus
And Jesus is satisfied with me

WORDS AND MUSIC BY JENNIFER ROTHSCHILD © 1990 ROTHSCHILD MUSIC (ASCAP)

Ten

LAUGH *at* YOURSELF

O ne afternoon, Joni's daughter came home from school after a long day of testing. Hannah was a first-grader, so this was her first experience with standardized tests.

"Well, Hannah," Joni asked, "how did the tests go?"

Hannah's response was tentative. "Fine," she said. But her face reflected her concern, and she quickly added, "Except that…well…Mom, I think I got an F in sex."

An F in sex? Joni asked herself. *What in the world is she talking about…and what in the world was on that test?*

When Joni questioned Hannah further, Hannah said that after she wrote her name at the top of the test booklet, the teacher came by and marked an *F* under her name next to the word *sex*.

"Honey," Joni said. "The F stands for *female*—not *fail!* They just wanted to know whether you're a girl or a boy. You're a girl, so your sex is female."

Hannah heaved a sigh of relief, and they both began to laugh.

What a perfect illustration of what it's like to be human! Often operating on incomplete information and with limited understanding, we do what is required of us, giving it our best shot. Yet when we're asked for a self-assessment, most of us cautiously respond, "Fine… I think I'm doing fine." Then all of a sudden…*wham!* A big F—failure! Even the smallest failure can take the steam out of our self-esteem.

So how do we keep our self-esteem intact when it's threatened by blunders that make us feel small or stupid? We all should have a plan because all of us will bungle something in life. Some gaffes are huge; others are small. But regardless of the size of the mistake, laughing is the wisest response. Archbishop Edward McCarthy once said that the ability to laugh at ourselves is a sign of maturity in the faith.

Why is it, then, that many of us find it so hard to laugh at ourselves? I think there are a couple of reasons. One is that we tend to take ourselves too seriously. Another is that we tend to give more weight to others' opinions of us than we do to what God thinks of us. Both things rob us of the humility that allows us to laugh when we feel humiliated.

Not long ago I had a makeup mishap that was really pretty funny—even though I sure didn't think so at the time!

The Key to Giggling at Gaffes

If you've ever had a bad hair day, you'll probably agree that we women tend to wear our self-esteem atop our heads. Now, you might assume that one of the fringe benefits of blindness is that you can't tell when your hair looks really bad. Not so! I don't have to see my hair in the mirror to know that it looks ugly—I can feel it!

I had just cut my hair. It had been pretty long and really big. One of my friends from Texas constantly commented that I had Texas hair. Oh, I did. It weighed as much as my first child and had gotten so big over the years that I needed to either get it cut or move to Texas. Well, I wasn't moving, so under the scissors I went! I was told that it looked cute, but I had trouble styling it.

This particular day I was preparing to speak at a local women's event. The hair was done—in fact it was over-done—and I knew it looked bad. Admitting defeat, I laid down my brush in frustration. Then I remembered something: A friend had given me lipliner and eyeliner pencils from the new cosmetic line she was selling. I don't usually wear liners, but under the circumstances I decided to use them. *It might give me a special look,* I thought, *and maybe no one will notice my hair.*

I meticulously applied the lipliner and then the eyeliner. I imagined how attractive I must look and, with bolstered confidence, headed for the door. As I passed through the living room, I spoke to my son, who was playing Nintendo. He obviously looked up at me when I spoke, because he said, "Mom, your lips are black."

"They are not black," I said. "This is raisin lipliner. It's just more dramatic than you're used to."

"Okay," he said, and went back to his video game.

Then I heard the garage door open. Phil had come to take me to my speaking engagement. He was a little late, and I ran to meet him. He came into the house just as I approached the door, and with more panic in his voice than I'd ever heard, he exclaimed, "Jennifer, your eyes are flaming red!"

Well, it was perfectly obvious at that point that I'd mixed up the makeup. Those were some excellent cosmetics. I had to scrub off the top layer of my skin to remove them. (Here's the practical application for the female reader: If you're having a bad hair day, just put lipliner on your eyes and eyeliner on your lips. I guarantee that it will give you a special look and that no one will notice your hair!)

Even though my mistake wasn't serious, I felt like a fool, and no one wants to feel that way. I couldn't laugh at my mistake because I took myself way too seriously.

Let's face it: We're all pretty serious about ourselves. Sure, we can sometimes struggle with a faulty self-image or low self-esteem, but believe it or not, deep down we still love ourselves. We all do! We love ourselves enough to care on some level what other people think about us. Don't panic—that's not an indictment of our spirituality; it's just part of being human. The problem occurs when we overdo it. Do you realize that taking ourselves too seriously is simply pride? *Ouch!* Now that *could* be an indictment of our spirituality!

Pride is our veiled attempt to protect our fragile ego from being exposed and feeling small. Deep down, what we really seek is honor. We want to be honored by others, and we want to know in our heart that we are worthy of honor. But pride never brings us true honor and respect...only humility does.

The Bible tells us that "a man's pride will bring him low, but a humble spirit will obtain honor"(Proverbs 29:23, NASB). Pride cannot laugh at itself. Only humility allows us to respond with a giggle to even the greatest gaffes.

Even though I always want to present a poised representation of who I am, sometimes that's just not possible, because I'm capable of doing some awfully embarrassing things. Proverbs 17:22 tells us that "a cheerful heart is good medicine," and believe me, I've made enough humiliating mistakes to learn that laughter really is the best balm for a bruised ego—even when my mistakes are a lot more embarrassing than just mixing up my makeup.

THE BEST BALM FOR A BRUISED EGO

I was on my way to Jacksonville, Florida, for a speaking engagement, and by the time my plane landed at the Atlanta airport for a short layover, I had a *big* problem.

My bout with kidney stones had occurred several months earlier, and anyone who has survived that torture will understand why I was determined never to let it happen again and why it's eight glasses of water a day for me. When the plane landed at 11:30 A.M., I had already consumed four of the eight and, well...*I had to go!*

No problem, I thought, *when the airport helper arrives, I'll ask her to take me to the ladies' room.* But when the flight attendant placed my hand on the arm of my escort, I knew something was wrong. *This arm can't belong to a female*, I thought. *The only thing fuller than this bicep is my bladder! My escort is a man!*

I decided that I would "hold it" rather than ask Mr. Muscle to take me to the ladies' room. I knew my layover was short, as was the next leg of my flight, so I began to pray for bladder grace. *Bladder grace?* Well, if you've ever needed it, you know exactly what it is. (Praying for bladder grace, however, includes a prayer of repentance for all the years you failed to do Kegel exercises.)

My escort and I arrived at my gate, and he seated me. Seconds after he left, an announcement came over the intercom: My flight was delayed! *Yikes!* My prayer for bladder grace became more fervent. As my sense of urgency intensified, so did my plea. But then it happened: I learned that there's a statute of limitations on bladder grace. I had reached it, and I was a desperate woman.

Because of my sight loss, my other senses are heightened, and as I sat there, I listened intently to what was going on around me. I felt certain that there was a restroom to my left across the thoroughfare. Desperate women do desperate things, and I flicked out my cane and walked gingerly (because of the bladder, not the blindness) toward the place where I heard all the voices trail off, as if they were entering somewhere. Soon I could hear suitcases rolling onto tile and the sound of running water. I was right! Relief was in sight…well, figuratively speaking.

Most airports have the same kind of setup for their facilities—a large opening in the wall with a bathroom to the left for women and one to the right for men. So I veered to the left, made the final turn into the restroom, and breathed a deep sigh of relief.

Then suddenly there was silence. Total, deafening silence.

Please tell me I'm not in the men's room, I prayed.

Make it so, I thought.

"I am not in the men's room!" I announced.

Maybe their left-brained circuitry had overheated from the shock, because at first all I heard in response were male voices stuttering, "Uh…uh…oh…uh…."

Then came the voices of three older women who had

quickly followed me into the bathroom. "Honey, honey," one of them cried, "you're in the men's room."

"Well, help her—she can't get out!" cried the second woman, who was obviously in charge of the rescue mission.

With seamless choreography, one grabbed my right arm, the other fastened herself fiercely to my left arm, and the two of them swept me away. The third lady stayed behind me, mumbling as she juggled the bags. Awkwardly, we shuffled around the corner into the ladies' room, where the Golden Girls led me to a stall. Three geriatric Rockettes and a blind woman hoofing it from the men's room to the ladies' room. We must have been quite a sight!

When I was once again seated at my gate, I felt my face flushed with humiliation. *The ladies at the senior center are going to hear about this for months,* I groaned. I kept thinking, *Oh no, I could be sitting next to the very guys from that men's room!*

But the longer I sat there, the funnier the bathroom incident seemed. I just kept picturing those men standing there like statues in a wax museum of the shocked and terrified. *Which was worse?* I wondered. *A blind woman watching them, or three women their mothers' age giving them the once-over?*

I began to laugh, and by the time I got back on the plane, my bladder wasn't the only thing that felt relieved— my heart did, too! Laughter truly is good medicine!

The Steam in Self-Esteem

When I had to be hustled out of the men's bathroom, my ego was bruised. I was very worried about what people would think of me and so embarrassed that I wanted to hide.

But guess what? In situations like that, God *wants* me to hide. He wants us all to hide—in Him! "You are my hiding place," says the psalmist. "You will protect me from trouble and surround me with songs of deliverance" (Psalm 32:7). When we hide in God, we realize that our sense of self is derived from His opinion of us, and that delivers us from fear of the opinions of others.

God takes each of us so seriously that He knows the number of hairs on our heads. He knew all the days we would live before they ever were. He knew that there would be bad hair days and days like the one in the men's room. He knew the times when we would look very silly and feel awfully stupid. But no matter how many embarrassing mistakes we make, God's opinion of us never changes. That's why our self-worth should never be based on how others perceive us or on what we see in the mirror. Instead, it should be based on the way *God* perceives us and on what we see in the mirror of His Word. True self-esteem comes from God's esteem, so when you feel humiliated, remember what God says about you:

    ~ You will never be rejected. (1 Samuel 12:22)
    ~ You are His very own. (Isaiah 43:1)

- You are honored and precious. (Isaiah 43:4)
- You are loved with an everlasting love. (Jeremiah 31:3)
- You are accepted by the Beloved. (Romans 15:7)
- You are purchased at great price. (1 Corinthians 6:20)
- You are a new creation in Christ. (2 Corinthians 5:17)
- You were chosen to be blameless in His sight. (Ephesians 1:4)
- You are His workmanship created for a great purpose. (Ephesians 2:10)
- You are defined by His righteousness. (Philippians 3:9)
- You are royal and holy. (1 Peter 2:9)

Do you see how serious God is about you? David was astounded by that realization:

When I consider your heavens, the work of your fingers, the moon and the stars, which you have set in place, what is man that you are mindful of him, the son of man that you care for him? You made him a little lower than the heavenly beings and crowned him with glory and honor. (Psalm 8:3–5)

Can you even fathom the truth that the God of the universe clothed Himself in humanity just to come find you because He loved you and you were lost? I believe that truly understanding how much God loves us and how committed He is to us will evoke true humility.

We may still struggle with feelings of inadequacy and embarrassment, but what we struggle with isn't the same thing as who we are! Part of the gift of being human is wrestling with the wrapping paper. Just because we sometimes feel inept when we blunder doesn't mean that we *are* inept! It means we're *human*. True self-esteem rests on who we are in Christ, and remembering what God thinks of us allows us to respond to our human failings with humility instead of humiliation.

Humility is the key to a healthy self-image because God is the One who puts the steam in our self-esteem. James reminds us that when we humble ourselves before God, He lifts us up (James 4:10). Realizing that God takes us so seriously that He hides us in Himself frees us from taking ourselves too seriously and from fearing what others may think of us.

And then we can laugh.

> *She is clothed with strength and dignity;*
> *she can laugh at the days to come.*
>
> PROVERBS 31:25

Find You Here

Here I am again
Back in the place I always run to
And I know that I will always find You here
I know that You will wipe away each tear

I know that in this place
I will always find Your grace
When I pray I know
I will always find You here

Captured by the moment of my prayer
Drawn by Your mercy to a place of gentle care
And I know that I will always find You here
I know that You will wipe away each tear

I know that in this place
I will always find Your grace
When I pray I know
I will always find You here

WORDS AND MUSIC BY JENNIFER ROTHSCHILD © 1990 ROTHSCHILD MUSIC (ASCAP)

Eleven

CRY WHEN *You* HURT

⁓

One dark, dreary January afternoon I received a dis-
heartening phone call. It was from Lori. When I
heard her somber, frail voice, I immediately
asked, "Did he die?"

Our beloved friend Thierry was valiantly fighting a losing battle with cancer, and we knew that a miracle was the
only remaining hope for healing this side of heaven. Our
hearts were heavy with sadness over his suffering, and they
were breaking for his wife, Diane, and their three small kids.

"Not yet," Lori whispered, "But Hospice tells us that it
will be sometime today."

Lori had faithfully attended to Thierry and Diane for many
months, so I specifically asked, "How are you, my friend?"

Finally she said, "I can't cry."

"Why not?" I asked.

"I don't know how to cry and still remain strong and hopeful, " she said.

Wow! I've felt that way before, and I bet you have, too. Lori echoed the sentiments a lot of us feel when our hope lies on a deathbed.

Over the years as I've struggled to learn how to handle all the emotions that accompany blindness—feelings of frustration, anger, loss, and sadness—God has tenderly taught me how to cry to Him, how to release my sorrow, and how to be strengthened by those very tears.

I think that I had to learn to cry because I misunderstood the purpose of tears. For a long time I mistakenly assumed that the weight of tears would undermine my strength. You've heard the phrase "reduced to tears." It makes it sound as though crying is the final, most debasing result of sorrow, as if our tears weaken us and make us smaller.

But that's not true.

Releasing our sorrow to God doesn't lead to weakness; it generates supernatural strength. Crying never washes away hope into an ocean of despair; it helps cleanse the eyes of our souls so we can more clearly see the source of our hope.

I'm learning that allowing myself to feel the weight of painful emotions—allowing myself to cry out to God even if I don't shed tears—enables me to roll the burden of those emotions onto Him. But before I could learn to cry, God had to open my spiritual tear ducts.

When Tear Ducts Are Blocked

When I was an infant, the doctors discovered that I was unable to cry. Oh, I went through the motions, but no tears ever came because my tear ducts were closed. The doctors had to surgically open them in order for me to cry.

As it turned out, I needed the same thing spiritually.

For years after I became blind, my immaturity and pride kept me from the healthy response of crying. I needed God to lay His healing hand upon me and open my spiritual tear ducts.

One day when I was in my early twenties, Darlene, my next-door neighbor and one of my best friends, came for one of her frequent visits. I had just finished vacuuming, and as Darlene settled onto the couch for a chat, I wound up the vacuum cleaner cord and turned to put the vacuum in the closet. As I swung it toward the closet, I did a full body slam into the open door.

"*Ouch!*" Darlene yelled.

I remained unusually silent.

"What? What?" she asked. "Are you okay? Why don't you say something?"

With bridled control, I calmly responded, "If I don't *act* like it hurts, it won't hurt so much."

Years later, I recall that painful moment and just shake

my head. *What was I thinking?* I had obviously overdosed on pop psychology. It's just plain silly to think that not acknowledging an injury will somehow ease the feeling of pain. Sometimes life hurts! And when it does, we can admit our pain and cry.

Now, let me be clear. When I speak of learning to cry, I don't necessarily mean only the physical act of shedding tears. I mean allowing ourselves to have an honest, heartfelt response of sorrow or grief when it is warranted. Some of us cry over Folgers coffee commercials, and some of us don't cry even at funerals. Crying is as individual as each personality. But in order to really experience life, we need to abandon our pride and reservations and humbly admit our sorrow, our pain, and our needs. All of us need God's touch on our spiritual tear ducts. To be tenderly in touch with our own humanity allows us to cry, and when we do, we feel the strengthening hand of our Great Physician.

Thierry went to heaven on January 16, 2002. At his funeral two days later, my friend Lori cried. She released her sorrow to God as she cried tears of sorrow mixed with tears of joy. And I have a feeling that as she cried, Jesus wept, too.

WHEN JESUS WEPT

"Jesus wept."

I take great solace in this, the shortest verse in the Bible (John 11:35). These two words, if correctly understood, can help us learn to cry.

The Gospel of John tells the story of Jesus' beloved friend Lazarus of Bethany. When Jesus was teaching beyond the Jordan, Lazarus fell gravely ill. His sisters, Mary and Martha, sent word to Jesus, but the Lord stayed where He was for two more days before setting out for Bethany. By the time He arrived, Lazarus had already been in the tomb for four days.

Martha greeted Jesus first. Consumed by grief, she said, "Lord, if you had been here, my brother would not have died" (John 11:21). When Mary's turn came, the Jews who had come to console the sisters followed her from the house. As they approached Jesus, they were all weeping, and Mary echoed her sister's words, "Lord, if you had been here, my brother would not have died" (John 11:32).

John tells us what happened next:

> When Jesus saw her weeping, and the Jews who had come along with her also weeping, he was deeply moved in spirit and troubled. "Where have you laid him?" he asked.
>
> "Come and see, Lord," they replied.
>
> Jesus wept. (John 11:33–35)

What a startling passage! Jesus not only allowed man's sorrow to enter Him, but He entered so deeply into man's sorrow that He outwardly expressed His deep emotion. What an amazing God!

You and I are no different from Mary and Martha. We all grieve. But Jesus understands our sorrow. Beyond that, He is *moved* by our sadness and grief. So trust Him with your tears. They are precious to God. "You keep track of all my sorrows. You have collected all my tears in your bottle. You have recorded each one in your book" (Psalm 56:8, NLT).

The Bible tells us that Jesus wept on one other occasion. He had just come down from the Mount of Olives, and "as he approached Jerusalem and saw the city, he wept over it" (Luke 19:41). Jesus' gaze extended far beyond Jerusalem's beautiful temple, busy marketplace, and bustling crowds. He saw into the future. He saw what would eventually become of the city. He knew that within decades Jerusalem would lie in ruins—its beloved temple demolished, its commerce destroyed, its citizens dead or scattered to the wind. He saw the needless, self-inflicted suffering of those who rebel against God's will—and He wept.

I think that the same is true today. I believe that when God looks into our hearts and sees the pain we have inflicted on ourselves by resisting Him and His gracious will, He weeps. God's tears always flow from a heart of compassion. "The LORD is good to everyone. He showers compassion on all his creation" (Psalm 145:9, NLT). Our God longs to protect us from unnecessary suffering. He longs to comfort wounded souls, heal broken hearts, and lovingly lead us. His tears are those of a brokenhearted and compassionate friend.

It would be difficult to trust our tears to One who never cried. But "we do not have a high priest who is unable to sympathize with our weaknesses" (Hebrews 4:15). Knowing that Jesus wept can minister deeply to us. But has it ever occurred to you that our tears can also minister to Jesus?

WHEN WE CRY

Let's join Jesus at a dinner in the courtyard of the home of a rich Pharisee named Simon. Back then, the houses of wealthy folks were often built around a courtyard in the shape of a hollow square, and when a rabbi came to dine, all sorts of people would come to learn from him. That would explain why a certain woman was at Simon's house that day. Luke calls her an "immoral woman" (Luke 7:37, NLT), which means that she most likely was a prostitute.

Jesus was reclining at the table, and when the woman approached Him, she was overcome and began to weep. Round her neck she wore a little bottle. It was called an alabaster, and she wanted to honor Jesus by anointing Him with the perfume in it. As she stood behind Him weeping, her tears fell upon His feet, and so she lovingly began to kiss them, pour the perfume on them, and wipe them with her hair.

That's a beautiful picture of abandoned love. For a Jewish woman to loose her hair in public was very immodest. Now I know that it might seem that a prostitute could easily disregard such a provincial view. But she was in the home of a religious man and in the presence of Jesus. I think that the picture we see of her loosening her hair to wipe His feet shows that she had forgotten about everything but Jesus. Mary of Bethany, who was not an "immoral woman," also anointed Jesus with oil and wiped His feet with her hair (see Matthew 26:6; Mark 14:3; and John 12:3). For both women, it was as if nothing and no one else really mattered at that moment.

What makes this scene so striking is the contrast between Simon and the prostitute. Although it was customary for the host to wash the feet of a guest, to give him the kiss of peace, and to anoint his head with a drop of attar of roses, Simon had done none of those things, as Jesus reminded him:

> "Do you see this woman? I came into your house. You did not give me any water for my feet, but she wet my feet with her tears and wiped them with her hair. You did not give me a kiss, but this woman, from the time I entered, has not stopped kissing my feet. You did not put oil on my head, but she has poured perfume on my feet. Therefore, I tell you, her many sins have been forgiven—for she loved much. But he who has been forgiven little loves little."
>
> Then Jesus said to her, "Your sins are forgiven." (Luke 7:44–48)

I think that if we look in the mirror, we'll find ourselves looking a lot like either Simon or that woman. Which of them really experienced the presence of Christ?

Some of us, like Simon, are religious, good, and moral. We invite Jesus in and are enlightened by His teachings, but we remain unmoved by His presence. We spread before Him all our achievements and wealth, much like Simon spread the meal before Jesus. Simon was pretty impressed with himself. He thought he looked good in the eyes of man and God, and since he was conscious of no need in his life, he felt little love for Jesus. Jesus came to Simon's house, but Simon totally missed out on His visit.

While Simon's self-sufficiency kept him from really knowing the One with whom he dined, the woman was overwhelmed with her need...and it opened the door to the forgiveness and love of God. That's why she cried. Her tears of gratitude were the outward sign that inwardly she had totally abandoned herself to Him. The woman came to Simon's house, and she left intimately connected to Jesus.

Don't ever think that your tears of repentance, gratitude, and love don't touch the heart of God. He is blessed and ministered to when you abandon yourself to Him. The religion of Simon did not minister to Jesus; the woman's love did. Don't allow your religion to be a shallow substitute for really knowing and experiencing the presence of Jesus in your life. Instead, cry out to Him. Your tears will not only be a sweet offering of worship, they will also promote the health of your soul.

WHEN THE SOUL CRIES

We often see tears as just the outward manifestation of an inward emotion such as sorrow, pain, anger, or even joy. But actually, tears promote the health of the human eye. In the same way, soul-tears—crying out to God—make an extraordinary contribution to the health of our souls. When you realize that God has a spiritual as well as physical purpose for the tears you cry, you'll understand why not one of them is shed in vain.

Tears cleanse

Physical tears wash unwelcome debris off the surface of the cornea of the eye. If you've ever been at the beach on a windy day, you know how true that is! Just one tiny grain of sand in your eye can cause the tears to gush. God has created a wonderful device to cleanse your eyes.

He has also created an amazing mechanism to cleanse your soul. It's what I call shedding soul-tears—allowing yourself to cry out to God in prayer from the bottom of your heart. Throughout the Psalms we hear the sound of David's soul-tears as he cries to God in prayer. "Give ear to my words, O LORD, consider my sighing," he writes. "Listen to my cry for help, my King and my God, for to you I pray" (Psalm 5:1–2). When David was rejected, slandered, pursued, and threatened on all sides, he chose to cry out to God in prayer. "Wicked and deceitful men have opened their mouths against me; they have spoken against me with lying tongues. With words of hatred they surround me; they attack me without cause. In return for my friendship they accuse me, but I am a man of prayer" (Psalm 109:2–4).

Sometimes the winds of life blow hard. Harsh words, rejection, and cruelty can rip a hole in our heart, and the debris they create can threaten to lodge there. That's why we need to cry—to allow soul-tears to flow from our heart to God's. David says that the Lord "is near to all who call on him" and that "he hears their cry and saves them" (Psalm 145:18–19). That doesn't necessarily mean that God removes the hard situation. But crying out to Him invites Him to begin to deliver us *through* the heartache by washing away the devastating debris so it can't lodge in our being.

Tears protect

Recently, Connor and I were attempting to display our patriotism by planting small flags along the front yard line. I showed him how to gently twist the wooden dowel as he pushed it into the grass. But we had no sooner finished planting the first pole than he quickly jerked it out of the ground. Well, I was still bent over him, so the jagged end of the flagpole jammed into my open eye.

Wham!

It was definitely a patriotic moment—I saw stars and stripes forever!

My eye began to flood in response to the dirt-covered invader. I had a scratched cornea, and for several days my eye seemed to produce enough tears to cause dehydration. But the doctor told me this was the best thing for my injury, because physical tears have an antibacterial effect on the eye that helps protect it from infection.

When our soul cries tears to God, we can be assured of the same kind of protection. Crying out invites the Great Physician to protect us from greater infection. If we cry tears of bitterness to God over a broken heart, that bitterness cannot become more deeply rooted or spread. When we cry tears of guilt to God over regrettable choices, that guilt cannot grow into depression and anxiety. To allow ourselves to cry to God the tears that only our soul can produce will bring healing as we release everything to Him.

WHEN WE COME AS WE ARE

One of the most poignant lessons I learned about crying happened in a Florida women's prison. A Bible teacher asked me to come to her class one Saturday afternoon to provide music for the inmates who attended the study. I was a little anxious to begin with, but after I was thoroughly frisked and my keyboard was almost completely disassembled, I was really nervous! What would these women be like? I had no idea what to expect.

After I set up my keyboard, the guard ushered in about twenty women. They were very quiet. There was no introduction. The Bible teacher just told me to "go ahead and start." I was so far out of my element that I started just as I would have at a church setting where everyone was eagerly responsive. Well, that went over about as well as an opera singer at a hoedown! I very quickly sensed that I needed to change my approach. So I took a giant leap outside my comfort zone and blurted out, "What would you like to sing?"

Silence.

Then a gruff voice called out, "Just As I Am"!

"You mean the old hymn?" I asked. I was a little surprised because it seemed to me that it wasn't a song that even most churchwomen enjoyed. It was one of those hymns they endured at the end of the service while they gathered their Bibles and purses and made covert plans for lunch.

The Bible teacher jumped in. "Jennifer, this is Sandy. She's been here for several years...."

"For manslaughter." Sandy finished the sentence.

"Yes," the teacher continued, "and since she came to Christ, 'Just As I Am' has been her favorite song."

Feeling very moved, I played the introduction, and as we began to sing, the weeping also began. Sandy was so overcome with emotion that she couldn't voice the words, and the Bible teacher pulled out a tissue and began to wipe away her own tears.

I've never heard "Just As I Am" sung more sweetly. On that day I understood Charlotte Elliott's words "Just as I am, without one plea" in a way I never had before. These women knew what it was to plead before a judge and jury. They understood what it meant to be declared guilty. I realized how little I really knew and understood about my own guilt and pardon. I also had trouble singing the words that day because I, too, wept. Just like Sandy, I was guilty—"without one plea, but that His blood was shed for me."

When we truly know how much we are forgiven, and when we embrace how much we are loved, we will learn to cry. Someday "there will be no more death or mourning or crying or pain" (Revelation 21:4). On the day we are released from our earthly shackles and stand before our Lord, He will lovingly cup each of our faces in His gentle hands and wipe every tear from every face once and for all. Until that day, our tears allow us to feel His healing touch every time we cry to Him.

The righteous cry, and the LORD hears
and delivers them out of all their troubles.
The LORD is near to the brokenhearted
and saves those who are crushed in spirit.

PSALM 34:17–18, NASB

Someday

Someday I'm gonna leave it all behind me
Someday I'm gonna fly where no pain will find me
I'm leaving all the suffering,
I'm leaving all the heartache
They won't confine me someday

Tears they fall so hard
They wound my tender soul
Taking me off guard
As if I'd never known
That someday this will be
Just a faded memory
And my eyes will finally see

Childishly I look at life
And scornfully I cry
Shaking of my fist
And wanting to know why
But someday I will be
In the place prepared for me
And my eyes will finally see

Someday I'm gonna leave it all behind me
Someday I'm gonna fly where no pain will find me
I'm leaving all the suffering,
I'm leaving all the heartache
They won't confine me someday

When I go I'll leave this world behind me
And then I'll know
I'll be free from all that binds me

Someday I'm gonna leave it all behind me
Someday I'm gonna fly where no pain will find me
I'm leaving all the suffering,
I'm leaving all the heartache
They won't confine me someday

WORDS AND MUSIC BY JENNIFER ROTHSCHILD AND CRAIG ALEA

Twelve

WAIT *on* GOD

When Phil and I had been married about a year, he was the director of student life at Palm Beach Atlantic College. Part of his job was to oversee the student body's formal banquets, so twice a year I had to squeeze some money from our tight budget to buy a formal dress. This time it was homecoming, and I was prepared! I'd just found a beautiful black dress at a bargain price.

The morning of the banquet, I got everything together. Shoes, earrings, hose…*yikes!* I only had white hose! I needed *black* hose! I called Phil at work to let him know about our latest family emergency. He was busy moving tables, dealing with caterers, and coordinating the student decorators, so to say that he wasn't available right then would be an understatement.

I realized that I'd have to wait. Now, it probably doesn't seem like a big deal at this point. After all, it was still morning. But on hectic days like this one, Phil often changed into his suit at the hotel. So I knew there was a good chance that I might not get my black hose in time for the six o'clock dinner, and I was already anxious.

By 5:45 P.M., I was fully dressed. My makeup was meticulously applied and my hair was done. I was a picture of well-groomed perfection—from the knees up, that is! I still had no black hose. All my waiting had been to no avail, and now I was really worried.

At this point any guy reading this is probably screaming, "Wear the white hose, lady! Wear the white hose!" Male logic is often ludicrous to a woman. I would go without hose before I'd risk being arrested by the fashion police for committing such a crime against good taste. No, I would wait it out.

Well, between moving tables and flower arrangements, Phil had evidently communicated my crisis to my friend Darlene, and at 5:56 she burst through my door.

"Black hose!" she proudly announced. I pulled the coveted hose from the package. Within seconds I had them on my grateful legs and, after a long day of waiting, I was on my way to the banquet.

Because of my sight loss, I've had to learn to wait. The

day of the homecoming banquet, I spent the entire afternoon wondering how I was going to get black hose and
wishing I could just jump in the car and go buy it. But I
can't drive. So when it comes to even the everyday needs of
life, I've had to master the art of delayed gratification. I have
to wait until someone else is heading to the store. I get my
needs and desires met according to someone else's schedule,
rarely my own.

I've learned that although waiting is never fun, it's always
healthy. It's like spiritual weightlifting: It strengthens us by
teaching us that our joy and peace and hope don't depend
on when our needs and wants are met. Instead, they come
from what we choose to do in the meantime, when life is
hard and so is waiting.

THE WAY WE WAIT

We all have to learn to wait for some things in life, and the
way I see it, there are three ways of waiting and three kinds
of waiters—and I don't mean the kind at a banquet! I bet
you'll recognize yourself in one of them.

First, there's the *worried waiter.* If you took a snapshot
of her, you'd see her wringing her hands and pacing the
floor. She's so busy calling her friends to bemoan her circumstances that she forgets to take them to God in prayer.
Then there's the *wishful waiter.* She never lives in the present moment because her energy is tied to "what if," not to
"what is." She spends most of her time speculating on

what it will be like when the wait is over, and until then she just aimlessly tries to get through each day. Finally, there's the *wise waiter*. She's focused on God's face, not on His hand—not on what He will do for her, how He will take care of her situation, or when He will end her wait. She is waiting only on God, and she is present, peaceful, and productive.

What kind of waiter are you? Are you present where you are, or do you pine away over things that are not? Are you wringing your hands, or bending your knees? Are you waiting on God alone, or waiting for the wait to end?

Many of us spend our lives "in the meantime," waiting for something we want or need: a better job, a less stressful time in life, a newer car. We endure the wait, and then, the prize—a promotion, a long vacation, a zero-percent car loan—only to have a new need, a new wait, and a new prize pop up in its place.

Sometimes the wait is much more difficult because the prize seems much greater.

For some of us, the prize is healing.

For others, deliverance from suffering.

For many, the lifting of a heavy financial burden.

The prize is often the thing that keeps us faithful while we wait. But what if all our joy isn't reserved for the award ceremony? What if there is something deep and precious in the in-between time? If our focus is on the prize alone, we can't help but see the waiting as a trial, and when we do, we can miss the joy of the journey and overlook the treasures along the way. Learning to wait for the small things or the big things in life is healthy because it teaches us that our joy doesn't depend on whether we have them or not. It teaches us to experience the strengthening effect of "in all" joy, not just "end-all" joy.

So what do we do while we wait? How do we make the meantime meaningful?

We can find great meaning during the waiting times of our lives by delighting in God. Psalm 37:4 says, "Delight yourself in the LORD and he will give you the desires of your heart."

I believe that's true when we delight in anyone. When I delight in my husband, I am mindful of and interested in his desires. In fact, they often become my desires. If I'm not delighting in him, there's no way I want to spend three long hours sipping coffee at one of those megabookstores, surrounded by books I can't even read. And besides, I don't even like coffee! But if I am delighting in him, I want to be there and sip right along with him.

Sometimes we look at Psalm 37:4 as a blank check. We think that if we delight in God, He will give us what we want. But the emphasis of the verse is on *delighting*. When we delight in God, He places in us the desires He wants us to have. "It is God who works in you," Paul reminds us, "to will and to act according to his good purpose" (Philippians 2:13). When our delight is in God, our desires will be what

He wants for us instead of what we want for ourselves.

God desires peace and contentment for all of His children, and I have found that the more I delight in Him, the more that becomes the desire of my own heart. Oh yes, healing would be an extraordinary prize—a treasure—and God may give it to me someday. But I would still ultimately lose if I were physically whole but lacking spiritually. Without peace and contentment, the joy of healing would be fleeting and shallow, but resting contentedly in Him reveals a depth of grace that I can still be reveling in ten million years from now in His presence, in His house.

Worry prevents us from experiencing peace and contentment. So if you happen to be a worried waiter, forget about calling up your friends to bemoan your situation. Here's the only phone number you need to remember: 1-800-CALL-GOD.

Jeremiah, the weeping prophet, knew God's number by heart: "Then you will call upon Me and come and pray to Me, and I will listen to you" (Jeremiah 29:12, NASB). Through the ages, God has urged all those who are worried and troubled to phone home. "Call upon Me in the day of trouble; I shall rescue you, and you will honor Me" (Psalm 50:15, NASB).

God's prescription for the worried waiter is "Do not be anxious about anything, but in everything, by prayer and petition, with thanksgiving, present your requests to God" (Philippians 4:6). If you do, "the peace of God, which transcends all understanding, will guard your hearts and your minds in Christ Jesus" (v. 7).

I am convinced that my deep desire for peace and contentment is a direct reflection of the heart of the God in whom I delight—a treasure He wants to give me in the meantime, while I wait.

Think about your own desires. What are they? If you could fulfill the desire of your heart, what would it be? The answer to that question will reveal where your delight truly lies.

Align your heart with the heart of God, and your desires will reflect His.

WAITING AND HOPING

I am not often overly emotional about my blindness. My usual approach is to face it with resolve. But one night was different. It was almost as if I'd been given permission to feel the loss more deeply, to wish that things were different, and to question why God had not healed me. It was like peeling back a Band-Aid very slowly from a tender wound, still sensitive to the touch.

That night I was returning home from singing at a prayer conference led by Dr. Waylon Moore. I was deeply moved in my spirit by what had transpired. Lori had gone with me, and on the way home we began to discuss why God had not healed me. Was it His will? Was it sin that had held back His hand of healing? Was it a lack of faith? Was it okay not to be healed? Didn't that reflect poorly on God? The ride home ended long before we exhausted the possibilities, so we sat in the driveway for another hour.

Feelings like these aren't easily plumbed or expressed, much less resolved, and at last we decided to explore them further when our bodies and spirits weren't so weary. I asked Lori to read me Psalm 63 before she walked me into the house, and by the dim light of the driveway she began to read: "My soul waits in silence for God only...."

"Oh," she said, "that's Psalm 62, not 63!"

"Read it again," I said, "that's the best mistake you ever made."

Lori continued to read. "My soul, wait in silence for God only, for my hope is from Him. He only is my rock and my salvation, my stronghold; I shall not be shaken" (Psalm 62:5–6, NASB).

On that night of painful questioning, those verses became the words that my spirit could not articulate alone. I felt as though I really had looked into the face of my Healer and come so close to Him that I'd heard Him speak to me. He told me that my hope for healing is in Him alone. Therefore, my soul can wait—wait as long as it takes, even if it never happens here on earth. He alone—not my healing—is my rock and my refuge. My deliverance from blindness is not my source of hope...He is.

When we pin our hopes on the fulfillment of our desires, we fall into the trap of wishful waiting. James has some advice for wishful waiters: "You do not know what will happen tomorrow. For what is your life? It is even a vapor that appears for a little time and then vanishes away. Instead you ought to say, 'If the Lord wills, we shall live and do this or that'" (James 4:14–15, NKJV). We can't know if our desires will be fulfilled or not.

Even if we could, we set ourselves up for disappointment when our focus is on the prize instead of on God.

The psalmist had learned where to place his hope. "Lord, where do I put my hope? *My only hope is in you*" (Psalm 39:7, NLT, emphasis added).

When our hope is in God alone, He becomes our prize. That's what Paul meant when he wrote, "I press on toward the goal to win the prize for which God has called me heavenward in Christ Jesus" (Philippians 3:14). Paul's desire was God's desire, his prize was Christ's will for him, and his hope was in God. Such hope will not disappoint us. "In you our fathers put their trust; they trusted and you delivered them" (Psalm 22:4).

If you're a wishful waiter, learn to trust the One who purposefully leads you through long desert stretches on your way to the Promised Land. Don't waste time daydreaming about how tasty the milk and honey will be. Enjoy the manna! God designed it just for you. Be willing to submit your longings to God and wait patiently on Him. Place your hope in the God in whom you delight and you will never be disappointed.

WORTH THE WAIT

Clayton has always been an intuitive thinker and a sensitive child. From the time he was capable of expressing abstract thought, he would say that he wished "Mommy could see." It was important to the little guy. Of course he wanted that for his mom. What child wouldn't?

So I wasn't surprised that one day when he was six, he said, "Mommy, I wish you could see." By then I had grown accustomed to such comments.

"Why do you wish that?" I asked.

"So you could play Nintendo with me," he said, "cause Daddy is really bad at it!"

At the time, Clayton's reasoning made me chuckle. But a year later he became a Christian, and one of the first evidences of his newfound faith was that, unprompted by his dad or me, he began to pray for my healing.

Then one spring day when he was in the third grade, we were playing a game together. I sat on the carpet and waited while he meticulously placed the pieces of the game on the game board. In most of the games we play, I roll the dice and he reads it; I ask him to move the pieces and he moves them. This game, however, was very tactile, and we thought it might be easier for me. He read my rolled dice, and I attempted to move my piece. But no matter how I tried, I just couldn't do it. I was frustrated and Clay was disappointed.

"Son," I said, "you need to choose a different game. This

one just isn't working." Without a word, he began to put the pieces back in the box. He was so pensive that I could almost hear the wheels turning in his mind. When he spoke at last, his comment was very different from the one that had made me chuckle two years earlier.

"Mom," he said, "I was thinking. I don't think God will heal you here on earth."

"Why not, son?" I asked. "Why don't you think God will heal me on earth?"

Clayton's answer has been my greatest lesson on learning to wait. *"If God healed you here on earth,"* he said, *"you might love earth more, and heaven is best."* The seeds of spiritual truth had already been sown in his young heart, and now they were springing up before me with the promise of fragrant blossoms of hope. A wise waiter can wait for what she knows is best—heaven!

I can't help but think of the Negro spirituals, growing out of the shameful practice of slavery in the early days of our nation. So often, these songs are focused on heaven. Life in bondage, life in the cotton fields from dawn till dusk didn't provide much material for songwriting. But heaven? What a richness awaited just over the horizon! What comfort and rest and beauty and freedom—and the Lord Jesus Himself, waiting with open arms! Lacking earthly treasure, their songs focused on the place where true treasures awaited... and that's where their hearts were, too.

When our eyes are fixed on temporal things, like illness,

financial strain, or difficult relationships, it's easy to get discouraged, because most of the time our burdens feel heavy and there seems to be no end in sight. When we keep our attention fixed on earthly things, we can easily lose heart.

But Paul says:

We do not lose heart. Though outwardly we are wasting away, yet inwardly we are being renewed day by day. For our light and momentary troubles are achieving for us an eternal glory that far outweighs them all. So we fix our eyes not on what is seen, but on what is unseen. For what is seen is temporary, but what is unseen is eternal. (2 Corinthians 4:16–18)

Like the psalmist, a wise waiter knows where to fix her gaze: "One thing I ask of the LORD, this is what I seek: that I may dwell in the house of the LORD all the days of my life, to gaze upon the beauty of the LORD" (Psalm 27:4). This is what allows her to redeem every moment of the wait and experience the joy of the journey.

Learning to wait for what is best from God is not the same as learning to wait for healing. To know Him and to allow our suffering to reveal His life in us is far better than the temporal prize of physical healing. Having that kind of perspective in even the most difficult places in our lives allows us to see them as temporary burdens that are fashioning for us a far greater—and eternal—weight of glory. It's as if somehow the suffering of today is immediately invested in a heavenly account that pays eternal dividends, even while we wait. When we fix our eyes on things that are unseen and view hardship through the lens of eternity, we can see that even the terminal is temporal.

Have you ever thought about "the end"?

You know, your funeral, the day your spirit celebrates its homecoming and your body is put to rest in the ground? Of course you have—we all have! One thing I know for sure is that when I die, I want to be buried facing east.

Now facing east might seem like a strange and minor detail to you, but I recently learned from my mother's genealogical research that most of my ancestors have been buried with their graves facing that direction. The reason, she discovered, was that they were sure that when Jesus returned and appeared in the eastern sky, the dead in Christ would rise first (1 Thessalonians 4:16), and they wanted to be positioned in such a way that their first glimpse with resurrected eyes would be the face of Jesus.

Wow! What a testimony—even in death.

That got me to thinking how much more meaningful it would be to *live* facing east. How sad it would be if His glorious appearing found us stuck in the meantime, wringing our hands and stressing out over the small things in life, or missing the joy of the moment by wishing for something other than God's best. We know that the sky can be rolled back at any second, so how much wiser it would be to live in such a way that everything we think and do positions us for His coming.

What a way to wait!

> *Those who wait on the LORD will find new strength.*
> *They will fly high on wings like eagles.*
> *They will run and not grow weary.*
> *They will walk and not faint.*

ISAIAH 40:31, NLT

When Faith Becomes Sight

I t's been more than twenty years now since I left the eye hospital knowing that I would be totally blind. But even on that day, I believed that just beyond my despair a doorway of promise was about to be opened by the merciful hand of God. It was the promise that *no matter what my circumstances, it could be well with my soul.* That's why even amid deep sorrow, I could go home, sit down at our old piano, and play "It Is Well."

God knows about great sorrow. He is a Father who watched His only Son suffer and die. When His beloved Son Jesus cried, "It is finished," the Father's heart must have been rent in half, just like the temple veil.

"It is finished" was so final, so certain.

Yet for us that cosmic closure became a gateway of hope.

On a hill called Calvary, God Himself made a way for us to have soul-wellness. When Jesus was suspended between heaven and earth on the cross, He made a way for it to be well with our souls once and for all. If we choose to receive His gracious offering of love, which He demonstrated through His death on the cross, His grace makes it well. Unfortunately, some of us close our eyes to the goodness of God and turn a deaf ear to His beckoning voice.

Joni Eareckson Tada was paralyzed in a diving accident when she was a young woman. Since then she has been confined to a wheelchair, and it has been there that God has taught her the greatest lessons about Himself. In her book *Diamonds in the Dust,* Joni recounts being asked if, given the choice, she would choose life in a wheelchair. Listen to her response:

I can't think of anyone who desires to be paralyzed. Who would be foolish enough to choose not to have the use of his legs and hands? Can you imagine someone wanting to be blind? Choosing darkness over the brilliance of a clear blue sky? And who would want to be deaf? Who in the world would desire silence instead of the beauty of a waltz or the soothing voice of a loved one? Yet there are people who choose to be handicapped.... Theirs are very serious disabilities, not physical ones but spiritual handicaps.[2]

Jesus Himself spoke of those with self-inflicted handicaps when He said, "You will be ever hearing but never understanding; you will be ever seeing but never perceiving. For this people's heart has become calloused; they hardly hear with their ears, and they have closed their eyes. Otherwise they might see with their eyes, hear with their ears, understand with their hearts and turn, and I would heal them" (Matthew 13:14–15).

The greatest handicap you can have is for it not to be well with your soul. To allow your circumstances to blind you to the infinite goodness of God is far more debilitating than physical darkness. To silence the voice of God who longs to tell you of His love and forgiveness is far worse than physical deafness. To be paralyzed by fear is far more confining than physical immobility.

We all have handicaps—flaws and weaknesses that remind us that we are clothed in humanity. Yet living with human handicaps is not nearly as difficult as living with the devastating consequences of a calloused heart. We can never experience what it really means to live if we harden our heart toward God and refuse to allow Him to make it well with our souls.

If I had to make the choice, would I really choose soul-wellness over physical sight? Having wrestled with that question in the deepest part of my longing, I can honestly answer that I would. Why? Because I've learned that I can function, even thrive, without sight, but I'm convinced that

I cannot live without soul-wellness. I know that I would barely function—and certainly not thrive. If blindness is the one illuminating force in my life that can reveal the depth of wellness I can possess, then I gratefully welcome it.

I'm convinced that to have soul-wellness, to have found the life I've dreamt of, has been worth the cost. To find such a life is worth *any* cost. God doesn't demand our suffering as an exchange for this blessing. Oh no, He is kind and merciful. Yet in His mercy, He sometimes allows us to suffer so we can shake off the things that crowd our thoughts, weigh heavy on our hearts, and keep us from Him. But giving ourselves completely to Him in utter abandon and faith allows us to receive life—life that cannot be shrouded by darkness, silenced by deafness, or stilled by paralysis.

I don't know what it's like anymore to look into people's faces. It's been many years since I saw a face clearly. I know that as a child I looked into my mother's face, with its soft olive skin, and I know that I looked into the sweetness of my dad's dancing blue eyes and watched his forehead wrinkle when he was in deep thought. I looked into the freckled faces of my sometimes annoying, but always adorable, brothers, and I looked into the wise eyes of my beloved grandparents.

What fascinates me is that even though I know I saw all those precious faces, in my memory they are now draped in shadows, blurred and indistinguishable. It's a strange phenomenon. Even so, it excites me—because unless God chooses to heal me here on earth, the very first face I'll see with clarity will be the face of Jesus. Awesome thought!

I'll always remember how Mike, my mobility instructor, wrapped up my first lesson of learning to walk in the dark. After he had walked me all around my neighborhood, he called my attention to some blooming hibiscus on the corner near my home.

"When you smell the flowers," he said, "you know you're almost home."

Always remember that for each of us there will come a day when we too will smell the flowers and know we're almost home. The closer we get, any kind of darkness here on earth—the depth of suffering it may represent, the difficulties that it may make us recall—will pale in comparison to the sweet aroma that will usher us into the presence of the One whose face we will clearly see. And when our eyes look into His face, we'll realize that, compared to the surpassing excellence of seeing Him, nothing else really mattered.

That's when our faith becomes sight.

And Lord, haste the day when my faith shall be sight
The clouds be rolled back as a scroll
The trump shall resound, and the Lord shall descend
Even so, it is well with my soul

Let's Keep in Touch

Thank you for allowing me to share part of my journey with you through the pages of this book. I would love to hear about your journey as well, and I invite you to visit me at JenniferRothschild.com, where we can keep in touch through my e-mail newsletter. On my Web site you can also find information about my music albums that contain the lyrics you have just read, along with a Bible study companion to this book.

Meanwhile, my prayer for you is that "the eyes of your heart may be enlightened in order that you may know the hope to which he has called you, the riches of his glorious inheritance in the saints, and his incomparably great power for us who believe" (Ephesians 1:18–19).

God speed you on your way as you learn to walk by faith, not by sight.

Jennifer

Multnomah Publishers

The publisher and author would love to hear your comments about this book. *Please contact us at:*
www.multnomah.net/lessonsilearned

Notes

1. Derek Redmond story adapted from *Experiencing God: The Musical* by Gary Rhodes and Claire Cloninger (Nashville, Tenn.: Genovox Music Group, May 2000).
2. Joni Eareckson Tada, *Diamonds in the Dust* (Grand Rapids, Mich.: Zondervan, 1993), devotional for February 15.

JENNIFER ROTHSCHILD

Multnomah® Publishers, *Sisters, Oregon*

LESSONS I LEARNED IN THE LIGHT
published by Multnomah Publishers, Inc.
© 2006 by Jennifer Rothschild

Cover photo by Randy Bacon
Interior design and typeset by Katherine Lloyd, The DESK

Unless otherwise indicated, Scripture quotations are from:
The Holy Bible, New International Version
© 1973, 1984 by International Bible Society,
used by permission of Zondervan Publishing House
Other Scripture quotations are from:
New American Standard Bible (NASB) © 1960, 1977 by the Lockman Foundation
The Holy Bible, New King James Version (NKJV) © 1984 by Thomas Nelson, Inc.
The Holy Bible, King James Version (KJV)
The Amplified Bible (AMP) © 1965, 1987 by Zondervan Publishing House.
Holy Bible, New Living Translation (NLT) © 1996.
Used by permission of Tyndale House Publishers, Inc. All rights reserved.
Revised Standard Version Bible (RSV) © 1946, 1952 by the Division of
Christian Education of the National Council of the
Churches of Christ in the United States of America
The Message by Eugene H. Peterson, Copyright © 1993, 1994, 1995, 1996, 2000.
Used by permission of NavPress Publishing Group. All rights reserved.
The Holy Bible, English Standard Version (ESV)
© 2001 by Crossway Bibles, a division of Good News Publishers.
Used by permission. All rights reserved.
Contemporary English Version (CEV) © 1995 by American Bible Society

Multnomah is a trademark of Multnomah Publishers, Inc.,
and is registered in the U.S. Patent and Trademark Office.
The colophon is a trademark of Multnomah Publishers, Inc.
Printed in the United States of America
For information:
MULTNOMAH PUBLISHERS, INC.
601 N LARCH STREET · SISTERS, OREGON 97759
ISBN 978-0-7394-7159-3

"One of my favorite things about the apostle Paul is the way he always shows us his hand. 'Not that I have already obtained all this, or have already been made perfect, but I press on...' (Philippians 3:12). Jennifer Rothschild teaches in the same way, using her life as a sincere and transparent example of what it means to press toward the goal—to live a thriving, courageous life in Christ."

—SARA GROVES
SINGER/SONGWRITER

"I love Jennifer Rothschild. I've not known her long, but it doesn't take long to see her as she really is: gifted, creative, insightful, charming, and full of the love of God. She shows how to see with new and different eyes. She walks in the light and takes us with her on that journey—in life and in her book."

—MARY GRAHAM
PRESIDENT, WOMEN OF FAITH

"Like the Renaissance artists of old, Jennifer Rothschild sees with her heart. Through self-discipline, acute observation, and Christ centeredness, the tapestry of her life has been woven together by an unshakable faith. I recognized this in Jennifer long before I read her book, but now even more so. Each story reflects a woman who not only teaches us how to live in the Light but how to trust the One who is our true vision."

—LUCI SWINDOLL
AUTHOR AND SPEAKER, WOMEN OF FAITH

"Jennifer writes with transparency and depth, weaving daily life lessons with firsthand spiritual truths. Where *Lessons I Learned in the Dark* covers our life by faith rather than sight, this sequel reminds us that we can bask in God's light—light that convicts of sin, but also frees us as we realize we are known by the Father of lights. This book is a must read!"

—DR. LORI SALIERNO
PRESIDENT AND CEO, CELEBRATE LIFE INTERNATIONAL

"Sit down to a cup of coffee and delightful conversation with Jennifer Rothschild. You will see truth clearly from God's Word, wrapped in beautiful life stories. You will laugh through tears as the Spirit's voice speaks through Jennifer's honest and open walk with God."

—ESTHER BURROUGHS
ESTHER BURROUGHS MINISTRIES, BIRMINGHAM, ALABAMA

"I'm a comedian. I love to laugh. But I have also experienced dark times. After reading Jennifer's book, I found myself humming the children's song, This Little Light of Mine. Humming in the dark? Yes! And there is no one more perfect to lead us out of the darkness than Jennifer Rothschild. Hold on to the rope, kids! It's time for recess!"

—CHONDA PIERCE
COMEDIAN, INO RECORDS

DEDICATION

―――――――

To Karen True
Because she loves and shines the Light.
No one could have a better friend.

CONTENTS

ACKNOWLEDGMENTS

To my husband, Phil. You are my partner in life and ministry. I love you.

To my editor, Larry Libby. You are my faithful friend and scribe. Thank you, my brother. Wasn't this fun?

To my son, Clay. I am proud to be your mom. Always cling to the Word, and the Lord will bring about great victories in your life.

To my son, Connor. While I wrote this book, you asked Jesus into your heart. May you always walk in the light of His Word.

To my writing and research assistant, Karen True. This book and this author are both the better for your wise and faithful offerings.

To my pastor, Dr. John Marshall. Thank you for your diligent and skilled handling of the Word. I am deeper and richer for it.

To my assistant, Kathryn McCall. Thank you for your tireless, loyal work and friendship.

To the Multnomah team. It was a privilege to partner with you. Thanks for being such good stewards of my message.

To Mom and Dad, Lawson and Judith Jolly. I am one lucky girl to have you. Thank you for shining the Light.

To Father God, who is my Light. How could I live without Your Word? Let it bring life to the readers of this book.

FOREWORD

Have you ever met someone and known instantly that the two of you would always be friends? That's how I felt about Jennifer Rothschild.

Of course, I can't imagine *anyone* not being drawn to this bundle of inspiration. If this book is your first introduction to Jennifer, let me give you a heads-up on what to expect.

First off, Jennifer is one of those rare individuals who is both honest *and* kind. She is delightfully candid while being tenderly aware of human frailty. I like that. I want to know the truth, but my experience has been that bottom-line frankness can loosen molars and separate friends.

But Jennifer has the ability to speak words into our lives that fit inside us as though we've been waiting a long time to hear them. They settle in like friends and they make sense. And gratefully, she's willing to open up her own humanity to make us more comfortable with ours. How hospitable. How vulnerable.

Jennifer's petite size and her darling ways may cause you to initially underestimate her, but trust me—she is one savvy gal. She is studied and current; she is relevant and well established in the Scriptures. I appreciate that.

Oh, and did I mention that Jennifer's blind? I almost forgot, because she so sees women for who they are and who they can become that her lack of physical sight is a non-issue for her audiences. And because Jennifer's perspective is so visionary and passionate, her sharing is as if someone finally opened a window and turned on a light in the cellar of our souls.

You'll instantly learn in Jennifer's presence that faith is her top priority, followed quickly by her love for and devotion for her husband and sons. And to watch their admiration of her is downright moving.

Don't get me wrong. I'm not trying to paint a perfect picture of Jennifer and her life. She struggles, she stumbles, and she suffers.

You will hear and see it in the pages ahead. But I want you to know that up close and personal, I find her stunning. Her faith is sterling, her commitment to her family is constant, and her determination to pass along to us the best of what she's learned is impressive.

But wait. I can't leave out the quality that captures my applause regularly when I'm with Jennifer: courage. She is one tenacious lady. But you'll figure that out in chapter 1, when you join her and her oldest son at an amusement park on a ride called The Accelerator.

I first experienced Jennifer's steady confidence at a Women of Faith conference when she was the featured speaker. Phil, her husband, escorted her on stage and left Jennifer on her own.

Picture a large, round stage, an audience of seventeen thousand, four cameras, no cane—and she can't see. Honey, she breezed around that stage like a sighted veteran using a network of carpets to alert her feet as to her whereabouts. It was fascinating. She spoke with the confidence of a lion and the gentle and playful heart of a kitten. I was mesmerized by her myriad gifts. Did I mention she sings beautifully as well?

If anyone's keeping score, I'm not certain it's fair that God has packaged so much in one vessel. Yet I, for one, don't want to miss one word that comes out of her lips and through her pen. I'm definitely a fan, and I believe you will be too. So cozy into your favorite reading place and prepare to be blessed.

Patsy Clairmont, author of *All Cracked Up: Experiencing God in the Broken Places*

INTRODUCTION

As I tucked our son Connor, who was three at the time, into bed one crisp fall night, he interrupted the routine with a challenging series of questions.

I'm used to this.

He's old enough to understand the art of stalling. It's usually executed with, "I need some water," skillfully followed by a well-timed, "I need to go potty!" When those pressing needs have been met, he may try a new tack:

"I'm scared."

"Lay down with me."

"Turn on the lamp."

"Crack open the door."

On this particular night, however, he brought out a previously untested weapon from his arsenal: three-year-old theology.

"Mommy," he asked, "does God smile like a frog or like a grandpa?"

That one stopped me in my tracks for a moment. Recovering, I told Connor that God could never look like a frog, so He must smile like a grandpa.

Then he asked, "What does God look like, anyway?"

I answered as best as I knew how, remembering 1 John 1:5: "God is Light, and in Him there is no darkness at all."

"Connor," I said, "as far as I know from the Bible, He looks like light."

Little did I know that I had just drawn the line in the sand. And so the litany of questions began.

"What kind of light, Mommy? Is He like the big, bright light in the kitchen that I like to dance under? Or is God like the lamp by the couch that's warm and snuggly?"

"I don't really know, Connor. All I know is that He's just big, beautiful, and bright!"

"Well, I like the kitchen light," he said, "because it's fun to dance under. But I like the couch lamp because it's yellow and warm."

I've found the best way to end the stalling game is to say, "Let's pray." So, we did. The day ended with an "amen" in unison and a sweet voice lifting up an "I love you, Mommy."

I went immediately into the kitchen and stood thoughtfully under the light. *Connor's right*, I thought to myself, doing a few dance steps across the tiles. *It is fun to dance here.* Moments later I walked to the couch and settled by the lamp with some hot tea. *It is warm and yellow*, I smiled.

How correct my little Connor was that night. Light can be comforting. Light can be clarifying. When I think about it, light can also be challenging. It warms us, guides us, calls us to leave our darkness, encourages us to persevere.

No wonder the psalmist compared God's Word to light in Psalm 119:105: "Your word is a lamp to my feet and a light for my path."

Perhaps the main reason the psalmist called God's Word light is because our world is dark. That's true of human beings, too. Without God in our lives, we can become very, very dark.

Paul put it this way: "For you were formerly darkness,

but now you are Light in the Lord" (Ephesians 5:8, NASB). What a statement. He isn't just saying you were in the darkness; you were the darkness.

Jesus shows us what a person in darkness is like. "But if anyone walks in the night, he stumbles, because the light is not in him" (John 11:10, NASB). "He who walks in the darkness does not know where he goes" (John 12:35, NASB).

In Romans 1:21 and Ephesians 4:18, Paul shows the impact of our darkness. Darkness involves futility of thinking, being darkened in understanding, exclusion from the life of God, and ignorance. No matter what you might think about philosophy, psychology, or higher education, none of these things can bring a human soul out of darkness. How about therapy? Self-actualization?

No, of course not.

The only remedy for darkness is light.

God's written Word is light. The psalmist declared, "The unfolding of Your words gives light; it gives understanding to the simple" (Psalm 119:130, NASB).

Just as a white cane guides me in my physical darkness, God's light guides me out of my spiritual darkness. God's light brings understanding, illumination, revelation, and gives direction.

I remember the Labor Day weekend I spent in Athens, Georgia, with my precious friend Katharyn. I love to visit her because she and her family are all treasured friends, and we have a blast when we're together. It had been a few years since my last visit and boy, had things changed. Katharyn had been busy redecorating her home and rearranging furniture.

It was nothing at all like I remembered it.

And for me, that's a big problem.

The piano was in a different room, couches were against new walls, and in some places there was new furniture that I was not yet acquainted with. Now, all of this only really matters because I can't see. I had a good mental map from previous visits, and now it was completely obsolete. The last few times I visited I enjoyed some independence, since I was so familiar with my surroundings. But this time, I realized pretty fast that I would have to pull out my cane to navigate all the new additions and changes.

I must admit, I don't really like to use my cane if I don't have to. But it was completely necessary that weekend.

I may not really like using my cane, but Katharyn's kids sure like it. Her daughter, Anya, was especially curious and it was all she could do to keep her little hands off of it.

One Sunday morning I sat down at the piano, resting my cane on the bench next to me. Anya made her way to my side and gently moved the cane so she could sit down. She held the cane in her hands, twirling it, pointing it, and thoroughly examining it. I could tell she was contemplating something.

Finally, she asked, "Are you ever embarrassed to carry your cane?"

I stopped playing to answer her sincere question.

"I used to be," I said. "Now I sometimes feel self-conscious, but I'm not embarrassed." I continued to explain. "To me, you see, my cane is my ticket to freedom. If I didn't depend on my cane, I wouldn't get to navigate or enjoy my world."

Anya was satisfied with my simple answer and left the room to play outside. But I couldn't stop thinking about what my cane represented to me—and what would happen if I refused to use it.

If I refused dependency, I would reject liberty.

In other words, because I choose to be dependent on my cane, I experience a kind of liberating independence.

It's a good picture, I think, of how we relate to Scripture. When we choose to be totally dependent on God's Word, it ushers in a freedom that we would never experience otherwise. When we rely on His wisdom and hold onto His precepts, we walk in freedom, not fear. When we fully lean on the promises in His Word, we find that we are freed from the wishing and worrying that so imprison us. The light of God's Word brings a brightness that allows us to dance. It makes clear that which could be fuzzy and dim.

Let's face it, life changes. Things are not always as we remember them. Loss happens, people we love leave, our inner worlds can get rearranged due to emotional changes. Sometimes the shadows of heartache overwhelm us and we just want to quit. We want to navigate and enjoy our world, but the only way is through dependence on a higher source of wisdom. Pure, utter dependence on God's Word truly liberates us.

God's light really is a clarifying beam that we can depend upon. And God's Word is light—a light that brings such freedom and joy that we really can dance.

God's light is warm. It comforts me and adds a sweet illumination to my darkness that is often more felt than seen.

God's light challenges me to be awake, aware, alert, careful, and ready to seize every opportunity He brings across my path.

God's light gives me the strength to stay in the race, even when I am weary. It encourages me to keep holding on, to keep moving forward, to keep reaching for His highest and best intentions for my life, no matter what my life circumstances.

It has been the light of God's Word that has compelled me to keep running my race with endurance, even in blindness. And I know that His Word will not return void in your life, either.

I love His light.

After all these years of walking in its illumination, my world would be a dark and desolate place apart from the warmth and freedom His Word gives. I'm pretty sure that when I see God someday, His smile will be that of a loving and kind Father. And our heavenly home will need no other light, because the light of the Lamb will shine there forever. Until then, I walk in the Light, learn from the Light, and depend fully on the Light to guide me home.

My friend, in the following pages you will be encouraged, equipped, and inspired from the lessons I've learned in the Light. I know they will bring you comfort, bring clarity to your path, and challenge you to never, never, never quit.

"The entrance of Your words gives light" (Psalm 119:130, NKJV).

CHAPTER ONE

Cling to His Word

They called it "The Accelerator."

For good reason.

Launching into the night sky, screams piercing the air in its wake, the great mechanical contrivance sent a surge of fear through my whole body. Just standing near it made my heart pound. And within mere moments, I would make its intimate acquaintance.

This wasn't the first time I've been stretched in such a way. In my attempts to relate to my teenage son, I have on several occasions ventured beyond the boundaries of sense and prudence.

One such excursion occurred the summer before Clayton's

sophomore year of high school. On a balmy August evening, our little family ambled through Celebration City, a theme park in Branson, Missouri. I held Phil's hand, giggled at a clown having some fun with six-year-old Connor, and sipped on my ice-cold Coke.

The night was dreamy. We were finally taking a badly needed family vacation, and my neck and shoulders felt more relaxed than they had in months. (But not for long, as it turned out). The fragrance of kettle corn and cotton candy mingled with music from the seventies and eighties, blaring from speakers throughout the park.

I found myself reminiscing to the sounds of "Dream Weaver" and singing along to "Saturday in the Park" when my perfect, relaxed mood was interrupted by Clayton's grip on my arm.

"Mom, go with me on that ride!"

"Which ride?" I asked.

Phil's slow, painful moan should have clued me in that I would not like the answer I was about to hear. My guys had stopped and were staring in awe at some midway monstrosity. Suddenly, it blasted off directly in front of us, the ground vibrating beneath our feet. I could hear the ride's quick ascent and felt the gust of wind in its wake.

And then came the screams.

I know my sounds, and I knew those riders weren't faking it. They were genuinely terrified.

"No way!" I said.

"Aw, c'mon, Mom," Clayton pleaded. "It's safe."

By this time, Phil was laughing. Little Connor emitted a

series of gasps and sighs as he watched the ride rocket abruptly heavenward, only to hurtle back toward terra firma.

"Mom?"

Okay, now I was in a real dilemma. My teenage son rarely requested my company (especially in public places)—in fact, I had the impression he didn't think hanging out with Mom was cool. And now...he wanted me to go with him. Not his dad...*me*. I felt a momentary elation that he at least thought I was cool enough to join him on a ride reserved only for the brave hearted.

The ride launched again, thundering off into what seemed to be the stratosphere. How high did that thing go? And what was a mom to do?

I knew that the more I thought about it, the more paralyzed I would become. So, feigning enthusiasm, I stepped forward, swallowed hard, and said, "Let's go!"

Phil whooped and cheered at my bravery. Then again, maybe he was celebrating the fact that it wasn't him who was about to lose his barbecue high over Branson.

Taking our place in line, I held my cane prominently in front of me. There was always the chance that the attendant would regretfully inform me that middle-aged blind women were not allowed on this ride. Then I would not only be spared the experience, but I would still collect the credit for my bravery.

No such luck.

We made it to the front of the line and were ushered to our seats. The Accelerator, I found out later, towers eighty feet in the air. It launches you suddenly into the sky before plunging you back down with back-to-back positive and negative G-forces. When the young man assisting me told me to remove my shoes so they wouldn't fly off, my breathing became shallow. What had I gotten myself into? I was already beginning to panic, and we hadn't even left the ground.

I learned later that the ride was circular in shape, and that all twelve riders were strapped in, facing out around the perimeter of the circle. At the time, however, without the benefit of sight, I really had no idea what I had so impulsively agreed to.

A cage-like set of two bars automatically lowered in front of me, and a set of belts fell down around my shoulders. The attendant helped me buckle in.

"Do you have any idea how *high* this goes?" he asked me with a chuckle. "Hey, if you're blind, maybe it's easier."

"Agghhh!" I shrieked.

"Mom," Clayton said calmly, "the ride hasn't even started yet."

I felt my "coolness" rating plummeting along with my valor.

Then the ride attendant gave instructions: "Everyone lift your hands in the air before we lift off. This helps you to relax."

I had no sooner obeyed that command than The Accelerator jerked us vertically at warp speed—and then dropped us like a stone. I screamed loudly. I mean, *really* loudly. Seizing the bars in front of me instinctively, I clung with all my strength, my hands becoming one with the metal. I held on so tight that my fingers hurt—just before they went numb.

After we landed for the final time, the attendant came to help release me from the harness. "How was it?" he asked, unfastening the buckle. He must have enjoyed the expression on my face; I could sense him trying to hold back his laughter.

I don't even know what I said in response. I was too busy catching my breath and thanking the good Lord that I was still alive.

After a brief hesitation, the attendant finally said, "Uh, ma'am? You need to let go of the bars so I can get you out."

My son was so embarrassed that he may not ever invite me to join him on a ride again.

Which is more than fine with me.

CLING

There are some things in life worth clinging to. And there are some times in life when all we can do is cling. Life has a way of presenting us with abrupt changes. Often, we can't tell whether we are being pulled up or down. Sometimes we just feel strapped, confined, and totally out of control. That's when we must cling.

Not long ago, I rediscovered a story in the Old Testament about a man who knew how to cling.

Boy, did he ever.

Eleazar was one of King David's mighty men...one of his three choicest warriors. Scripture tells the story of Eleazar's role in an amazing battle with the Philistines.

One time when the Philistines were at war with Israel, [Eleazar] and David dared the Philistines to fight them. Every one of the Israelite soldiers turned and ran, except Eleazar. He killed Philistines until his hand was cramped, and he couldn't let go of his sword. When Eleazar finished, all the Israelite troops had to do was come back and take the enemies' weapons and armor. The LORD gave Israel a great victory that day. (2 Samuel 23:9–10, CEV)

The Philistines had been Israel's nemesis for generations—a thorn in the side of God's people. Time and again through the years, they had raided and harassed the towns and villages of Israel, spilling the blood of countless young Israelite soldiers.

On this particular day, the enemy seemed unbeatable. Overpowering. They were so intimidating that the Israelite army turned tail and ran.

All but one.

The Bible says that one soldier refused to retreat. Eleazar. He stood his ground, clung to his sword, and fought like a one-man wrecking crew. One translation says he "struck the Philistines until his hand was weary and clung to the sword."

The enemy came in like a flood, and Eleazar didn't flinch. How did he prevail? The sword. He clung to the sword with such dedication, such desperation, such determination that his fingers actually "froze" around its hilt.

Can you see that in your mind's eye? The returning soldiers, probably sheepish from running away and allowing their comrade to stand alone, saw him standing there, maybe leaning up against a big rock, sword still in hand, surrounded by the dead.

"Eleazar," you can hear someone say gently, "you can set your sword down now. It's okay. The battle's over. You've won the day. The Lord has given you a great victory."

And Eleazar replies, "I would if I could, but...I can't let go."

I can imagine one lone soldier tentatively approaching the mighty man, kneeling before him, and then peeling each of Eleazar's cramped fingers from the hilt of his weapon. It was hard to see where Eleazar's skin ended and the sword began. He had wrapped every fiber of his being around that weapon. It was as if the two had become one, cemented together in those great moments of terror, courage, battle, and victory.

What a beautiful picture of what it means to cling.

Here's my question for you, my friend. When is the last time you clung to your sword—the Word of God—with *that* kind of desperation, that kind of determination?

The Bible calls itself a sword.

For the word of God is living and active. Sharper than any double-edged sword, it penetrates even to dividing soul and spirit, joints and marrow; it judges the thoughts and attitudes of the heart. (Hebrews 4:12)

Take the helmet of salvation, and the sword of the Spirit, which is the word of God. (Ephesians 6:17, NASB)

It is the weapon God gives us to fight our enemies, to overcome in any battle in our lives. Because of Eleazar's determination to cling to his sword, "the LORD gave Israel a great victory." And it's the same for you and me. Hold on tight to God's Word, and the Lord will enable you to pre-vail—to utterly defeat the forces arrayed against you.

But you have to cling. You have to stand your ground and hold onto that sword with everything you've got.

As in so many other areas of life, Jesus shows us the way.

JESUS AND THE SWORD

As much as I hate to admit it, sometimes God intends for us to face battles and endure wilderness experiences so we can learn to use the valuable weapon He has entrusted us with. This is the example that Jesus set for us. Matthew records that He was "led up by the Spirit into the wilderness to be tempted by the devil. And after He had fasted forty days and forty nights, He then became hungry" (Matthew 4:1–2, NASB).

Never doubt that when Satan and his demon army move to attack you, they pick the time and the battlefield. Have you noticed that? The attacks seem especially heavy when we're hungry, hot, tired, discouraged, depleted, or lonely. Our trials ensue just when it seems like we're least capable of handling them.

Why does God allow those dry wilderness wanderings and the ongoing battle with evil? Why doesn't He protect us from such times? The fact is, He sometimes *leads* us into such times.

Why? Because we will be weak, vulnerable, and useless kingdom soldiers if we never train with our swords.

Is there danger in these encounters? Of course there is. This is a dangerous world, and these are dangerous times. But He has given us a wondrous weapon to wield against the "father of lies." And God assures us that no temptation will come our way beyond our ability to handle it and emerge victorious. We have His word on it.

> But remember that the temptations that come into your life are no different from what others experience. And God is faithful. He will keep the temptation from becoming so strong that you can't stand up against it. When you are tempted, he will show you a way out so that you will not give in to it. (1 Corinthians 10:13, NLT)

When Jesus faced the enemy in that desolate place, He could have used any weapon at His disposal to knock him out with a humiliating defeat. Besides the fact that Jesus was God incarnate, possessing unlimited power, consider what else He had going for Him in the weapons department.

First, He was a rabbi—a religious "professional," you might say. Familiar with the Law and the Prophets, He led a tidy, good, religiously upstanding life. He could have pulled out the "religion" weapon from His arsenal during that duel in the desert. That's what we do at times. When the battle gets hot, we pull out our religious experience or our good works or our own virtue in order to deflect the enemy's attacks.

Bad idea.

Scripture says that "all our righteous acts are like filthy rags" (Isaiah 64:6). We can't fight a fierce enemy with a filthy rag, my friend—and that's what empty religion is.

Second, Jesus had a great personality. The Gospels portray Him as a kind teacher, compassionate friend, popular speaker, gentle leader, and compelling storyteller. He was obviously persuasive in His speech. Perhaps He could have convinced His enemy not to hit so hard, or to join Him in a peaceful singing of "Kumbayah." He could have pulled out the weapon of personality-plus and fought, but He didn't. Not for a moment. And neither should we.

How often do we muster all our strength and the collective attributes of our personality and try to stand against the enemy of our souls? But it won't work. We can't fight spiritual battles with weapons of the flesh. Our great personalities and charisma are not weapons; only truth is a weapon.

Jesus could have fought with any implement of war at His disposal, but He chose wisely. He engaged the enemy with the only weapon that guarantees victory: the sword of the Spirit, the Word of God.

Read the full account in the book of Matthew. Satan attacked three times from three different angles. He tried ridicule, he tried subtlety, he tried a brazen frontal assault.

And all three times Jesus countered the assaults of hell with "It is written...." The living Word of God quoted the written Word of God to beat back the enemy's attack. How can you and I do any less when it comes to our battles? "It is written" should be our weapon of choice. We should never counter the attacks with "It is my religious experience" or "It is my personality." Those weapons will always disappoint us, but God's Word never will.

If God has allowed you to be in a wilderness of trial or temptation, if you find yourself, like Eleazar, on a battlefield utterly alone, don't lose heart. Don't quit. God's Word is the weapon that will bring you victory, comfort, and provision. Cling to it, for your King considers you worthy to possess it.

SWORD OF HONOR

Along with millions of other Americans, I look forward to my favorite weekly television program: *Antique Road Show*. It's a marvelous parade of old collectibles and vintage treasures found in the attics of ordinary people. Sculptures, paintings, jewelry, and even toys make up the potpourri of antiquities that are carefully examined and exclaimed over by seasoned appraisers each week for all to see.

One night I was watching the show on location in Charlotte, North Carolina, when a certain item caught my attention. It was a sword. Normally, antique weapons don't pique my interest. But this time was different. I think it was the appraiser's reaction to what he saw that caused me to sit up and take note.

With childlike exuberance and a touch of reverence, Mr. Mitchell, the appraiser, exclaimed, "This is the most exciting military find I've ever seen come into the show." As he held the jewel-adorned heirloom, he asked its owner to explain the sword's origin.

Pleased and proud, the man told the story of a ceremonial blade that had been in his family since 1848, when it was presented to one of his ancestors, a general who fought in the Mexican War. The appraiser quickly noted that at the time of its presentation, such a sword was considered the highest honor bestowed by the United States government.

The impressive scabbard was beautifully engraved, indicating that the President himself had presented it. Because the blade bore such an inscription, the dealer placed an incredibly high value on this rare find.

I own such a sword.

No, better—infinitely better than that old piece of metal.

My sword, too, has been passed down through many generations. I'm not sure that I had really recognized that it was such a symbol of honor. I don't keep my sword in the attic, though. I hold onto it for dear life. I pick it up every day and notice its beautiful jewels.

You have the same sword. The sword you and I possess is God's Holy Word, inscribed by the very finger of God. It's filled with promises, hidden treasures, and powerful truth, making it an incredibly rare find.

What an honor that God Himself would entrust us with such an extraordinary gift. Hold your sword in high regard, for it is a reminder that God Himself holds you in high regard. If yours is in the attic, get it down, dust it off, test its edge, and examine its jewels. Feel its comforting weight in your hand. Hold it with reverence and cling to it with confidence.

Remember Eleazar, who became so attached to his sword he couldn't let it go. Don't let anyone or anything pry your fingers—or your heart—from the Word of God.

CHAPTER TWO

Say Farewell to Ducks

It was the eleven o'clock worship hour, and my pastor was on a roll.

As usual, I was hanging on every word of his message. But this Sunday he was outdoing himself. Call it eloquent, call it passionate, call it anointed, call it whatever you like, but it was just about the best sermon I'd ever heard on the virtues of God's Word.

And there I was (in my usual spot in the second row), saying "Amen! Amen!" with practically every breath he took. I was in full accord with every word he spoke about the Bible and its inestimable value in our lives. After all, I spent a lot of time studying the Word. I was busy teaching it—and even writing books about all I was learning. There were moments in the message when I had to restrain myself from jumping out of my pew to stand behind the pulpit and finish the sermon for him.

He was dancing my dance, singing my song, humming my tune. Imagine my surprise when he hit a discordant note near the end of his remarks.

I had been riding along on his thought train, happy and content, and suddenly it was as if the train derailed. He spoke some words that were, to my mind, highly questionable.

He had been pleading with us as his congregation to spend daily time in God's Word. But as he was bringing his thoughts to a close, he paused for a moment and said, "Listen to me. If you're not having daily time in the Word, then you have a pride issue."

What did he just say? A pride issue? Oh, I don't think so!

The amens lifting from the second row went suddenly silent. For the first time all morning, I did not agree with my beloved pastor.

He's wrong, I thought. *I certainly have issues that keep me from daily time in the Word of God, but pride is NOT one of them.*

I quickly began my mental rebuttal. *I don't have a pride issue. I have other issues—like ministry, motherhood, and just plain hard circumstances.*

The pastor was still speaking, but I had tuned out, reviewing my "ministry issue." My life had changed since I entered full-time ministry. I had manuscript deadlines, I traveled several weekends every month—I was practically a "professional Christian"! How could he expect me to carve time out of every busy-sometimes-crazy day to spend time in the Word? It just wasn't always easy to do.

Warming to my own argument, I thought about a second issue that made setting aside time for Bible reading almost impossible: motherhood. Our little Connor was in the midst of potty training, and things were tough around my house. I was sleep deprived, frazzled, and numb from listening to endless episodes of *Barney* and *Veggie Tales*. I was a worn-out woman. Some days were so busy that I had to decide between a shower and reading the Bible. So, for the good of humanity, I showered.

You know, I mused, *it's not as easy for the rest of us as it might be for you, Pastor. We don't get paid to be a Christian like you do.*

But I wasn't done yet. I had one more issue that topped them all.

Blindness.

Yes—that's the mother of all issues. It's pretty hard to read the Bible when you can't see it. Yes, I have the Bible on CD. But if I place it in my little CD player and accidentally bump it, I can go from Matthew to Revelation in a nanosecond. Ah, yes, my cup runneth over with issues, but pride spilled out a long time ago.

I felt pretty satisfied with my list of excuses...and maybe just a little bit smug. Yes, all my ducks were in a neat row. So, continuing to ignore the sermon I now found offensive, I decided to take a closer look at my little feathered friends.

The Ministry Duck

This little ducky had neatly platted feathers and a smile plastered upon her beak. Beneath her feathered wings were her study Bible, prayer journal, worship CDs, and, of course, her Day-Planner. Her wings, in fact, were so full that they could never be lifted in praise or opened before God to receive what He might want to give her.

The Mama Duck

Another ducky waddled into view. When this mama duck saw her reflection in the pond, it wasn't nearly so polished as the ministry duck. The feathers atop her head were disheveled because she hadn't had time for a shower—and were in desperate need of a trim and a highlight. Her webbed feet hadn't had a pedicure since before her first little duckling hatched. Her eyes were bloodshot from lack of sleep since her duckling was now teething. She paddled dizzily through her day, from one end of the pond to the other, just trying to keep the family afloat. Privacy is a distant luxury for mama duck. She just can't squeeze any more time out of her day to spend alone with God.

The Blind Duck

Oh, this was a sassy one. When it was her turn to appear, she waddled up with her white cane and attitude to spare. Sauntering into the line beside mama duck, she took her place in a long, long row of duckies, extending as far as my imagination could see.

~ ~ ~

What a lovely set of excuses. No one could ever shoot them down. They were so innocent, so sincere, so full of worthwhile pursuits, and swimming in a stream of service to others.

Then it happened. *Bam! Bam!* Duck hunting season began.

Just as I tuned back in for my pastor's final words, he shot right through my thoughts and sent my feathered excuses flying.

"I call this a pride issue," he was saying, "because at the core of your neglect of the Word is the belief that *you really don't need God.*"

His aim was perfect, knocking all three lame-ducks right out of the sky. Unable to fly against the truth, my duckies were down to stay. He was right. Neglecting my time in God's Word—whatever my excuse—was like telling Jesus I really didn't need Him.

Terrible thought. I knew better...didn't I? I *did* need Him. I will *always* need Him. As I examined my heart, I readily affirmed that I could never navigate life on my own. And didn't want to! So why was I so smugly acting as if I could?

Resuming my internal dialogue, I told myself *It's high time you started acting on what you believe, girl. You don't have ministry issues, motherhood issues, or even blind issues. You have one issue...pride.*

I had been wounded that day for sure, but it was the right kind of wound. One that would lead me to wholeness.

We all have "issues," don't we? You've got ducks, I've got ducks, all God's children got ducks. Your ducks are any excuses that you allow to keep you from the one thing you most desperately need in life.

How many ducks have you lined up? Are your excuses really worth more to you than God's Word? Nothing has really changed in my life. I still face ministry pressures, responsibilities as a wife and mom, and yes, I am still blind. But instead of allowing those life issues to become roadblocks keeping me from my time with God and His Word, I want them to become pathways to His presence. Reminders of my profound, constant, moment-by-moment need.

We should never allow the demands of life—which admittedly seem so urgent at the time—to keep us from what is the most important. In fact, the demands of life that seem so quickly overwhelming should push us right into His arms.

Which ducks are quacking up your schedule, and keeping you from your time with God? I have found that no matter how much we love the Bible, it still takes discipline to be in the Word every day.

INDEFATIGABLE DISCIPLINE?

Clayton groaned after dinner as his dad pulled a familiar book off the kitchen shelf. "Not again," he moaned. "Why do we need to read this every night?"

"Well," Phil said simply, "you never know when you might need to know these."

The book which drew such protest from our high school freshman is *100 Words Every High School Graduate Should Know*. And even though Clayton was a few years away from graduation, we pulled out the book each night following dinner and tried to guess definitions. His dad and I think it is fun and stimulating; Clayton, on the other hand, thinks it's the very essence of cruel and unusual punishment.

Last night, for instance, we learned what it meant to be *feckless*. Perhaps you know someone who meets the qualifications. The word means lacking purpose or vitality, feeble or ineffective, careless and irresponsible. What a great adjective. But what an awful label to wear through life.

We recently unearthed a buried treasure in the word *bellicose*. Even though the word sounds so beautiful and kind of rolls off the tongue, it actually means warlike or hostile. I'm not sure about Clayton, but I still remember wonderful words from weeks ago...words like *enervated* or *indefatigable*.

Now there's a mouthful. The first means to be drained of energy and the latter means to be tireless. Aren't words magnificent, grand, spectacular, and sublime?

Lover of words that I am, I do understand my young son's antipathy (there's another gem) toward learning new terms. It takes discipline to grow a vocabulary, and discipline is neither natural nor easy.

I understand because I have felt that way about investing regular time in the Word each day. It takes discipline to grow a spiritual vocabulary filled with memorized truth.

I guess that's why it's so easy to allow the merely urgent in my life to crowd out the truly important. When it comes right down to it, I don't like discipline any more than my son Clayton does. But I'm learning something I pray that he learns in the coming days: Discipline will always lead to delight, and delight will always lead to desire. Did you get that? If you and I dedicate ourselves to the Word, discipline ourselves to read and memorize it, then we can expect the fruit of that discipline to bring us delight.

And don't we desire those things in which we delight?

The prophet Jeremiah experienced the delight and desire of God's Word. He wrote, "Your words were found and I ate them, and Your words became for me a joy and the delight of my heart" (Jeremiah 15:16, NASB).

Sometimes we moan when it comes to discipline. In fact, we become downright feckless and enervated. But be indefatigable and pick up the Book each day and night and learn something from His Word. One day you will realize that what began as discipline has now become pure, perfect, genuine, absolute, complete delight.

Listen to how a simple shepherd boy named David tried to wrap words around his elation.

> The precepts of the LORD are right,
> rejoicing the heart;
> the commandment of the LORD is pure,
> enlightening the eyes;
> the fear of the LORD is clean,
> enduring forever;
> the rules of the LORD are true,
> and righteous altogether.
> More to be desired are they than gold,
> even much fine gold;
> sweeter also than honey
> and drippings of the honeycomb.
> Moreover, by them is your servant warned;
> in keeping them there is great reward.
> (Psalm 19:8–11, ESV)

Yes, it's a beautiful psalm, and most of us would nod our heads and say, "How true. How true." But if I can become very personal for a moment—almost more personal than I want to be—I'd like you to think what your life would be like if you could never, for the rest of your life, read a Bible at all.

IN ONE MOMENT OF SIGHT

In an interview not long ago, I was asked, "If you could see just one thing for one moment what would it be?"

The question took me aback. I really hadn't been expecting her to surface the subject at all—I have so many other things I'd rather talk about than my blindness. But since she asked, I paused for a moment to consider an answer.

After a few seconds I said, "I'd reject the offer. To me, it would be like Lay's Potato Chips. You can't eat just one!"

The interviewer laughed as I continued. "Truly, I would hesitate to choose one thing because—I'd be so afraid of later regretting my choice. I'd fear that a moment of sight might awaken something within me that has long been at rest under the blanket of contentment. I'd be afraid to arouse the desire to see."

The interviewer gave a long, contemplative sigh and moved to the next question.

Hours and even days later, however, the question haunted me. It nagged at me and began to erode what I thought had been a secure fortress of contentment. Part of the problem was that she had hit me with that question during a season of what I call "life fatigue." Ever felt like that? Just worn out by life.

I was tired of being blind. I guess that's why the question unsettled me. It felt like the sting of a bandage being torn away too quickly. I didn't *want* to be able to see for "a moment." I wanted to see for a lifetime.

Even so, it perplexed and frustrated me that I couldn't come up with an answer to her question. *If I could see for just a moment, what would I choose to see?* In spite of myself, I began to catalog all the things I might choose.

My parents' faces. *They were so young when I last saw them. What a joy it would be to see how they have aged in grace and beauty.*

My own children. *What would it be like to see their faces? What a gift that would be.*

My husband. *He was such a good-looking young man when we married. How do I know he was good-looking? He told me.*

Sunsets. *When I was a girl growing up in Miami, I saw some amazing displays at the beach. Oh, to see the ocean, or a sunset, or a seashell.*

I continued to ponder the array of possibilities, but no thought brought satisfaction. Then, at last, my discontent gave way to peace as I thought of the one thing I would choose.

If I could see for just one moment, I would open a Bible and look upon Psalm 63.

O God, You are my God; I shall seek You earnestly;
My soul thirsts for You, my flesh yearns for You,
In a dry and weary land where there is no water.
Thus I have seen You in the sanctuary,
To see Your power and Your glory.
Because Your lovingkindness is better than life,
My lips will praise You.

So I will bless You as long as I live;
I will lift up my hands in Your name. (vv.1–4, NASB)

Surprised by my choice?

Oh, my friend, how do I explain this to you?

Even as I write these words I am overwhelmed by the thought of actually seeing those eternal words. Why? Because His lovingkindness truly is better than life, better than sight, better than anything. Nothing in my life has been better to me than His lovingkindness. And I have experienced His lovingkindness from reading His Word.

I am convinced that nothing else would be worthy of my momentary gaze.

I don't want to over-spiritualize or be dramatic. It's just that the depth of emotion I feel about this makes it hard for me to put it into words.

I can understand that my choice might seem strange to you. After all, I can still access the Word because of my computer and CDs. I can listen to it being beautifully read by actors, I can hear it read by my children, my husband, and my pastor. So why would I want to use the only moment of sight to see something I can hear anytime?

I know that God's Word is much more than written words on a page.

It's much more than ink on India paper. But there's just something about the *Book*...that's how I used to experience the Word. And no longer can.

Do you realize what a privilege it is to be able to pick up your Bible and open its pages to read *anytime you want to*? It's a liberty that you may not realize until it's lost. It's a comfort that you can't fully appreciate or understand unless the privilege has been removed.

I have never seen the faces of my boys or my husband, so I don't feel the loss in the same way. But I did see my Bible. My eyes lingered on its pages from early childhood. As a young girl, I remember my red leather Bible that I read on my own out of curiosity and even childlike desire. As a young teen curled up in my bed in Miami—unsure of myself, insecure, afraid—I would read my Bible late into the night.

It was mine. I underlined it. I marked the pages. I held it. Even though it was merely ink on paper wrapped in a leather binding, it represented something physical and tangible. And to hold it again and see it...would be to experience it in a way that was precious to me, and in a way to which little else compares. It was a privilege to see it with my own eyes. I wish I had taken even more advantage of that privilege. Now, it's gone. And I miss it.

I loved my Bible so much that even years after the onset of my blindness, I still carried it to church with me. Holding the book, smelling the leather, hearing the thin rustle of the pages was to me a bit of security—like holding hands with heaven. But I finally stopped doing even that, because of the curious questions.

Even now, when I am with my precious friend and writing assistant Karen, I feel a tinge of jealousy and long to be able to pick up the Word and read it like she does. Her Bible is well worn, and she has her history marked and jotted in the margins. She loves the Word and she treats her Bible accordingly.

I envy that. I would love that. I miss that.

Oh, my friend, of course I would love to see the precious faces and sunsets and magnolias, but I know they will all eventually fade. After all, the flowers faded a long time ago in my world. The grass does wither, as the apostle Peter put it, and faces age and change. Flowers wilt away; sunsets wane. But the Word...it's the same—just as glorious on earth as it will be in heaven. God's Word will never fade, wither, or return void.

To see the Scripture is a foretaste and a settling reminder of what is truly, eternally mine. The Word was my love before my kids were born, and the Word will be my love after my husband and parents go home to heaven. It's my companion. It's forever reliable; I am dependent on it.

Right now, in faith, I cling to the Word as I receive it, but I long for the day when my faith becomes sight.

I know I will see my kids' faces in heaven. In fact, I can't wait. I know I will see my parents—overflowing with life. My memory of an earthly sunset will be dull and colorless compared to the vibrant, transcendent glories of heaven.

If only given a moment of sight, how could I really choose a sure thing? How could I really make a choice I would never regret? Seems like the Bible is the only choice I could make that wouldn't disappoint me. A choice I could never regret. I would be able to hang onto that memory as a beautiful piece of my past and a joyous foretaste of my future.

And so, farewell to ducks. They are no longer welcome to waddle into my world. How could I have ever allowed my ducks to keep me from the discipline of a daily time in the

Bible? How could I neglect my exposure to the light of God's Word when it is the only light I really have? His Word is worthy of my discipline; it is worthy of my devotion. And it is worthy of yours.

Your eyes may see sunsets and faces. Your eyes may squint at the brightness of a steamy summer day, but you still need light. Deeper light. A light so radiant it touches blind eyes and pushes aside the shadow of death. It is the light of His Word that really allows you to see, to run, to grow, to finish strong.

David wrote: "For with You is the fountain of life; In Your light we see light" (Psalm 36:9, NASB).

Nothing else comforts me, guides me, and illuminates my darkness like the light of His Word as the Holy Spirit opens it to my understanding. It is His Word alone that compels me to keep on running the race even when I am fatigued by life. Even when loss stuns me and scrapes against the bottom of my soul, it is the Word that I run to so I can make sense of it all.

That, my friend, is desire.

When we discipline ourselves in the Word, it will lead to delight. And delight will always lead to desire. To long for the Word more than we long for life is to never be disappointed.

———◦◦———

CHAPTER THREE

Be a Risk Taker

Most of us approach hot dogs with a pretty traditional mindset. We slip it neatly in a bun, douse it with ketchup and mustard, and then top it off with sweet pickle relish. Some of the more adventurous among us cloak the mystery meat in chili or layer it over with sauerkraut.

When I was pregnant with both our sons, I actually craved hot dogs. I couldn't get enough of them, personally downing a minimum of a pack a week. For all my experience with the fabulous franks, however, I apparently completely missed out on the *right* way to eat them.

Yesterday, as I placed Connor's lunch before him, I told him that he needed to eat his hot dog and carrots, and then he could have some strawberries and whipped cream. As motivation, I set the plate of strawberries and the bowl of whipped cream on the table above his plate.

The strategy was apparently working. My little guy began to rapidly consume his hot dog, proclaiming that it was the best he'd ever had.

I finally figured out why his ordinary dog was so delicious. He was doing something only a four-year-old would do: dipping every bite into the whipped cream. He offered me a taste of this new culinary sensation, and I casually declined, trying not to gag.

My point is twofold. First, never dip your strawberries in whipped cream which has once belonged to a four-year-old hot dog connoisseur. Second, we must all learn to think outside the bun. According to Connor, if you don't put whipped cream on your hot dog it will taste "plain." And he let me know that he was *really* tired of plain hot dogs.

Sometimes our lives are simply plain, and we can grow weary of the "same ol', same ol'."

That's not the way God would have it.

Jesus came that we might have life, and not just plain life, not just vanilla, one-size-fits-all, run-of-the-mill life, but life that is abundant.

"The thief comes only in order to steal and kill and destroy," He told a man who had sought Him out one windy night. "I came that they may have and enjoy life, and have it in abundance (to the full, till it overflows)" (John 10:10, AMP).

What are we talking about here? The kind of life that is dipped in sweetness and smothered with all the good things of God. But in order to experience all that abundant life has to offer, we may have to climb out of some completely familiar, perfectly comfortable ruts...and venture into the territory of risk.

RELUCTANCE

Christmas dinner had long since ended and we were still visiting around the table.

"Why don't we go sit in the living room?" I suggested.

My sister-in-law quipped, "Because we fear change!" We erupted in laughter over such a dramatic answer to my simple question. But there was a bit of truth in her humor.

Most of us feel a tinge of reluctance when it comes to change, because it means we must take a risk and release some of our control. Children feel it on the first day of kindergarten. Outwardly confident teens sense it when they step foot on their new high school campus. Most of us experience it on the first day of a new job. Lots of us cringe when we contemplate a new hairstyle—and our hearts race if a move is on the horizon.

But where is our spirit of adventure? Why is it that change and letting go invokes hesitation? Is it that the predictable and familiar make us feel safe? Robert Frost shaped our misgivings into a poem he called "Reluctance."

> Ah, when to the heart of man
> Was it ever less than a treason
> To go with the drift of things,
> To yield with a grace to reason,
> And bow and accept the end
> Of a love or a season?

I guess what he's saying is that we are all clingers. We wrap ourselves around what we know and love and are reluctant to release. But if we cling to God's Word, then we are more willing to take risks in this life because we realize that we were made for adventure. Jesus Himself invites us to risk our preconceived notions and our comfort, to gain the ride of a lifetime—an eternal lifetime. "For whoever wishes to save his life," He declared, "will lose it, but whoever loses his life for My sake, he is the one who will save it" (Luke 9:24, NASB).

Adventure, you see, demands that we risk letting go.

Sometimes what we attempt to hold so tightly really has a tight hold on us. Have you ever thought about that? When we try so hard to be in control, we can often find that it is our own insecurity that really controls us. An unwillingness to let go simply keeps us bound. It's only as we risk and release that we truly receive.

RISK

Sometimes I only play in the key of C, color inside the lines, and look out the window instead of going outside. You know what I mean. I have seldom jumped in the water without first sticking my toe in to check the temperature. Why do I play it safe?

I call myself an edge dweller. Do you know what that is? An edge dweller is the person who stands right at the line, peers over, analyzes the risk, wishes to jump, takes a deep breath...and turns the other way and *runs*.

The reason I like to hug the edge is because I have taken some risks in my life, and, well...sometimes they've turned out, and sometimes they haven't. Let's face it—life offers us lots of opportunities to risk. Just by rolling out of bed and putting our feet on the floor in the morning, we are invited to experience the adventure of growing, learning, failing, and myriad other thrills.

Relationships fall into that category. Every relationship is something of an adventure—because every relationship involves risk. That risk, however, carries with it magnificent rewards, even if the outcome isn't what we would have chosen.

Several years ago I took a big risk with my (now) friend Karen. I had known who she was for some time, but we had never met. At the time, I was preparing to write my first book proposal, and I needed someone to help me. I really had no idea of Karen's personality, skills, or even her interest. But I had observed her life, and felt strongly led to call her and ask her to consider joining me on the project.

To call a perfect stranger on the phone and ask her to help me do something that I wasn't even confident about launching into in the first place felt like a big risk to me. I remember psyching myself up, praying, trying to control my nervous breathing...and then dialing Karen's number.

"Hi, Karen," I said. "You don't know me. My name is Jennifer Rothschild and I am trying to write a book. I know this sounds crazy, but...I felt led to call you and ask if you would be interested in helping me?"

I will admit, I was expecting an awkward silence from Karen...followed immediately by a gracious escape from the phone call. I just knew she would hang up and immediately call her husband: "Gerry, you won't believe the weird phone call I just got. I'm afraid that wacky blind woman suffers from delusions of grandeur. Either that, or she's really needy for friends—and I'm her new target."

But none of that happened. Instead, she said, "Oh, I know who you are. That sounds so interesting. I would love to talk to you about writing a book!"

Little did I know that the nerve-racking, risky step out of my comfort zone would land me in one of the best friendships and partnerships I've ever experienced. Don't you love it when risks pay off like that? What a great reward.

But not all risks turn out roses and sunshine. Otherwise...they wouldn't be risks, would they? I took another risk within what I thought was a very secure friendship, and the reward was not what I expected.

After almost a year with a precious friend whom I will call Julie, I took a big risk and confronted her about her depression. I had watched her moods change over the many months of our friendship. I had seen her become less able to snap out of her valley times—and I knew she had once been on medication to help her with the chemical imbalance that caused her downward spirals. So one fall day as we drove to lunch, I decided that if I were really her friend, it required some truth telling.

One of the reasons it was risky for me to confront Julie was because I wasn't quite sure how she would receive my comments. I didn't want to hurt her feelings or our friendship. She was special to me.

But even so, it was worth the risk. *She* was worth the risk.

"Julie," I began, "I've watched you change gradually over

the last few months, and I'm concerned. I think you might need to be back on your medicine."

That was it. That was all I said. And my statement was met with silence. Cold, loud silence. As I prodded, she maintained her iceberg composure—and came up with an excuse to cancel lunch. The weeks that followed were very painful for me. Julie systematically removed me from her world. No matter how gently I questioned her, no matter how persistently I confronted what was happening, I met with a cold, unyielding brick wall.

I had taken a risk to tell her what I thought was necessary truth, and I had come up a loser. She wasn't going back on her meds, and as far as she was concerned, our friendship was over.

So was it worth the risk?

I will admit, I was plagued with questions. Did I really know her as well as I thought I did? Was I out of line to confront her?

I lost the friendship, but really, I still gained. The reward of my risk was greater wisdom, a more tender heart, and the affirmation that risk is always worthy, even when the result isn't what I would have chosen.

Years later, we reunited at a women's conference and the walls fell as the tears flowed. Restoration was the final result. Risk carries with it both the potential for great loss and great reward.

But there are no rewards apart from risk.

Are you willing to risk? A lesson I learned in the Light has helped me to be more of a risk taker. It's found in the book of Matthew.

RELEASE

Jesus addressed the potential adventurers of His day, calling them to be risk takers rather than hole makers. Well, that's not exactly what he said, but you'll see what I mean. His parable in Matthew 25:14–27 tells us a lot about ourselves. There were three servants, each given a portion of their master's money. Two were risk takers. They invested and had more to offer their master. The third, however, was a hole maker. Fearing risk, he took his portion and buried it.

The master's response to the hole maker was basically, "No risk, no return. You could have taken at least a small risk by investing. After all, the money I gave you didn't come with a shovel. It was granted to you so you could make some choices and take some chances."

Here's the way Eugene Peterson paraphrased the words of the Master in *The Message*: "That's a terrible way to live! It's criminal to live cautiously like that! If you knew I was after the best, why did you do less than the least? The least you could have done would have been to invest the sum with the bankers, where at least I would have gotten a little interest. Take the thousand and give it to the one who risked the most. And get rid of this 'play-it-safe' who won't go out on a limb" (vv. 26–28, *The Message*).

Oh, my friend, our lives were given to us so *we* would make some choices and take some chances. Are you a risk taker or a hole maker? Do you risk, release, and gain reward in spite of reluctance? Or are you an adventure avoider? Do you stand at the edge of abundant life, grasping your shovel, digging a safe place to hide? Don't trust your shovel and shallow hole more than you trust God. He is worthy of your release.

The ultimate adventure happens when we risk release—when we dare to let go. Consider what the Word tells us about those who dared to let go...or not.

THOSE WHO DARED...NOT

When the Israelites began their wilderness sojourn, God positioned them for risk taking. Actually, He provided a test to see if they viewed their trust in Him as a risk. Each day, God told Moses, the people would receive all they needed to eat. Their new delicacy was called manna. Here's what God told Moses:

> "I will rain down bread from heaven for you. The people are to go out each day and gather enough for that day. In this way I will test them and see whether they will follow my instructions." (Exodus 16:4)

There was one condition to God's provision: no hole making. "No one," He commanded, "is to keep any of it until morning" (Exodus 16:19). But some of the Israelites did not obey or trust—or whatever you want to call it. (There is rarely a separation between trusting and obeying.) Some people grasped their shovels and dug, dug, dug. Instead of doing what God said, these hole makers hid away some manna for breakfast...just in case God didn't come through the next day. They saw trusting and obeying as too big a risk.

The hole making didn't pay off though. By morning the manna had become putrid.

God chose to make the people of Israel live in daily dependence upon Him. The wilderness was provided to make risk takers out of the hole makers in the crowd. It was an opportunity for the Hebrew children to live in utter dependence on God.

Perhaps, if you find yourself in a wilderness, it's for the very same reason. So that you may "not live on bread alone, but on every word that comes from the mouth of God" (Matthew 4:4).

God allows wilderness in our lives so we can experience the liberating adventure of trust. You don't learn these things lounging by the fire in an easy chair. He expects us to walk through our dark valleys with open hands of trust and praise, rather than hands sweaty and weary from grasping our shovels.

Just to keep everything in the proper perspective, I'd like to let you in on a little secret: *We're not really in control of our lives anyway.* To acknowledge this and then step into life with confidence in a loving God is to taste the sweet, spicy, and satisfying flavors of adventure.

In our darkness, God's light guides us.

In our wilderness, God's manna feeds us.

It is no risk to trust the One who is totally trustworthy. It is no risk to place our faith in the One who is Faithful. Why cling to our shovels when we can cling to His Word? Seems to me that being a hole maker is a far greater risk than being a righteous, redeemed risk taker. Try as they might, hole makers will never find the abundant life tucked away in the back of a secure tunnel. No, life overflowing is reserved for those who cast themselves on the goodness and lovingkindness of God, refusing the temptation to hold back and self-protect.

After thinking about these hole makers, it made me want to drop my shovel and walk right off the edge of my map into unknown regions. Are you like the manna-hoarding Israelites who dared not, or are you like the risk takers below?

THOSE WHO DARED

Letting go led Abraham to risk his security and leave his country.[1]

> The LORD had said to Abram, "Leave your country, your people and your father's household and go to the land I will show you".... So Abram left, as the LORD had told him. (Genesis 12:1, 4)

> By faith Abraham, when called to go to a place he would later receive as his inheritance, obeyed and went, even though he did not know where he was going. (Hebrews 11:8)

When you and I think of a move, we think about pulling up stakes from one side of town and landing a few miles away. Or trading one American city for another. Or maybe leaving the Midwest for the West Coast.

When God called Abraham and Sarah to leave Ur of the Chaldees for a land He would show them, it was more like a transfer to Mars. The world was young and wide and full of mysteries and perils.

On the word of an invisible God, however, here is a couple that abandoned their home, their familiar city, their friends, their extended family, and their way of life, to start off on a journey with no map, no directions, and no stated destination.

Imagine! And please don't think of these people as super-religious, stained-glass saints. They were as real, as human, as vulnerable, and as full of fears and feelings as you. But when God called, they simply risked everything and followed.

Letting go led a reluctant Moses to risk catastrophic failure—*again*.[2]

The LORD said, "I have indeed seen the misery of my people in Egypt. I have heard them crying out because of their slave drivers, and I am concerned about their suffering. So I have come down to rescue them from the hand of the Egyptians.... So now, go. I am sending you to Pharaoh to bring my people the Israelites out of Egypt." (Exodus 3:7–8, 10)

When you're young and you make a colossal mistake, you are sometimes allowed to "take your licks" and bounce back, fully reclaiming your life. But what if you made a huge mistake, ran to another country, gave up everything you'd ever known, and took a job as a minimum-wage laborer? *And then stayed there for forty years.*

Imagine that (if you can), and then picture yourself receiving a divine summons to return to the very scene of your terrible failure and to confront the very people who had been involved in your sudden departure. Oh...and add one more small variable: You're asked to take on the job of leader and representative of several million people.

How would you feel? Shocked? Scared? Incredulous? Insecure? Of course! But because God said so, you walk straight out of a forty-year exile and head back to the scene of your greatest defeat...in order to lay hands on what may be your greatest victory.

Letting go led Hannah to release her dream and give up her little boy, Samuel.[3]

> "Sir, do you remember me?" Hannah asked. "I am the woman who stood here several years ago praying to the LORD. I asked the LORD to give me this child, and he has given me my request. Now I am giving him to the LORD, and he will belong to the LORD his whole life." (1 Samuel 1:26–28, NLT)

What woman who has yearned for years on end to cradle a baby of her own in her arms can imagine giving him away as a toddler? Hannah, who had wept before the Lord pleading for a child, had her prayers answered. But keeping the terms of her promise, she released the little boy to the Lord's service with the priest at Shiloh, believing all would be well for both her and her son.

Walking away from that worship center, leaving the desire

of her heart behind, must have been the most wrenching, heartbreaking thing she would ever do. But the Lord honored her for her faith by both richly blessing her boy and by granting her additional children—three boys and two girls.

And so it goes through Scripture. The pages of the Bible list man after man, woman after woman who—because of their faith in a faithful God—were willing to let go of what they had in order to gain what had been promised.

Young David risked his very life to challenge a blasphemous giant.[4]

At God's commands and for God's mysterious purposes, the prophet Hosea released his expectations of a happy marriage and home to marry a woman who would break his heart again and again.[5]

Peter and Andrew risked their very livelihood, released their nets, and followed Jesus.[6]

Onesimus risked punishment, reproach, and reenslavement by obediently returning to his master, Philemon.[7]

Jesus released His royal rights as God's Son, relinquished His very life, and became obedient to death on a Roman cross.[8]

And what did they receive? They received far more than they risked. They gained much more than they lost. The same odds are in your favor, my friend. There is no risk when we release our control to God. The Word tells us that "he who promised is faithful" (Hebrews 10:23).

So embrace the adventure of completely trusting Him, for He is completely trustworthy.

Trust in the LORD forever,
for the LORD, the LORD, is the Rock eternal.
(Isaiah 26:4)

The Israelites received their manna until the day they arrived in the Promised Land (Exodus 16:35). Likewise, you and I have the Bread of Life to sustain us until we reach our Promised Land. It nourishes us and equips us to trust God completely, drop our shovels, and step out in obedience. So, when you're challenged to change, when you're called to leave the old or embrace the new, when it's time to let go or step out of your comfort zone, be a risk taker. Overcome your reluctance. Drop the shovel, trust Him, and release your control to God.

Trust GOD from the bottom of your heart;
don't try to figure out everything on your own.
Listen for GOD'S voice in everything you do, everywhere you go;
he's the one who will keep you on track.
(Proverbs 3:5–6, *The Message*)

CHAPTER FOUR

Have Courage, Not Confidence

On the heels of turning forty, I ran smack into a fashion crisis.

Should I continue to wear the same style of clothing I'd worn for the past decade? Or was it time for a fresh breeze to blow through my stale wardrobe?

Well, I knew the answer to that question.

I just didn't want to face it.

The world had turned round and round, seasons had fled, and styles had changed, while the contents of my closet remained comfortably the same. I was settled into a snug, easy, but admittedly dull pattern. You know what I mean. Certain colors. Particular lines. Similar styles. But now, as I stepped into my fourth decade of life, it seemed like the right time to reassess. My hair was now a different color, and my body was hosting the latest and maybe not the greatest new lines. And the old wardrobe? Well, it needed a little lift since this new decade brought with it the tugging effects of gravity.

I needed a little spice. It was time to step out.

But it isn't that easy to simply step out of a deep rut. You have to *climb* out hand over hand. It's a major effort and investment of emotional energy.

Right at the front of my closet, I had four identical suits, all safe and traditional. I say they were identical, but in reality they were different colors. And even the colors weren't that adventurous...black, gray, brown, and, you guessed it, the ever exciting navy.

So at the urging of my most honest and loyal friends and with the full support of my family, I finally went shopping. That's when I discovered that I not only had a fashion crisis, but I also had a confidence crisis. I had no idea what to buy. I was uneasy in this venture toward a new look. I really wasn't sure of what I even liked.

I was also unsure of *how* to update my style. Remember that the last fashion I saw with my own eyes as a young teen was that of the Lady Diana Spencer before she became the Princess of Wales. So I was stuck with mental images of white stockings, linebacker-like shoulder pads, and stiff tailored suits. I also had the image of the ever-stylish Jacqueline Kennedy Onassis seared on my memory. I loved her classic look and clean lines.

These were my only points of reference, so you can imagine the building anxiety I experienced as my friends started piling clothes into the fitting room. There were tiny ruffles and bits of lace. Long shirts, short skirts, low-waisted pants, and high heeled shoes. My confidence waned with each selection I tried. The clothes my friends brought into the fitting room were cheery, bold, and colorful. As only good friends can, each reassured me that I too was cheery, bold, and colorful.

I felt very little confidence in venturing out into the world of hot pink and leather, especially when both were located on the same piece of clothing. Even so, I swallowed hard and made up my mind to be brave. Instead of gravitating to the classic Jackie O clothes that I would normally have chosen, I laid aside my insecurity and added a splash of trendy J-Lo to my wardrobe. Now I am the proud-yet-slightly-insecure owner of a pair of leather pants and a hot pink suede jacket. Whew!

In the days that followed, however, my new purchases remained neatly and safely tucked behind my closet door. Well...wasn't it daring enough just to buy them? Did I have to *wear* them, too?

What's keeping me from debuting the new look? I whined to myself. When I chose to be honest, I had to admit that a lack of confidence is what kept me from wearing them. I just didn't feel confident. If I just felt a little more confident, then I could exercise courage. Or so I thought.

After weeks of encountering my leather pants hanging in my closet, however, I decided I would not wait until I felt confident. Instead I would, at the first opportunity, slip my forty-year-old self into those sassy pants and be courageous. In other words, I would have courage even if I didn't have confidence. Think about that. Do you realize that those two concepts are often mistaken for each other?

Courage and confidence are not the same thing. Confidence is a feeling; courage is an action. Let me put it this way. In our spiritual lives, lots of us simply wait for feelings of confidence before we exercise courage. The Bible never tells us to *feel* something and then act. No, it tells us to trust Someone and then act. Rather than feeling our way into a right action, we must act our way into right feelings.

Waiting for confidence to arrive can only make us more uncertain, because when we fail to act, we lose hope. If we are to persevere through our faith walk, we must be brave even when we don't feel self-assured.

That is one of the most liberating lessons I have ever learned in the Light. The Bible demonstrates this through countless examples of those who had no confidence in the flesh, but who did what brave believers do. *They stepped out with courage—even when they lacked confidence.*

WHAT DOES GOD REQUIRE?

Do you think Abraham felt confident when he climbed Mt. Moriah with a sharp knife, a stack of firewood, and his only son—with no alternative sacrifice in sight?

Did Moses' mother feel totally confident when she laid

her sweet baby in a basket to float down the Nile?

We can all identify with how the grown-up Moses wore his own lack of confidence on his sleeve when God asked him to confront Pharaoh. He stuttered his way through all his insecurities.

I think of the woman with an issue of blood. How in the world could she have felt confident? There she was, in the middle of a crowd. She was ceremonially unclean. It would have been practically criminal for her to touch a Rabbi. She didn't reach for the hem of Jesus' garment out of a sense of confidence. No, it was courage. Pure, raw, desperate courage.

Esther didn't march boldly into King Xerxes' throne room and confidently state her case. Instead, it took the persuasive arguments of her beloved cousin Mordecai, three days of prayer and fasting, and a couple of dinners with the king before Esther could muster the courage to tell Xerxes why she had risked so much. She lacked confidence. Of course she did. I'm sure I would too if I had to stand in her slippers. But she acted with heroic courage and saved her people as a result.

God doesn't require confidence; He asks only for courage. If we wait for a feeling of confidence to settle in before we step out, we may never act. We must be willing to get out of our comfort zone and experience the uncertain adventure of exercising courage in spite of our lack of confidence. When we do, then we find that an amazing confidence results. Yes, a confidence in God and in His promises.

THREE GIFTS OF COURAGE

God did not give us the spirit of timidity or fear. Second Timothy 1:7 tells us exactly what He has given us. "For God has not given us a spirit of timidity, but of power and love and discipline" (NASB). I want you to grab hold of the three things that Paul claimed as gifts from God in this verse, because God has given us these same three gifts. These three things will bolster your courage and renew your confidence.

Power

What has God given you in place of timidity? He has given you power. Yes, He has! He said so. The Greek word for *power*, "dunamis," refers to the kind of power that exists in something or someone inherently—within its very nature. It's a power that shows itself through exertion. We get our word *dynamite* from this word. This kind of power requires our cooperation. Just as a stick of dynamite needs a touch of fire to release its great power, so it is with our will. When we recognize that God's power is our gift, we simply ignite its potential in our lives by stepping out and applying it.

Paul wrote to the church in Philippi about this kind of power when he said, "I can do all things through Christ who strengthens me" (Philippians 4:13, NKJV).

"All things" kind of power is indeed dynamite.

What are you timid about? In what areas of your life today do you lack confidence? No matter what answer pops into your mind, it falls into the "all things" category. Why? Because all things means *all things*. That means even when you don't feel confident, even when you lack courage, you can do those things...through Christ. You *do* have the power to accomplish all the things that God calls you to accomplish, and you *can* do it through Christ who is your strength. Yes! It's as true as the morning sunrise, and as near as your next heartbeat.

What intimidates you? It is no match for the power of Christ in and through you. My friend, it isn't even close.

Love

What else did God give you instead of timidity? He gave you love. The times in my life when I have been the most timid and lacking in self-confidence have been those seasons when I was least secure in my husband's love. It's not that Phil ever intentionally held back his love for me. It's just that in our mutual immaturity during the early years of our marriage, he didn't always express his love for me in a way I could readily recognize. But as the second decade of our marriage began to unfold, there was no doubt of his loyal, kind, committed love for me. It had been there all along, but after ten years, he learned how to communicate it and I learned how to recognize it.

Can I just say that the result was, and still is, wings? I am secure enough to be vulnerable, secure enough to risk, secure enough to fail. That is a result of love.

If imperfect human love can overcome the effects of timidity, how much more can the perfect love of God?

"There is no fear in love," the apostle John tells us. "But perfect love drives out fear" (1 John 4:18). The Greek word for love in both 2 Timothy 1:7 and the verse you just read is *agape*. It is the perfect, unconditional, unmerited, unreserved love of God lavished on each of us. It is not based on our deeds; neither is it awarded according to our worthiness. Agape is from God to you...just because.

How can you and I allow fear to govern us when we've received this extravagant kind of love? We should be emboldened by agape love, which says, "I love you when you fail. I love you when you succeed beyond your wildest imagination. I love you, and My love is stronger than your insecurity. My love for you is bigger than your fear, stronger than the timidity that binds you, and deeper than your deepest insecurity."

It makes me want to shout with the apostle John, "Behold what manner of love the Father has bestowed on us!" (1 John 3:1, NKJV). Receive the over-the-top love of God. He longs to lavish it upon you. He wants you to have wings—and be brave enough to spread them and soar.

Self-Discipline

The third and final gift God gave you in place of your timidity is self-discipline. I remember the first time I met Beth Moore. It was in the early 1990s and I was in my late twenties. We'd both been invited to participate in a conference in south Florida.

She and I clicked from the start. I was mesmerized by her handling of the Word and thought she was absolutely genuine and loads of fun. And so I picked up the few speaking tapes she had available at her table. The message I most wanted from our weekend together was one she gave on self-control. It resonated with me, and over the years God has used it to continually teach and guide me.

Recently, as I was preparing one of my Bible studies, I retrieved my beloved tape. As I sat in a comfy chair listening to her introduction, I was struck again by the profound truth she was unfolding. Then as I continued to listen, something else struck me...*the amount of food I had consumed during her thirty-minute message.*

During the introduction, I ate a handful of dark chocolate. I actually stopped the tape mid-message to go get a cup of coffee with the nicest French vanilla cream you've ever tasted. Near the end of the tape, I found myself dropping leftover Easter jelly beans into my mouth. I did pause my indulgence a few times throughout her teaching, just long enough to record a verse...and then resumed eating.

That's when it struck me. As I listened to a message on self-control, I was myself absolutely out of control.

Second Timothy 1:7 uses the word *self-discipline.* It reminds us that we are positioned for a life of moderation, soundness of mind, and yes, self-control. The good news is that what God calls us to do, He equips us to do. In Galatians 5, one of the fruits of the Spirit that should blossom from our yielded life is none other than self-control. God knows our weaknesses, and He provides through His Spirit the self-control we need. Our part is to so walk in the Spirit, that we will fulfill the desires of the Spirit.[9]

When we have this kind of self-control (Spirit controlled self-control), it will penetrate every weakness that intimidates us. If it is our thoughts that bind us to a life of timidity, then we need to bravely proclaim that we can hold "every thought captive to the obedience of Christ" (2 Corinthians 10:5, NASB). If it is an action or addiction that intimidates us, continually overpowering our will, then we can agree with the truth that "no temptation has seized you except what is common to man. And God is faithful; he will not let you be tempted beyond what you can bear. But when you are tempted, he will also provide a way out so that you can stand up under it" (1 Corinthians 10:13).

Oh my friend, don't wait to feel confident about your ability to control all your weaknesses. Recognize that God has given you the *gift* of self-control. Be brave and exercise it. As you act with courage, watch how feelings of confidence will follow. And don't miss where your real confidence will come from. It will be a confidence in God Himself, and in His Word. The prophet Malachi reminds us that God's Word never will return void.[10] It will always accomplish what God intends. So be confident in His Word, and exercise courage.

Shortly after the explosion of the shuttle Colombia in 2003, I heard an interview on the evening news. The anchorman was questioning a former astronaut, probing the man's feelings on future space travel. The question that caught my attention went something like this: "Aren't you afraid to venture back into space? Surely your confidence in NASA has been shaken."

The astronaut's response reminded me a lot of the difference between courage and confidence, and how fear or timidity impacts the two. He solemnly answered that his fear of *not* doing it was greater than his fear of dying doing it.

In other words, the astronaut's decision to step out in courage had nothing to do with confidence. That's why fear did not impact his willingness to persevere.

I want my faith journey to be so precious to me that my fear of not pursuing will be greater than my fear of dying as I pursue. Don't you? Quitting is what I fear most, because quitting represents the ultimate death. *To finish well, we must fear quitting more than failing.* We must fear giving up more than we fear giving our all.

So don't ever let fear keep you from stepping out in courage. Don't wait for your confidence to exceed your fear. Quite honestly, that may never happen. But recognize that God didn't give you fear; He gave you love, power, and self-control.

Love will motivate your courage, power will give muscle to your courage, and self-control will help you maintain courage. Now those are some reasons to feel confident.

So, step out. Don't let a confidence crisis keep you from running your race with perseverance. After all, you are not of those who shrink back!

10:39!

I've always tried to find quick and creative ways to communicate with my sons. As a mother of two boys, I learned very long ago that their DNA does not predispose them to lengthy conversations, meaningful talks, or many words. So early on, I made a habit of simply saying "4:13!" to them.

You see, "4:13" is a reference to Philippians 4:13, the beloved Scripture I mentioned earlier: "I can do all things through Christ who strengthens me" (NKJV). So each time I yell, "4:13!" after them as they leave for school or a soccer game, they know what it means...that they can do all things as Christ gives them strength. It's a great way, in very few words, to boost their confidence.

In the last few months, however, a new phrase has replaced the "4:13" mantra.

10:39!

"But we are not of those who shrink back." Those are the first words of Hebrews 10:39. It's what the writer told the worn-out Jewish believers enduring persecution, and it's what I tell my boys. It's my way of reminding them to have courage and not give up. And it seems those eight little words are making a big impression on my five-year-old Connor.

As a type A personality, I'm ashamed to admit this, but my video cabinet is a disaster. Videos and DVDs are all mixed together, and none of them are stored in their correct cases. It's almost impossible to find what you're looking for. Connor was recently searching through this mess for one of his favorite DVDs. After about ten minutes, my little man began to lose heart, so he came and asked me for help. I began to dig through the video cabinet, pulling out empty containers and old videos. I also began to lose heart, and commented on how hard it was going to be to locate his DVD of choice.

"Mom," he announced, "we are not of those who shrink back."

"You're right, Connor," I replied, getting to my feet with a smile. "So you just keep on looking." As I took my first step toward the door little Connor yelled, "Mom! WE are not of those who shrink back! WE means both of us!"

I laughed, did a 180, and knelt again before the video cabinet. Thankfully, by some miracle, Connor instantly put his hand on the exact DVD he was looking for. "I found it! I found it!" he squealed, running to pop the disc into its player. I was relieved that the search had ended, but was grateful for what I discovered in the process—that "we" really does mean both of us.

Sometimes it's easier to have courage and persevere when you have a buddy. Every football player needs to hear the fans chant, "*We* will, *we* will, rock you!" just when he's starting to feel weak-kneed and defeated. Every kid needs a soccer mom who yells "Good try!" when the goal is elusive.

One of the most reliable companions for your journey, a companion that will always cheer you on, is God's Word. It provides all the cheers and encouragement you need to keep on stepping out in courage.

Scripture says, "For you have need of endurance, so that when you have done the will of God you may receive what is promised" (Hebrews 10:36, ESV).

In other words, we don't ever give up. We don't quit. Because we are not of those who shrink back. We keep searching even when treasures are hard to find. We keep helping even when the situation seems hopeless. And we keep believing even when the mission seems impossible. So my friend, let those eight words fill your tank and provide fuel for your journey. I'm just one of the many voices you'll hear cheering you on.

Don't wait until you feel confident to exercise courage. God's Word reminds us that we are given all we need for life and godliness.[11] You too are cheery, bold, and colorful, so live like it! As you do, you will find that a small risk is far more exciting than a big rut.

"Have I not commanded you? Be strong and courageous! Do not tremble or be dismayed, for the LORD your God is with you wherever you go" (Joshua 1:9, NASB).

If you see a forty-something lady walking down the street with leather pants, a pink suede jacket, and a white cane, just chalk her up to the ranks of those who can't quite manage confidence...but have enough courage in Jesus to make up for it.

CHAPTER FIVE

Carry No Baggage

I was given a lovely bracelet at a recent speaking event in Lawrenceville, Georgia. In fact, all five hundred women attending the ladies' night out received the very same bracelet.

Just above the knives at each woman's place setting lay a stretchy, shiny, silver charm bracelet. They're the kind I call "happy bracelets." You know what I mean. They clink and clatter and jingle when they are jostled. They sound happy just to be on your wrist.

The bracelet was strung with charms resembling women's shoes—stylish stilettos. I loved it, especially since my wrist was the only place my body would ever safely wear such fashionable footwear.

The bracelet was a creative way for the host church to communicate the evening's theme: *walking by faith*.

I thought it was a fabulous idea.

But there was one problem.

Between each shoe on the bracelet hung a woman's purse. Yes, it was cute, but what do purses have to do with walking by faith? To my linear way of thinking, it diluted the whole theme of the evening. The cute purses, trendy and tiny as they were, detracted from the message of the bracelet.

Then, as I slipped it on my wrist, it hit me.

Purses have everything to do with walking by faith. The shoes are an obvious reminder to do as Paul tells us in 2 Corinthians 5:7—to walk by faith, not by sight. And the purses are an equally important reminder to carry no baggage.

BAGGAGE CLAIMS US

The person who thrives in a dark world and perseveres cannot be encumbered by the heavy things of life. Most of the things that weigh us down are the things we pick up along the way. This kind of baggage might seem attractive at the time— unforgiveness that seems justified, selfishness that seems harmless, prayerlessness that seems warranted, envy that we keep to ourselves.

Most of the baggage we gather is grabbed on impulse. We think we can afford it. It doesn't seem expensive until we realize we never quit paying for it. We convince our- selves we can own and manage it, until it dawns on us that our luggage owns *us* and we are managed by it.

So here's my confession: I've had to clean out my spiritual closet once or twice a season because I collect so much baggage. Are you a baggage collector like me?

A friend of mine who hadn't traveled much told me about finding himself weighted down on a rare business trip. He had been sick a few days before the trip and felt weak anyway; he also had a garment bag over one shoulder, a laptop computer in its case strapped over the other, a bag in one hand, and a briefcase in the other. (Clearly, no one had ever shown this guy how to pack.)

He was waiting for the bus at an airport kiosk to transport him to the rental car facility. When the bus rolled up, the doors opened and—he couldn't move. While the bus driver and people standing behind him waited, he found himself without the strength to lift his foot to the first step. His mind said "move," but his body just wouldn't.

That's what it's like when you're trying to move through life with heavy, bulky baggage biting into your shoulders and cramping your hands.

Thankfully, God has made a simple way to purge our lives of the harmful totes and heavy carry-ons we have collected. In the New Testament, the wise old apostle John tells us that if we confess our baggage, God is faithful and just to forgive us our baggage (see 1 John 1:9).

Actually, the Bible uses the word *sin*. But really, isn't that what baggage is? Don't let what seems like cute, trendy baggage keep you from walking well. It will weigh you down, immobilize you, and cause you to stumble.

You can't carry as much as you think. Things like unforgiveness, selfishness, and prayerlessness are really very heavy bags to haul. Sometimes we have no idea of how heavy that heaped-up load has become until we finally release it...and feel that wonderful sense of lightness, rest, and relief.

Sinful baggage manifests its ugly self in all sorts of ways. No matter what form it takes, however, it always bears one completely predictable element: It is rooted in self, not God. Ouch. I know that is not pleasant to hear, but deep down, you know it's true. At the center of any sin, all sin, is the letter "I." *Me, my way, mine.* No matter how you spell it, it all sounds the same. The letter "I" will always be at the center of sin.

THE KING—AND "I"

As pagan kings go, Nebuchadnezzar is definitely one of my favorites. At least, he's one of the most intriguing. Nebuchadnezzar was the notorious ruler of the great Babylonian Empire, and he began his reign four hundred years before the King of kings stepped onto our planet. He ruled over the world capital of Babylon for forty-three amazing years, and during his tenure he beautified and fortified his great city. Temples, waterways, and the wondrous hanging gardens—one of the seven wonders of the ancient world—were all of his royal doing. The historian Herodotus claimed that the outer walls of the city were 56 miles in length, 80 feet thick, and 320 feet high.

King Nebuchadnezzar, the greatest and most powerful of

all Babylonian kings, was a proud and boastful man. You might remember him from the Old Testament book of Daniel, when he was so impressed with himself that he erected a magnificent, ninety-foot-tall image of gold—almost three times higher than your average telephone pole—in his own honor. It was kind of like a fourth-century-B.C. Trump Towers. This king had absolutely no self-esteem issues. *Me, mine, my,* and *I* were undoubtedly his most frequently used words.

And then one night he had a very troubling dream. Something told him this was more than the cold pizza he'd eaten before bedtime. The dream came from God Himself.

After consulting all his counselors and advisors, Nebuchadnezzar remembered Daniel the Hebrew, a man on his staff who was known to walk with God.

Daniel interpreted the dream and didn't mince words with his boss. Unless something changed in the king's life, unless he got rid of his heavy baggage of sin, it was going to drag him down. *Way* down.

Here's what Daniel said: "So, king, take my advice: Make a clean break with your sins and start living for others. Quit your wicked life and look after the needs of the down-and-out. Then you will continue to have a good life" (Daniel 4:27, *The Message*).

It was good, hard-hitting counsel—and certainly not the kind of flattery he was used to. And maybe he thought about it for a while. But eventually he shrugged it off and became enamored again with his own pride and power.

That all changed, however, one fateful day. His pride

finally caused him to cross the line and fall under God's judgment.

Where was the line? What was the last piece of luggage that finally pulled him off his feet? Only God knew. And one fine day as the king was strolling on the high balcony of his royal palace, looking out over the marvelous city, he said to himself, "Look at this, Babylon the great! And I built it all by myself, a royal palace adequate to display my honor and glory!" (Daniel 4:30, *The Message*).

Just that quickly, in a moment of swelling pride, Nebuchadnezzar lost it. In an instant. The lights were on but no one was home. He went crazy. The ancient Greeks called this kind of madness *lycanthropy*. The victim imagines himself a beast. He leaves all human activity and takes on the lifestyle and demeanor of an animal.

For seven unbelievable years, Nebuchadnezzar was struck with this strange malady. From a palace to a pasture, the confused king made his abode among the cows and donkeys, "eating grass like an ox."

The king's pride weighed more than he knew, and that was some pretty costly luggage to carry. The baggage weighed him down—way, way down. It pulled him off his throne, out of his palace, out of the city, and literally down on his hands and knees like a four-footed beast.

His sin cost him far more than he ever thought he would have to pay. That's what pride does.

Pride makes the spotlight on me, myself, and I shine so brightly that everything and everyone else falls into the shadows.

If, before his fall, the king had been speaking in today's vernacular, he would have said: "My way, my looks, my brains, my rule, my skill, my clout, my stuff."

Do you ever sound like that? I will be the first to admit that this self-appointed monarch sits on her throne and spouts the same from time to time. We all struggle with sin. It's ugly and it's dangerous. Just look what it did to this high-and-mighty world ruler.

Baggage is heavy to carry, costly to store, and expensive to own. Maybe it's time to clean out the closet?

GETTING RID OF THE UNMENTIONABLES

For about ten years now, Katharyn, Lori, and I have met for a girls' weekend. Beach condos, New York City hotels, and even our homes have all played host to our once-a-year estrogen-charged escapes.

This year, we chose Kansas City for our latest installment. We arrived late Thursday night to discover that our lovely suite overlooked the Country Club Plaza. My expectations and excitement were brimming. The only thing I anticipated more than the shopping was the emptying of my brimming bladder. It had been a *long* drive.

After checking in, I raced into our hotel bathroom and quickly shut the door. Well, I tried to shut the door. Something had lodged beneath it and the door was jammed. I reached down to dislodge the assumed washcloth, grasped a wad of fabric in my fist—and screamed.

Katharyn and Lori rushed to the scene for a "sight" inspection. I knew for certain when Katharyn yelled, "Gross!" and Lori groaned.

I held an anonymous pair of men's underwear in my hand.

We all marched from the restroom to the phone. I pressed zero and connected with the young man at the front desk.

"How may I help you?" he said in a smooth, professional voice.

"There's *men's underwear* in my bathroom!" I exploded.

"I'm sorry, ma'am." (What else could he say?)

I stumbled and stuttered until he interrupted with "I'll send someone up." And so we stood near the door as far from the offending garment as possible, and waited for the attendant.

Five minutes...ten minutes...twenty minutes passed—and no one came to our rescue.

I could no longer restrain my righteous indignation. This was not right. Girls' weekend had been violated. The "strictly forbidden" list included testosterone, remote controls, football, and yes, men's underwear.

As Katharyn and Lori sat by the door, I quickened my pace back to the bathroom, picked up my cane, and stabbed those "whitey tighties" with the tip of my walking stick.

Like a spear gun in the belly of its prey, I proved to that mass of cotton who was boss. I marched toward the door, with cane pointed toward the heavens, and commanded, "Katharyn, open the door!" She did, and out flew the skivvies into the hallway. We roared with laughter as I again picked up the phone and informed the delinquent desk clerk that the underwear were now in the hallway.

Katharyn watched through the peephole, and sure enough, hotel personnel arrived in five minutes to disinfect the hallway.

So what's the point of this story? That there are some things in our lives that simply don't belong. Men's Fruit of the Loom underwear do not belong in a girls' bathroom on girls' weekend. It would be out of place, out of order, out of bounds, out of sync, and out of the question for us to leave them lying around. I guess that's pretty obvious. But it should be just as obvious that a child of the King would never tolerate such unmentionables as pride, envy, gossip, hidden malice, or any other such baggage lying around in her personal life.

It doesn't fit. It doesn't belong. It's an offense.

These things get in the way of what God has planned for you. Instead of enjoying the pleasure of the palace as God intended, the baggage of sin weighs you down and you end up in a pasture—becoming something and someone you were never intended to be.

That's when it's time for real righteous indignation.

Don't hover and huddle by the door, waiting for sin to march itself out of your life. Instead, stride forward by faith. Stare it down, use the tools God gave you to conquer it, and then fling it out of your life. You might need someone to open the door for you, or walk beside you, but don't let precious plans and your purposeful life be derailed by something that doesn't belong there.

TOOLS FOR BAGGAGE REMOVAL

Now, my friend, you really ought to listen to me because I have more experience with sin removal than I would like to admit.

I have found two particular tools from God's Word especially helpful. So just in case you've got some excess baggage—or perhaps discovered a few unmentionables that need to be "flung"—let me open the door and guide you through it.

The first tool in the box might be a surprise. It's the law. Yikes! Don't be nervous. The law wasn't given for your condemnation; it was given to lead you to real life.

The law makes us "conscious of sin" (Romans 3:20). Without the law we'd never know the standard, the rules. Life would be a game in which we haphazardly move the pieces without knowing how to reach the real destination. God's law lays a foundation for life by making us aware of the sin that keeps us separated from our Father and Creator.

The law also makes us accountable for our sin (Romans 5:13). Now, you might not believe me at first, but this truth really should lighten your load. Sin separates us from God, and if God did not hold us accountable for our sin, we'd never be able to find an approach to Him at all. Knowing the truth about our sin paves the pathway to His presence. And remember what Jesus told us about the truth: It sets us free (John 8:32). (I feel a little lighter already.)

Lastly, the law leads us to Christ (Galatians 3:24). Jesus is the real destination of life. He is the pinnacle at the end of the pathway. He is our pursuit, our longing, the desire of nations. All we could ever want or need, we find in Him. But without the law, we'd never know the way. The law is the tool that leads to life and clarity because it shines the spotlight on our unmentionables. It makes us aware of our sin, exposes our need, and leads us to grace. The law is like a road map that leads to the cross. And that's the only place you can leave your baggage.

The second tool in the box is repentance. This is what God empowers us to do. *We don't have to carry those heavy bags around from place to place.* He has provided a way for us to drop that ugly luggage, turn from sin, and fling it out of our lives. The Greek word for repentance is *metanoeo*. It means to change one's mind, one's direction. In what direction are you walking?

Proverbs 28:13 says, "He who conceals his sins does not prosper, but whoever confesses and renounces them finds mercy." First John 1:9 reminds us that our God is faithful. If you do confess your sins, He will forgive you. He will cleanse you from all the unrighteousness your baggage represents.

It simply takes agreement with God.

What He calls dirt, you call dirt.

What He labels excess baggage, you label the same way.

What He names as an offending garment that has no place in your life, you agree and pitch it out.

It's an about-face, a 180. Nebuchadnezzar came to that place after seven long, humbling years, and both his kingdom and his sanity were restored (Daniel 4:34).

Do you need to change your mind? Do you need to turn around and walk in the other direction? Do you need to wield this tool of repentance? In order to finish well, in order to run with endurance, you must be heading in the right direction—and carrying no baggage.

God's Word is the light that guides us; it's the laser beam that focuses on our need, the warm glow that beckons us to come. The tool of the law guides us to repentance. The tool of repentance grants us restored relationship with God through the grace of Jesus Christ. It is God's amazing grace that leads us through the twists and turns of this life.

Ultimately, it is the grace of God that takes us from darkness to light. In the words of John Newton, "'Tis grace that brought me safe thus far, and grace will lead me home."

You don't need any baggage for that trip Home, however long it may be. God Himself will provide you with everything you need.

Travel light, my friend.

———◆———

CHAPTER SIX

Obey the Grace Rules

"Miss, where is she seated?"

When the gentleman seated in first class spoke up, the flight attendant who was guiding me down the cramped aisle of the 737 paused.

Where was *I* seated? I immediately quipped, "Not up here!"

The flight attendant replied that my seat was near the back of the plane. Hearing that, the businessman grabbed his carry-on bag and excused himself over the other passenger in his row. "I'll take her seat," he told the attendant. "She can have mine."

"Are you sure?" I asked. I could hardly believe my ears.

After all, he had paid good money for a first-class ticket. He had the opportunity to enjoy china dishes, cloth napkins, hovering flight attendants, and pampering. I was destined for peanuts, leg cramps, and a can of lukewarm Coke.

He patted my shoulder as he walked back toward my seat. "I want to," he assured me.

I was humbled. "Thank you," I said, sinking into the wide leather seat—the very lap of airline luxury.

What a great surprise! What grace.

GRACE RULES

According to the rules, my coach-class ticket bound me to coach seating. But grace has its own set of rules. And when the grace rules overrule the regular rules...well, that's what we call unmerited benevolence, undeserved favor.

Grace has nothing to do with fairness or equity. Grace gives to the undeserving, forgives the guilty, and covers the unworthy. Grace sits in the back of the plane so you can have the front seat.

The law, on the other hand, judges strictly, shows no mercy, demands compliance, and exposes guilt (Romans 8:2). Which set of rules would you rather be under?

The sons of Aaron the priest were under the rule of law rather than the rule of grace. Because of His white-hot holiness, God instituted a protocol—strict step-by-step procedures—by which man should approach Him.[12] But one day Aaron's sons chose to freelance a little, presumptuously stepping outside the protection provided by God's set of rules.

Now Nadab and Abihu, the sons of Aaron, took their respective fire pans, and after putting fire in them, placed incense on it and offered strange fire before the LORD, which He had not commanded them. And fire came out from the presence of the LORD and consumed them, and they died before the LORD. (Leviticus 10:1–2, NASB)

Aaron's sons showed up in the presence of the Lord with their own manufactured worship, not as the Lord had required. It wasn't that God was angry or out to make a point. As twentieth-century evangelist Vance Havner put it, "We do not really break the laws of God, we break ourselves against them. We do not break the law of gravitation by jumping from a skyscraper, we break our necks."

In other words, Nadab and Abihu simply fell under the law of the holiness of God—something that cannot be trifled with or taken lightly.

Aaron's sons aren't the only people mentioned in the Bible who suffered the consequences of the law when they tried to pave their own roads to God. God rejected Cain's sacrifice of fruits and vegetables because it did not meet His requirements.[13] Uzzah helped carry the ark of God back to Jerusalem. But when he touched the ark, he was immediately struck dead. Why? Because the law forbade anyone to touch the ark of the covenant, which represented the presence of God among His people.[14]

Aaron's sons, Cain, and Uzzah all learned the harsh reality of the law when they violated its unbending rules:

Sinful man simply cannot stand before holy God on his own terms and live.[15] Period. End of discussion.

When I consider truths like these, I sometimes wonder why I'm still around—why I haven't been fried on the spot like Nadab and Abihu. Why aren't we consumed or rejected when we clumsily approach Him? Why aren't we instantly vaporized when our sinfulness collides with His holiness? Why aren't we subject to the same law as Aaron's sons? After all, He is the same God. And we are much like the sons of Aaron. We offer to God our own versions of *strange fire*. We show up in the presence of the Lord with hypocrisy or indifference, pride or disregard. Simply put...sin. Sin that cannot stand safely before the holiness of God. God will always exercise justice concerning sin. He has to. His holiness will permit no less.

So how can we stand before God? One of the most poignant lessons I have ever learned in the Light is...grace. Jesus absorbed the penalty for sin that should have been directed toward us.[16] That is the very heart of the issue. That is the essence of grace.

Because of His death, we live.[17]

Because He became poor, we are now rich.[18]

God gives His grace so we can meet His demand of holiness—and live. And serve Him and walk with Him and approach Him and enjoy Him.

GRACE IN A GOURD

There once was a well-known prophet who might have taken a refresher course on the grace rules. His graceless prejudice led him down the path of a prodigal. God called Jonah to be His man, His prophet, and chose to sign him up for a much needed lesson on the rules of grace.

God told Jonah to alert the people living in the Assyrian capital of Nineveh to the imminent destruction of their city. But Jonah hated the Assyrians for their arrogance and cruelty and atrocities against his people; instead of heeding the Lord's call, he sprinted away from God and Nineveh and fell fast asleep in the belly of a storm tossed ship. Then he stepped forward to be thrown overboard, exchanging a ship's belly for a fish's belly. (That's the CliffNotes version of the story. You'll find all the details in the Old Testament book of Jonah.)

Jonah's journey from a fishy fortress to a hillside hideout tells us a lot about the meaning of grace. In the well-worn story of Jonah's deliverance from the fish, God puts His undeserved kindness on display by saving Jonah's life and renewing his calling, even though Jonah was unworthy.

After reluctantly carrying out his duty, Jonah set up camp on a knoll overlooking the city he despised. There he waited—sulking and yearning for God to annihilate the people who had just turned *en masse* to the God of Israel. Then he had the audacity to whimper and whine and rant and rave at God, who had hurled him to and fro through the digestive juices of an anonymous but very great fish.

Jonah wanted the Ninevites to feast on a banquet of just deserts. He savored the idea of God's justice raining down fire and brimstone upon the people. I imagine him sitting back with a bowl of popcorn and waiting for the fireworks to begin as God gave the people of Nineveh what they deserved.

Funny, isn't it? Jonah didn't get what he deserved...but he certainly wanted the Ninevites to. Only trouble was, the fireworks display got called off. The brimstone never fell. The disaster passed them by. Deep down, Jonah knew it would turn out that way. And it made him boil over with anger.

Thoroughly disgusted, he told the Lord, "I knew that you are a gracious and compassionate God, slow to anger and abounding in love, a God who relents from sending calamity" (Jonah 4:2).

God demands justice because He is judge, but He offers grace because He is good. When it came to the Assyrians, Jonah wanted God to be one-dimensional. He wanted harsh justice and vengeance. Earlier in the book, Jonah had claimed God's grace. But there was no way he wanted to share that grace with Nineveh. Jonah, who had received grace, was unwilling to grant it.

If I were God, I think at this point I would have lost it with that prejudiced, ungrateful prophet—maybe turning him back into fish bait. Wouldn't you? That's just like me to think in those terms—but it's not how God responded. Rather than returning Jonah to his sunken sanctuary or pitching out a few well-placed lightning bolts to teach him a lesson, God cultivated a living parable to instruct Jonah in the profound schoolroom of grace.

> The LORD God provided a vine and made it grow up over Jonah to give shade for his head to ease his discomfort, and Jonah was very happy about the vine. (Jonah 4:6)

Jonah once again received grace. Grace in a vine, which the King James Version describes as a "gourd." The prophet was glad for the vine, but he was not grateful. He took comfort in its shade when he could have found ultimate satisfaction in the shadow of God's wings.

The prophet, who had over and over been the recipient of God's amazing grace, became the judge. And the almighty Judge became the patron of grace.

Sadly enough, I can relate to Jonah. I understand his perspective far better than I can comprehend God's incomprehensible grace. However, I also agree with something Vance Havner once said: "I do not understand all about electricity, but I don't intend to sit in the dark until I do." That's how I feel about grace. Grace calls prodigals to be prophets and turns pagans into parishioners.

One thing is for certain: If not for grace, our world would be dark, merciless, and...exactly what we deserve. As Scripture says, we would be without hope and without God in the world.[19] The hymn writers have fittingly called grace amazing, wonderful, marvelous, matchless, and greater than all my sin. Grace is all those things and more.

But it is never fair.

THAT'S NOT FAIR!

Grace by its very nature is unfair. We don't "deserve" such bountiful excess—not even close.

The apostle Paul understood very well the staggering unfairness of this grace. He also knew it was sufficient to meet his every need, though it took a thorn for Paul to learn that lesson. Paul asked God, in 2 Corinthians 12:8, to remove the painful thorn in his flesh. He evidently struggled with some difficult circumstance that he really wanted changed.

His thorn could have been anything; physical, emotional, spiritual. The Bible doesn't clarify exactly what his thorn was. Why not? Maybe so that we could all better identify with the results of that affliction—pain, discomfort, and a longing for it to be removed.

We all have thorns. For me, blindness is a neverending, constantly challenging, fatigue inducing thorn. I can't deny it: It hurts. I've often longed for it to go away.

What is your thorn? What makes you, like Paul, beg God for a little divine surgery?

I wonder whether Paul considered his thorn unfair. We do know that Paul asked God to remove it and God responded. God, who is always fair and is well qualified and quite capable of "thorn removal," answered with something even better than immediate release or deliverance. That something was His grace.[20]

We can all imagine how Paul must have felt. We tell ourselves, *If only my thorn would be miraculously, instantaneously removed, that would be enough for me.*

But as much as we would like to convince God that thorn removal would be sufficient, God knows best that only one thing is sufficient: His grace.

Trust me, my friend, the longer I live in physical darkness yet in the light of His Word, the more convinced I become that healing is not sufficient.

Deliverance is not sufficient.

Restored relationships are not sufficient.

Finding a life partner is not sufficient.

Material provision is not sufficient.

Fame and popularity are not sufficient.

Perfect health and a sculpted body are not sufficient.

Each of these things is a joyous blessing in itself, but they are not enough. *Never* enough.

If healing or "thorn removal" in and of itself were sufficient for the apostle Paul, then surely heaven would have granted it.

But God had something wider, higher, deeper, broader, more miraculous and enduring in mind. Paul wouldn't get what he asked for because he didn't understand what he needed more than anything else. If he had simply and instantly been healed of his malady (whatever it was), he would have missed something far greater than he could have conceived.

Healing can't be compared to the grace of God, alive and at work in our lives. Comfort and stress relief and health and paid bills can't even be recorded on the same ledger with the power of God surging through our brokenness, want, and need, and becoming perfect in our weakness.

The grace of Jesus Christ is better than anything. God's lovingkindness is better than life itself. Don't settle for a merely adequate and temporary answer to your prayer, when God may be granting you the lasting and deeper gift of grace.

And sometimes, perhaps even most times, that grace is best realized in our thorns.

Grace will not take you away from the pains and disappointments and limitations and heartaches of life on a broken planet. But it will sustain you, deepen you, strengthen you, change you, and overflow your life in a way that simple deliverance from pain or hardship never could.

Grace is enough. It is enough to sustain you when the thorns hurt, enough to cover you when you bow before Him in your sinfulness. The psalmist said:

If you, O LORD, should mark iniquities,
O Lord, who could stand?
But with you there is forgiveness,
that you may be feared.
(Psalm 130:3–4, ESV)

God's grace truly is amazing, unfair, and sufficient. The reason God's grace is sufficient is because it is both priceless and practical.

Priceless

When my friend Karen returned from England, she told me about visiting the Tower of London and beholding the stunning crown jewels of Great Britain.

"I asked an attentive and well-accented Beefeater about the value of the crown jewels," she told me, "and instead of an answer, I received an education."

The guard explained to Karen that the jewels lend their splendor to coronations and jubilees as symbols of royalty, authority, justice, and spirituality. They remain a tangible link, he said, between modern-day England and the kings and queens of long ago. He told Karen that the jewels have been housed in the Tower for nearly a millennium and pointed with pride to the 530.2-carat Great Star of Africa, the world's second largest cut diamond.

The Beefeater's final bit of information, however, came as a shock to Karen: As to stated value, the storied jewels have none. That's hard to believe until you ask, How could you put a price on such magnificence? The jewels possess far more than a superlative intrinsic value. Their symbolism, history, and tradition cannot be appraised. They are irreplaceable and without comparison; no price tag could do them justice.

So it is with grace, though perhaps we don't have eyes to see it or hearts that truly understand it. Grace has no equal, and its value goes far beyond imagery, history, and tradition. Grace was "...bought with a price" (1 Corinthians 7:23, NASB). Philip Yancey wrote that grace "contains the essence of the gospel as a drop of water can contain the image of the sun."

What does grace cost? Well, it cost Jesus His very lifeblood.

> For you know that it was not with perishable things such as silver or gold that you were redeemed from the empty way of life handed down to you from your forefathers, but with the precious blood of Christ, a lamb without blemish or defect. (1 Peter 1:18–19)

If the worth of the crown jewels—basically a pile of shiny rocks, when you think about it—cannot be measured, then what of the blood of God's own Son? It is a question that confounds even the angels.[21]

Grace Shows Up

Karen's husband, Gerry, showed the practical side of grace while shopping with his kids at Target recently.

As Gerry made his way through the aisles picking up a few essentials, he tried to demonstrate the concept of grace to his two children. He told them that grace is God's "unmerited favor." When that phrase generated a blank stare, he explained that it's getting something we don't deserve and haven't earned.

He illustrated his point by taking a detour from the usual aisles lined with laundry detergent and paper towels and heading straight for the toy department. His wide-eyed children quickly decided that if grace had something to do with toys, it must be worth learning about.

He knelt beside his little ones and told them they could choose any toy they wanted—up to ten dollars. (Daddy's grace may be without limit, but his checkbook isn't.) Neither Maddie nor Mason asked any questions. They searched the toy-strewn lanes for just the right prized possessions, and then gleefully watched as their daddy paid the bill and handed over the goods—which they received with joy.

Gerry tells me that he knows his kids got the message because now whenever they see a Target sign, Mason asks, "Daddy, can we have a little grace?"

In the Bible, the Hebrew word for *gracious* is used almost

exclusively of God.[22] It denotes the action which springs from His free, unmerited kindness toward us. God's ultimate expression of grace was in Christ, through whom grace and truth came to us.[23]

Grace is no abstract quality or starry-eyed lover dreaming fanciful dreams. It is an active, personal principle showing itself in the way we deal with others and in the way God deals with us.

In other words, grace shows up.

Grace shows up when "[God] causes his sun to rise on the evil and the good, and sends rain on the righteous and the unrighteous" (Matthew 5:45). Grace arrives to show us that He "does not treat us as our sins deserve or repay us according to our iniquities" (Psalm 103:10).

Grace showed up when Jesus restored a demon possessed man.[24] Grace revealed Jesus as Messiah to a Samaritan woman.[25] Grace gave dignity to another woman shamed by adultery.[26] Grace reinstated Peter, who had openly denied Christ.[27] And Grace called Saul, the persecutor of saints, to become Paul, the preacher of the gospel.[28]

Grace is priceless and practical. And it's also paid for. When we sing "Jesus paid it all," we're really saying that grace covers our debts, credits our account, finances our investments, yields a capital reserve in the depository of eternity, and then bestows "an inheritance that can never perish, spoil or fade—kept in heaven for you" (1 Peter 1:4).

Before I lost my sight, I remember curiously staring at those 3-D stereogram pictures. They look like a bunch of random nonsense until you stare at them long enough to see the real image pop right out at you. Then, once you see the image, you can't *not* see it.

Grace is like that. It might not seem to make any sense at first, and it might take some time and focus to perceive it correctly. But once you do, there's no going back.

Grace is the great surprise of salvation. It's an unexpected trip to the toy department, an undeserved seat in first class. Where the law demands, grace delivers. When the law hands down a verdict, grace sets us free. It is a gift, not a payment. It is benevolence, not reimbursement. It is kindness, compassion, generosity, and goodwill.

When situations fail us, when the familiar ground crumbles away beneath our very feet, grace mounts us on eagle's wings. When daily issues confront our sensibilities, grace carries us to the heights. When disappointment, suffering, or thorns hurt us, grace is the gentle covering that blankets our lives with everlasting incorruptibility.

Grace doesn't fluctuate with the stock market or fly away when the winds blow hard. It doesn't fade, diminish, or hesitate. Grace stands the test of time.

It is unmerited favor.

It is undeserved kindness.

It is sufficient, unearned, priceless, practical, and unreasonable.

And yes, completely, blessedly, eternally unfair.

The LORD longs to be gracious to you; he rises to show you compassion. For the LORD is a God of justice. Blessed are all who wait for him! (Isaiah 30:18)

CHAPTER SEVEN

Become Meek and Mighty

After my new guide dog, William, and I had been home together for a few weeks, I realized we had a big problem. William—my bouncy, eager, loyal yellow Labrador—could not get over his food obsession.

When we were in training at the "dog school," William and I went through rigorous behavior-modifying techniques to help break him of his food focus. But even after several daily doughnut walks (you'll have to read *Lessons I Learned in the Dark* for the doughnut drama), William still had an appetite for the forbidden.

So I left the dog school with specific training instructions to help William with his food issues. Since there were no canine support groups where dogs stood on all fours and confessed,

"My name is William, and I am a foodaholic," the burden for his recovery rested on my shoulders. That meant each morning, when he was good and hungry, I would set William's food before him. But then I would instruct him to *stay*.

The trainers at the school told me to continue this until my dog showed a degree of self-control. Ah, poor William. He would sit six inches away from his brimming bowl, his nose extended as far as possible, his neck completely contorted. He would quiver all over and whine piteously until I gave him the "go" sign.

Every day William and I performed this difficult task, and every day it got a little better than the day before. Each day he would whine less, quiver less, and control himself more. One day I began the usual routine, called William, told him to sit and stay, poured his food, and left the kitchen.

I waited around the corner and listened. No chomping. No whining.

Good, I said to myself. *He's recovered from his addiction.*

Just as I was rounding the corner to give him the "go" sign, the phone rang. I picked it up and became engrossed in a long, soap opera–style conversation. After I hung up, I realized how late it was getting and quickly made my way into my room to get dressed for the day.

When I was all dressed, I walked back into the kitchen for a glass of water. And there sat William. Alert. Hopeful. Obedient. Forgotten. I had left him there in front of his food for almost an hour. Of course I gave him the go-ahead and praised him profusely. I think I even gave him seconds that morning. William, even without his harness, acted with a bridled will, obedient and under control.

William was meek.

Not weak, but meek.

Someone has said, "Meekness does not identify the weak but more precisely the strong who have been placed in a position of weakness where they persevere without giving up." In other words, a meek person bears and wears his or her yoke.

A WELL-FITTED YOKE

There once was a humble carpenter who lived in ancient Palestine. He enjoyed the reputation of making the best yokes in all of Galilee. As a skilled craftsman, he would measure an ox, and then fashion a customized yoke for the animal from a piece of wood. Once the yoke was completed, the ox would be summoned to try on the masterpiece. If adjustments were needed, the carpenter would work a little more to make sure it fit just right.

People from all of Palestine came for his yokes. The carpenter worked daily in his little shop and used only the finest materials. From dawn to dusk he sculpted yokes of unparalleled craftsmanship. Farmers came from miles away for this gentle carpenter's handiwork, because none fit better. Anyone who came to Nazareth needing a well-fitting yoke could find his shop, because above the door hung a sign that read "My Yokes Fit Well."

I know about the little carpentry shop in Nazareth,

because I know the Carpenter. I happen to wear one of His yokes, and it does fit perfectly. In fact, His yoke is easy.

The yoke Jesus offers each of us is easy. Well fitting. I would walk millions of miles just to have the privilege of bearing it. You see, to be beneath the yoke of Christ is to enjoy a meek, submitted life.

When the ancient Jews spoke of "the yoke," they referred to one placing himself under submission. They were accustomed to submitting to the yoke of the law, the yoke of the kingdom, the yoke of the commandments, and the yoke of God. And to be honest, the yokes of which they spoke burdened and constrained them, and were a frequent source of discouragement.

That's why the words of Jesus the Carpenter must have felt as free and refreshing as a summer breeze: "Take My yoke upon you and learn from Me," He said, "for I am gentle and lowly in heart, and you will find rest for your souls. For My yoke is easy and My burden is light" (Matthew 11:29–32, NKJV).

Can you imagine what His Jewish audience must have thought as they listened to such inviting words? Can you imagine how they must have felt? When you personalize His words, you will find that His yoke is an invitation to enjoy a meek will.

When Jesus used the word *easy* to describe His yoke, the Jewish listeners heard something very different from what you and I might perceive today. When we hear the word *easy*, we might think of "simple" or "uncomplicated." But the Greek word for *easy* in this verse can mean "well fitting." His yoke is crafted, not by an earthly carpenter's hands, but from your heavenly Carpenter's heart. It fits perfectly, because He knows how a yoke feels. He wears the yoke of His Father.

MODEL OF MEEKNESS

As Jesus passed through Capernaum, a Roman centurion flagged him down. I can just see the powerful official gasp, trying to catch his breath as he ran to tell Jesus, "Lord, my servant is lying at home paralyzed, dreadfully tormented" (Matthew 8:6, NKJV).

Jesus must have gazed with great intention into the eyes of the concerned yet confident centurion when He graciously offered to go to the officer's home and heal his beloved servant.

> The centurion answered and said, "Lord, I am not worthy that You should come under my roof. But only speak a word, and my servant will be healed. For I *also* am a man under authority, having soldiers under me. And I say to this one, 'Go,' and he goes; and to another, 'Come,' and he comes; and to my servant, 'Do this,' and he does it." (Matthew 8:8–9, NKJV, emphasis mine)

The centurion's big faith usually takes center stage in this story, but I want to shine the spotlight on one little word: *also*. You read it in verse 9. The centurion acknowledged that just like himself, Jesus was a man of authority and also a man under authority. The centurion knew he possessed power because he had submitted himself to the powerful Roman authority.

The centurion recognized that Christ possessed authority because He bore the yoke of His Father. His authority was supreme, because He was submitted to ultimate authority.

Jesus had been telling His disciples as much while they traveled the dusty miles together.

> "For I did not speak on My own initiative, but the Father Himself who sent Me has given Me a commandment as to what to say and what to speak.... Do you not believe that I am in the Father, and the Father is in Me? The words that I say to you I do not speak on My own initiative, but the Father abiding in Me does His works.... So that the world may know that I love the Father, I do exactly as the Father commanded Me." (John 12:49; 14:10, 31, NASB)

The centurion acknowledged both Jesus' inherent authority and His submission to authority. That's the most remarkable part of this story as far as I'm concerned, because this Gentile man had clued in to what few others had even noticed. Jesus possessed all power and authority but at the same time, submitted Himself to the power and authority of Another.

Beautiful, isn't it? Jesus is the ultimate picture of meekness.

To be meek is to recognize our own personal power and willingly submit it to the authority of another. That's what our Savior did. And in His meekness was majesty.

In the Sermon on the Mount, Jesus made a radical proclamation concerning the meek. "Blessed are the meek, for they will inherit the earth" (Matthew 5:5). Only meekness can make that possible. To be meek is to have control over sin and self. If we were truly meek—our wills bridled to the extent that we had mastery over ourselves and our sin— how strong we would be. God would be free to bless us and use us to our full potential.

MEEKNESS HAS A BACKBONE

Rosa Parks was a God-fearing, churchgoing seamstress in Montgomery, Alabama. As she boarded the city bus one evening after work, she settled into a seat near the front. When a white man boarded, it was expected that she, a black woman, would willingly surrender her seat. After all, segregation on the public transit system in the South in 1955 was the law.

When Rosa quietly refused, she violated a city ordinance and, in her meekness, changed the course of American history. Certainly she had no idea that her gentle defiance on behalf of human dignity would spawn the civil rights movement.

That same night, forty black pastors came together and vowed to fight the segregation that plagued Montgomery's public transportation system. The Reverend Martin Luther King Jr. was chosen to lead the boycott. African Americans all over Montgomery walked and carpooled to work, enduring hatred and harassment.

One year later, the U.S. Supreme Court ruled that segregation violated the Constitution. History was forever altered, and it began with a quiet, gentle, meek refusal to obey that which was wrong, and a willingness to bravely take a risk for what was right.

Meekness is not simply doing what you are told. The person who is ordered to do something wrong or evil and automatically complies isn't meek. That's just cowardice.

True, God-ordained meekness can move mountains. Meekness was Jesus washing the feet of His disciples—and it was also Jesus clearing the temple with a whip. Meekness was Moses showing intolerance for his wayward people at the base of the mountain; meekness was a humble seamstress refusing to give up her seat.

Meekness is not passive. It is active restraint, bridled control, and humbly motivated action. Meekness is the backbone of Christianity. It is a gift from the Holy Spirit (Galatians 5:22), yet it is up to us to unwrap it. Failure to receive the gift of meekness results in debilitating weakness.

WHEN WE AREN'T MEEK

Sometimes you hear that people who have been married a long time become so close they begin to take on one another's characteristics.

Well, maybe.

But I am rock-solid sure that there are some things about my husband and me that will never change. Phil, for instance, is a die-hard, card-carrying, fully committed, lifelong pack rat. And me? I tend toward the tightly wound, type A, *Good Housekeeping* Seal of approval—bearing neat freak.

As the years have gone by, however, I have become cheerfully resigned to our differences. Pack Rat and Neat Freak have made a go of it by learning to give and take—and with massive infusions of grace from the God who delights in marriages.

Late in the summer of 2003, however, in our seventeenth year of wedded bliss, we hit a speed bump. That's when I began nesting. I wasn't expecting a baby, but I was due to deliver a book manuscript to the publisher in a few months.

Knowing the months of labor that lay ahead, realizing what an all-consuming task waited just around the corner...I got the urge to purge. I simply felt like there was no way I could write my book if our storage room was in such a mess. (Only the type A reader will fully understand that statement.)

And so I attacked our basement storage room like a sugared-up, out-of-control child in a tae kwon do class. Don't stand in the way of a nesting woman with fire in her eyes. I marched in with steel determination and began kicking boxes outside and pitching old lampshades over my head and out the door. I really got into it. Let me just tell you, sufficient drive makes up for insufficient eyesight. I hung tools and filled boxes while my assistant filed papers from 1985.

In my frenzied cleaning, I ran my hand across the dusty speakers from an old sound system we had purchased when we were first married. I had traveled with that cumbersome system for five years, setting it up each time I sang. It hadn't seen the light of day for years.

The urge was strong upon me.

I *so* wanted to give it away.

I knew I had room in the truck. I knew Victory Mission would be blessed by such a generous donation. And I would be blessed to be rid of it.

And so, without consulting anybody and with no thought for Phil's opinion, I dragged three thousand dollars' worth of Yamaha, Peavey, and Bose equipment up the basement stairs and shoved them into the back of the truck.

After the delivery was made, I felt cleansed.

The cleaning compulsion had burned itself out for the time being, and now...I would be able to write that book. My muscles were sore but my head was clear, and my storage room was clean, clean, clean!

The next morning at 4:30, however, I awoke with an uncomfortable feeling. All I could think about was the sound system I had given away the day before. And then the questions came rolling along. *Why didn't you ask Phil before you gave the system away? Don't you think he'll notice it's gone? Whose sound system was it, anyway?*

I tried to mount a defense against the pangs besetting me. *I didn't ask him because he wouldn't have gotten rid of it. Anyway, did he ever sing over those microphones? No. It was my system...my decision.*

My defense wasn't cutting it. I was losing ground to a growing conviction. I tried to fall back asleep, but the thoughts kept hounding me. Finally rescued by my alarm clock, I jumped up and threw myself into the busy morning routine. But as soon as the last child left for school, the house became quiet...and my thoughts drew me back to some painful conclusions.

My actions had been unbridled. Out of control. I had wanted it my way and on my timetable. My mantra had been "I'd rather ask forgiveness than permission."

Oh, so clever. I hadn't been willing to consider anything or anyone outside of my will...not God, not Phil. And now, I was alone with my consequence. It wasn't the storage room that was dirty. It was my heart.

I went down to my writing room and knelt before the recliner where I often listen to God. I knew I had really blown it and needed to be cleansed. I asked God to forgive me for my intentional deceit and selfishness. He did...and then He prompted me to do what I dreaded most.

Call Phil at work.

Oh Lord, You know he'll never notice that it's missing. I threw stuff out of that room that he hasn't thought about in fifteen years!

But there was no getting around it. I knew I was to call, so I did. I told Phil what I had done and asked for his forgiveness. He was so disappointed, but even so he forgave me.

I hung up and decided that what I had wanted wasn't worth what I got. I wish I had stowed that bulky, outdated sound system in the back corner of my storage room so I could enjoy an uncluttered relationship with Phil. My former mantra was a lie. It's *not* easier to ask forgiveness than permission. No, not at all. You see, I love Phil and I love God's Word, and I violated both in a single act of willful volition.

Now I realize that it's good that the sound system is

gone. Not for the extra space in the storage room, but for what it exposed in my heart that desperately needed to go—an unbridled will.

Unbridled volition screams to the world, "It's my way or the highway," "I will because I can," and "I'd rather ask forgiveness than permission."

A surrendered will sings a different song. It isn't loud, it isn't shrill, it isn't flashy. But there's something about its understated melody that reaches into the deep places of the soul, satisfying at a whole different level. Meekness says, "I will seek permission so I won't have to seek forgiveness," and "Just because I can doesn't mean I should."

Unrestrained volition—a rampant, out of control will—invites wasted energy, frustration, and eventual self-destruction. However, meekness—a will bridled and cooperative—experiences a clean, uncluttered heart.

When I attempt to shrug off His perfect yoke, determining to go my own way and march under my own banner, I'm headed for a big fall. I will hurt myself, hurt others, and grieve the Lord's Spirit within me.

I'll be self-willed, and weak as a woman can be.

Our Lord's gracious invitation to submit to His well-fitted yoke still echoes through the ages, and resonates through the pages of Scripture. Strength is not the answer to power, control, or triumph. Meekness is. "It is not by strength that one prevails" (1 Samuel 2:9). When we unburden ourselves from the heavy weight of our own power, then we can bear the well-fitting yoke of Christ, and within His yoke, we learn meekness.

You can be strong willed and meek willed at the same time. A strong willed personality is a gift from God, and it serves those of us who have it very well. But it should never be an excuse for a lack of meekness.

Meekness marries the two virtues of strength and compliance.

And the benefits? Well, they simply never end. David tells us that God will personally guide the meek and teach them His way (Psalm 25:9). The Lord even told Isaiah that He values and *esteems* the man or woman who has learned the way of meekness (Isaiah 66:2).

Add to that, then, the promise of Jesus that the meek will inherit the world.

So why in the world do I expect to win by fighting for my own way? In fact, that is the surest path to defeat. And that's one of the best and hardest lessons I've learned in *the Light*.

CHAPTER EIGHT

Pray Like Crazy

Back in college, I remember being on a worship team with a friend named Paul. He was the most spiritually mature guy my age that I knew. Each week, our little team practiced our praise songs together so we'd be ready to lead the two hundred college students that gathered every Thursday night in the student center—Paul on the guitar and me on the piano.

I will never forget the time we had finished our rehearsal and began a time of prayer. This was our normal custom, to finish each session with prayer. But this time was different. The bass player and drummer had already left, and Paul and I were there alone.

Paul began to pray in a way I had never heard before. He

stretched himself across the floor, nose so close to the ground that I was sure he was inhaling carpet fiber. There I sat, head bowed, startled and still, sitting on the piano bench. How could I pray with this guy? He was obviously more connected with God than I was. After all, he had taken the "lying prostrate before the Lord" position.

In my mind, my posture of crossed legs and hands was not nearly as spiritual, and therefore not nearly as acceptable, to God. If my position wasn't sufficient, then there was no way that my words would have been.

Besides, who can pray when your mind is filled with comparison and self-analysis? I just listened to Paul, agreeing with his heartfelt words. When he finished, I muttered something like "Me too" or "I agree, Lord." I was a ball of mixed emotions and conflicting thoughts.

Prayer had left me feeling confused and silent instead of secure and conversational, as God intended. Was it Paul's fault? No way. It was all about my being more concerned with the method and mechanics of prayer than the motives and meaning.

The truth was, I was intimidated. Intimidated by prayer. I had become so preoccupied with my own perceived deficiencies that I lost the joy of simply coming into the presence of my heavenly Father who loved me.

Prayer *still* intimidates me at times.

There. I said it. That's my confession; do with it what you will. Hesitant as I may be to admit it, I have to own up to the truth. In fact, I've been known to work myself into a spiritual frenzy of hesitation and second-guessing before I say the first word to God. ...*How much prayer is enough? Are my motives pure? Are my petitions selfish or shallow? Will God be offended if my mind wanders?*

Do you ever ask yourself those kinds of questions? I suspect we all do. But the great lesson I've learned in the Light is profound and simple.

Are you ready?

Just pray.

Pray anyway. Pray constantly. Pray right through all those doubts and questions. Yes, intimidated or not, pray...pray like crazy. Vance Havner boiled it all down when he said: "If you can't pray like you want to, pray as you can. God knows what you mean."

OUR INTERPRETER

God knows how we struggle in prayer. Of course He does. He's never overlooked anything, ever, and He never will. The word *overlook* isn't even in His vocabulary.

He knows our situation... He knows that we are flawed, fallen-yet-redeemed human beings on a rebel planet that is temporarily under the control of the evil one.

He knows our weakness... David assures us that "He Himself knows our frame; He is mindful that we are but dust" (Psalm 103:14, NASB). God is totally aware of our physical, mental, and emotional struggles when we attempt to pray.

He knows our circumstances... There isn't a single event, concern, worry, or pressure in our lives that slips His notice. Job reminds us that "He knows the way I take" (Job 23:10, NASB).

Knowing all these things, understanding that you and I will sometimes find prayer difficult or discouraging, God gave us some powerful help. Paul writes, "The Spirit helps us in our weakness; for we do not know how to pray as we ought, but the Spirit himself intercedes for us with sighs too deep for words. And he who searches the hearts of men knows what is the mind of the Spirit, because the Spirit intercedes for the saints according to the will of God" (Romans 8:26–27, RSV).

I love how those verses acknowledge that we don't always know how to pray. I find that very reassuring. Don't you? But did you also notice that verse 26 highlights the truth that we "ought" to pray? As the poet has put it, "Prayer is the Christian's native breath." In other words, if you need to breathe, you need to pray.

But just as our breathing can become shallow or labored in times of weakness or stress, so it is with our praying. We are weak, we labor in prayer, sometimes we feel like our prayers are shallow, and often we can't catch our spiritual breath. But the Holy Spirit accepts our small, feeble, human offerings and takes them to the throne as deep, eternal, and appropriate sacrifices. He transforms our shallowness into worthy requests before the Father because He knows the deep things of God. Amazing.

That's why you can still pray even when you can't (or think you can't).

That's why you can still pray even when you don't feel like it, and don't seem to have a single worthwhile word to say to God.

That's why you can still pray even if you don't have confidence in your ability to pray. It doesn't matter. You *can* have confidence in the ability and faithfulness of the Holy Spirit to interpret your prayers.

So, pray. It is the true mark of a Christian.

THE MARK

Making good time down the Damascus Highway, Paul eagerly anticipated his next opportunities to hunt down and persecute followers of "the Way." Known as Saul the Pharisee at that point, he had rightfully earned a reputation as the most dreaded and brutal oppressor of the newly formed Christian faith.

But Saul's travel plans were interrupted. It wasn't a flat tire on his chariot or road construction and flaggers by the Syrian Department of Highways. Saul was stopped short— knocked flat, to be precise—by a sudden encounter with "the Light." Literally blinded, he was led by the hand into the city, where he awaited the further instructions Jesus told him to expect.

In the meantime, the Spirit of God spoke to a believer named Ananias, saying, "Go to the house of Judas on Straight Street and ask for a man from Tarsus named Saul, for he is praying" (Acts 9:11). God gave Ananias a distinct clue about the spiritual condition of Saul, the persecutor. He pointed out only a single quality and action as living proof of Saul's conversion. God simply said, "He is praying." The

New Living Translation version translates those words, *"He is praying to me right now."*

I love that. That is the mark of a true believer. God didn't acknowledge *how* Saul was praying. He just told the reluctant Ananias that the man who used to persecute followers of Jesus was now praying to Jesus.

I doubt that Paul's prayer was worthy of canonization at that point. It may not have been eloquent or even very coherent. He had to have been shaken to the core. Just think, he was now praying to the very Name he had scorned, hated, and tried to wipe off the map. In his distress, he may have prayed the simple psalms he'd memorized as a child at synagogue. He may have knelt there in his new blindness, saying over and over again, "I'm so sorry, Lord, I'm so sorry. I didn't know...I didn't know."

He may have prayed the simple prayers of a child or of a traveler who has lost his way in the wilderness. But don't miss the profound point: *He prayed.* I'll bet he prayed like crazy. I know I would have. Paul's simple act of praying became the visible evidence of his changed heart. We don't have any record of those prayers, but God does.

And that's what matters to God. That's all God wants: our sincere prayer. It doesn't matter whether we're on our knees, stretched out facedown on the carpet, or sitting in a car; whether our hands are folded in reverence or soaked in dishwater. All that matters is that we learn to pray. And in so doing...we learn to fall.

WE ALL FALL DOWN

I remember a busy Wednesday morning that commenced a "fall-down day." I opened my eyes that morning and felt the weight and worries of the day descend on me before I could even get out of bed. My schedule was packed: errands, responsibilities, back-to-back appointments, and a constantly chirping cell phone consumed every moment.

As the minutes passed, so did any assurance that I was going to pull off all the demands of the day. By 9 a.m. I had greeted my assistant, paid the garage door repairman, and taken phone calls from the preschool, church, and my husband.

And then...*I fell down.*

But that was a good thing.

In fact, I even fell with two other people—at the same time. I often fall alone, but on that day, I needed someone to fall with. So down in my basement, before I left for my first appointment, I grabbed Dotty and Tammy (the housekeepers who sneaked in behind the garage door repairman) and announced, "Put down your mops, girls. We need to pray."

You see, when I speak of "falling," I am talking about laying it all out before our Father. To me, falling means that I bow in my heart, falling before Him in weakness and worship. I've learned that "When I bow to God, God stoops to me."[29] So when I fall, I then rise in joy and strength and I'm able to walk on. In fact, the Bible recommends these "group falls." James 5:16 says that we should "pray for one another," and Matthew 18:20 reminds us that where two or three are gathered in His name, He is there also.

On that particular morning I'd felt my need for God's strength so keenly that I knelt in the hallway, holding hands with Dotty and Tammy. Maybe in some cathedral somewhere at that moment, some priest in embroidered vestments was kneeling before an altar with fragrant incense wafting through the air. But down there in my basement hallway with the housekeepers, it was the scent of Clorox and Pine-Sol that filled the room. And we fell down together in our hearts as we stood in a circle of unity. I thanked them and my Father and then left the house.

On the way to my first appointment, Katie, my assistant, told me about her husband's job dilemma. "Jennifer," she suddenly interjected, "we need another fall. You pray while I drive." After I said a concluding "Amen," she said, "Well, Jennifer, I think this is Fall with Your Friends and Family Day.'" We chuckled as we parked in front of the hair salon.

After I shed some burdens and a whole lot of extra hair with my precious stylist, Paulette, she teared up as she told me about her latest heartache. Again, I grasped her hands and we fell. In the middle of a busy salon, on a busy day, we met together with Jesus. We gave Him our weakness, and He gave us His strength.

The day continued, and so did the falling. A man named John, my neighbor Lori, my husband, and an entire staff from a Christian publisher via conference call were eventually added to the Falling Friends and Family roster.

Have you had one of those fall-down days lately? Sometimes we may be reluctant to fall with others because we're intimidated or embarrassed. But when we catch a glimpse of our profound need for God and our need for each other, we become willing to risk embarrassment in order to receive strength.

Besides, it's not just for ourselves and our own needs that we fall with our friends. No, we fall for the sake of others, too. We share in their weakness and join them in their search for strength and guidance. Prayer ushers each of us before the very throne of God Himself, and in that place, we are changed.

If you want to keep running your race with endurance, fall to your knees on that race track and connect with your heavenly Father. So many of us fool ourselves into thinking we'll get more done and go farther if we keep running, running, and running all day long. But in the Christian life, falling down gets you further in the race than running.

If you want to walk by faith, always choose to fall. Fall down for your needs. Fall down for the needs of others. Fall down in repentance over sin. Fall down in reverence. Fall down in thanksgiving and praise. If you need to fall alone, do so. But never forget the power and joy of a group fall. And as you fall, you'll find your burdens falling, too, because "the LORD upholds all those who fall and lifts up all who are bowed down" (Psalm 145:14).

It's really true: God does lift up those who fall down. Peter said, "Humble yourselves, therefore, under God's mighty hand, that he may lift you up in due time" (1 Peter 5:6). I've felt that lifting-up hand again and again in my life. I've even noticed some fellow fallers in the pages of God's Word.

A WHOLE LOT OF
FALLING GOIN' ON

I decided to see how some of my spiritual predecessors prayed and what they prayed about. And what do you think I found? A whole lot of falling going on.

We spoke about Paul earlier. Suddenly curious to know how he prayed and what he prayed, I began searching through his New Testament letters. In so doing, I learned a lot about the purpose of prayer. Check this out.

Paul asked the church in Rome to pray that he would be able to come for a visit, that he would be rescued from unbelievers in Judea, and that his service in Jerusalem would be acceptable to the saints.[30]

He asked the Corinthian believers to pray that he would be rescued from deadly peril.[31]

He asked the church in Ephesus to pray that he would fearlessly advance the Good News.[32]

He called on the believers in Colosse to ask God to open a door of ministry for him, and that he would be able to proclaim the gospel clearly.[33]

He asked the Thessalonian church to pray that the message of Christ would spread rapidly, and that he and his companions would be delivered.[34]

The writer of the book of Hebrews asked the Jewish believers to pray that he would lead an honorable life, and that he would be restored to them.[35]

Here's what I find fascinating. These "falling" letter writers didn't ask for comfort, luxury, or self-gratifying conditions to prevail. If you review again what you just read, you'll see their requests falling into four categories:

- Future fellowship
- Favor from God
- Clear and fearless proclamation of the message
- Furtherance of the gospel

What a model for us to follow. Their prayers weren't self-centered; they were God-centered. When our prayers are merely self-centered, they lead us to a self-centered faith. In other words, a dead end. But if our prayer requests are God-centered, they direct us toward God. This kind of God-centered faith doesn't run out of steam and quit when the road grows long.

God-centered praying focuses our attention on His purposes. Notice how often the apostles requested prayer for themselves. And with each request, they sought to fulfill God's plans and desires. Praying for yourself, then, is not necessarily self-centered. As your desire becomes God-centered, so will your praying. And that's a way to thrive.

Consider with me, how many of your requests fall into the category of seeking God's favor? How about fearless proclamation or fellowship? Or what about furthering the gospel message in your neighborhood, your city, and out across the world? I have considered these things—and it's made a difference in the way I pray, and in the way I ask for prayer from others.

And guess what? That kind of New Testament praying

is infectious. It sets an example for all who pray *with* you.

We need each other. We need someone to fall with. But sometimes our prayers for others seem a little shallow and surface-y—like a simple recitation of their latest wants and needs. How do you pray for your loved ones more deeply?

Fortunately for us, the New Testament writers recorded more than just their requests for prayer. They also wrote down the actual prayers they offered up for others. So let's see what happened when they fell for others. You'll love this.

Paul prayed that the Corinthian brothers and sisters *would grow in maturity*.[36]

For the believers in Ephesus, he asked the Lord that *the eyes of their hearts would be enlightened*, so they could better understand their hope and their inheritance in Christ. Pleading with God for these saints, Paul asked that *they would be strengthened in their inner man*, and that *Christ would dwell in their hearts through faith*. He prayed that *they would have power to grasp the love of God*, and that *they would be filled to the measure of the fullness of God*.[37]

For the Philippians he prayed that *their love would abound in depth and insight*.[38]

And for the Colossian believers, Paul got really cranked up. He asked God that *they would be filled with the knowledge of God's will and have spiritual wisdom*. He prayed that *they would live a worthy life, bear fruit, and grow in the knowledge of God*.[39]

Opening his heart to heaven on behalf of the young church at Thessalonica, the apostle prayed that *they would be supplied with all they lacked, that God would count them worthy, and fulfill their every good purpose and act of faith*.[40]

For his Ephesian friend, Philemon, Paul prayed *that God would help him actively share his faith so he would have a full understanding of every good thing we have in Christ.*[41]

Do those prayers sound like the prayers you pray for your friends and family...your children...your spouse? Do you pray for their growth and maturity and their enlightenment to see spiritual things? Do you pray that they will have strength in their innermost being or that they would be filled with the knowledge of God's will? Do you petition God that they would have spiritual wisdom and live a worthy life?

SWIMMING FOR THE DEEP END

As I reviewed these prayers of Paul and others, I didn't see anything about Demetrius getting a better job, or Hannah finding "Mr. Right," or Apollos getting along with his mother-in-law, or Lydia finding relief from her arthritis, or Gaius passing his chariot driver's exam. Now there's nothing *wrong* with any of those requests. God cares about what we care about, and He's interested in every detail of our lives.

But these prayers of the apostles made me think about going deeper in my petitions for others. Too often I ask God for superficial things, either for myself or others. I splash around in the shallow end of my prayer life, but God invites me to dive into the deep end.

Oh yes, we know that we ought to pray. The apostle James reminds us that "you do not have because you do not ask" (James 4:2, NKJV). Too often we go without simply because we neglect to bring our requests to God. We are stuck within our spiritual poverty, our loneliness, and even live without blessing just because we don't pray.

God meets our deepest needs through prayer, but even more magnificently, *He* meets us in prayer. Prayer allows us to cooperate with the work He's doing in us, and it offers a rendezvous through which we can know Him.

Prayer isn't meant to be intimidating; it's supposed to be inviting. But there are times when life is just simply too big, too complex, too overwhelming, and we don't know what to say or what to ask for. That's when I remind myself that even though I may be overwhelmed, the Holy Spirit is not. He can take my wordless longings, my unnamed fears, and my jumbled thoughts and weave them into a lovely, seamless intercession before the Father.

Those life-is-too-big moments are also times when I choose to "trade places."

"TRADING PLACES" PRAYER

Sometimes, when I pray, I can't see the forest for the trees. My prayers sound more like gibberish than well-thought-out petitions. Drowning in the sea of my own problems, I feel like I'm flailing and grasping, tossed by the waves, never able to clutch the life preserver just beyond my reach.

That's when I shift my prayers to someone else.

And what a difference. I can see *their* forest and *their* trees with perfect clarity. I can lean over the edge of my boat and toss a life preserver into their reach with exacting precision.

I remember unloading my frustrations on my friend Karen while we talked on the phone one day. Sometimes blindness just scrapes against the bottom of my soul and makes me tired, and it was one of those days. My thoughts were fragmented, and I was so overwhelmed by circumstances that I could barely articulate my heart.

Then it was Karen's turn. She poured out her concerns about her mother's recent diagnosis of cancer. Like me, she was so overwhelmed that her thoughts had become patchy, and she could barely make sense with her words.

And then Karen hit upon the solution. "I know!" she said. "I'll pray for you today, and you pray for me. I can handle praying for your situation much better than I can figure out how to pray for mine."

I was struck by the intuitive wisdom of her suggestion. Sometimes I just get worn out in my prayers. Subjectivity skews my ability to petition wisely. Yet objectivity brings a great advantage to prayer. My deep love and concern for my friend Karen caused me to seek God diligently on her behalf. Because I was a spectator I was able to see her playing field more clearly.

Of course God wants us to seek Him for our own needs. He says so time and again. But to show that kind of persistence on someone else's behalf invites God's power to overwhelm them. And catch this—His power splashes over into our own lives, our own situations. As we become a channel of His grace, mercy, kindness, wisdom, and provision, God lets that channel overflow the banks, flooding our own lives.

On that day of "trading places" prayer, I didn't feel empowered because my own circumstances had changed. Somehow, God's grace and power swept through me as I poured myself out for Karen. Paul said as much to his friends in Corinth. "For we rejoice when we ourselves are weak but you are strong; this we also pray for, that you be made complete" (2 Corinthians 13:9, NASB).

Sometimes I feel God's presence most mightily when I am freed from the shackles of self. It is empowering to carry another's burden to the throne. When we do, it strengthens our spiritual muscles and invigorates our spiritual stamina.

We are stronger and sturdier because of our persistent pleas before the throne of grace. Left to myself and my own needs, I become weary and hopeless. But praying for someone else emboldens me and gives hope and confidence that my own needs will be met. "Prayer always works. But beware: through it God may work upon us in ways we would never have anticipated."[42]

Oh my friend, bearing another's burden will certainly lighten your own load. "Carry each other's burdens, and in this way you will fulfill the law of Christ" (Galatians 6:2).

If you're getting worn out or feeling intimidated or powerless in your prayers, maybe you should trade places or fall down with your friends and family. You can certainly experiment by imitating the way the early apostles prayed. But most important...just pray. Pray for others, pray with others, pray by yourself and for yourself. But keep on praying and never stop.

Corrie ten Boom summed it all up by asking, "Is prayer your

steering wheel or your spare tire?" God just wants to hear from you. He loves you and longs for you to call upon Him so He can direct your every step. It is your life's breath to pray, so *breathe.*

"Pray to Me," our God tells us, "and I will listen to you" (Jeremiah 29:12, NASB).

What could be intimidating about that?

CHAPTER NINE

Hold Onto Hope

Hope was as elusive to me as a black leather watchband with a silver clasp.

Okay, I know that might sound strange to you. But after three exhausting hours of searching, I was starting to lose hope.

I had just purchased a new Braille watch that I was crazy about. It was silver rimmed with a midnight-blue face. The only problem was that its black leather band was too big. So I set out to get it adjusted. My pilgrimage began at a likely place to fix a watch—the jewelry counter at the largest department store in the mall.

A nice older gentleman offered to help me while I waited. As I handed him my watch, he fumbled, and his hands shook as he tried to hold it in his grasp. *Oh no*, I thought, *this is not going to work out well.*

I was right. An hour later, I was still standing there.

Finally, the aged salesman handed my watch back to me in its original condition, regretfully informing me I would need another band—and his store didn't have one that would fit.

So my friend Pat and I left the store and ambled through the mall. We popped into a jewelry store and asked if they sold black leather bands with silver clasps. "None here," a disinterested clerk mumbled. (If you're not there to buy diamonds, you're definitely a second-class customer.)

In the next jewelry store we encountered, the salesman examined my watch and told me he thought it was fixable.

"No way," a gruff female voice interrupted. "Can't be done." That's when I was introduced to the other sales-woman. Ignoring his comrade, the first salesman still held out hope. "But you will have to wait thirty minutes for my manager to return," he said.

Pat and I decided to get some lunch while we waited for the manager. After grabbing a quick bite in the food court, I was armed with a better attitude, better blood sugar levels, and renewed hope. We returned to the jewelry store and found seven customers ahead of us in line for service.

When she saw us, the crude-sounding saleswoman who had discouraged me earlier yelped, "The manager isn't back yet."

"We can't wait," I replied. Just as we turned to leave...the manager arrived. *Hope at last!*

The salesman explained my situation. I could feel waves of irritation radiating from the manager's person. He stretched and twisted my watch, peered at it, unbuckled it, and then went behind the counter. "Can't be adjusted and can't be replaced" was his pronouncement. "You should go to the leather repair shop. Maybe they can cut it down."

At this point, my desperation was growing and my optimism was shrinking. The parade of watch experts was not amusing me any longer. I was glad I was with my friend Pat, who was a fairly new Christian. It made me more mindful of guarding my tongue and testimony.

So, with fading optimism and growing frustration, we trooped into the leather repair shop. By that time, I had my speech down, and handed the repairman my troublesome timepiece.

Still barely hanging onto hope, I waited for him to emerge from the back with a well-fitting watch. But it wasn't to be. Instead, he held out the watch and exclaimed, "I'm not touching this." Pat gasped at the now dangling buckle which the repairman had broken. He said it would have broken anyway and there was nothing he could do.

"Take it back to the jeweler," he suggested.

Without responding to him, I slung my cane out in front of me and turned toward the door. I didn't even risk holding him responsible for the broken clasp since I was so irritated. Pat's view of godliness might have been compromised by my verbal explosion. Now my favorite watch wasn't even wearable.

We searched out the last jewelry store in the mall in hopes of finding a new band. And again, no black bands with silver clasps were available. Finally the Zales salesman told us to try the department store around the corner. "I think they have bands," he said.

"You think? Or you know?" I pressed.

"I know."

"Okay, Pat," I sighed. "Let's try one last time." So we entered the department store and found the watchbands. Pat told the salesgirl, who sounded like she was about twelve, that we needed a black band with a silver buckle, size 14. The girl rifled through a basket with Pat's help, occasionally giggling and pulling out bands one by one. The scenario went something like this:

Girl:	Here's a cute one!
Pat:	Yes, but it's a size 16.
Girl:	Oh. Here's another one. It's to die for!
Pat:	It's a size 12.
Girl:	Oh, well. I love this one!
Pat:	It's a size 16 also.
Girl:	(*Giggles*) I don't really know what those numbers mean!

I am intentionally omitting my own thoughts from this exchange. You don't need to know those. It wouldn't be good for my reputation. Let's just say, I stayed quiet...and tried to hold onto *hope*.

I finally bought the only black size 14 watchband with a silver clasp in the store. It was on clearance and cost three dollars. It was plastic and very tacky, but at least I could wear my watch.

I asked if the salesgirl could please attach it to my watch. "No," she responded, "I don't know how. You should try the Watch Doctor."

"The who?"

"The Watch Doctor. He's at that little kiosk just outside the entrance."

By the time I arrived at the Watch Doctor's clinic with my oh-so-tacky band, I had lost all sense of decorum. I was spent, and not nearly so concerned about Pat's opinion of my testimony anymore. And so, like a crazed, worn-out, hopeless woman, I whined loudly and all in one breath, "Help me! I just need a new band, or an adjustment on my old one, or at least I need this tacky one attached to my watch. No one can help me. It's taken three hours and nothing is working."

Somewhere in my hapless account I must have mentioned the watch was Braille. "Braille?" the good doctor gasped. "Are you blind?"

"Yes," I answered.

"Can I pray for you?"

"Yes," I moaned, "but sir, I really want you to fix my watch first."

"What can I pray for?" he asked as if I'd never mentioned the watch.

He took out a pen and paper, ready to write. "What's your name?" he asked. I told him my name, introduced him to Pat, and learned that his name was Rick. As gently as I could manage, I relaxed and tried to refocus him on the watch. He asked me if I knew Jesus.

"Yes," I replied. "Know Him and love Him."

"Hallelujah!" he shouted. "I love people who love my Lord!"

"Me, too," I said. But what I was thinking was, *Now,*

brother, fix the watch. We talked about Christ and our salvation as he and Pat tried to find a new band. When Pat found the perfect one, she lamented, "But it has a gold buckle, and we need a silver one."

"No problem," the doctor smiled. "I'll just switch it. Only take a minute." No one else during the earlier watch wars had even hinted that such a maneuver was possible. But Rick just kept raising the praise and working on the watch. He was my brother, and he was making sure that his sister's watch was just right.

When he finished, I paid him and buckled the watch. He then grasped my hands, and there, in the middle of the mall, Rick prayed for me. And I thanked God for my newly discovered brother. I told him how he was my last hope and that he redeemed the whole day for me, and he just laughed as if he knew exactly what I meant.

In Romans 5:5, Paul tells us that hope will not disappoint us. What the apostle doesn't say in that verse, however, is that hope may take you down some interesting paths. Hope most certainly will require perseverance, but it will also help you remain focused on the prize.

HOPE HOLDS YOU

We must hold onto hope. But if you are weary, you can allow hope to hold onto you.

Phil and I celebrated our nineteenth wedding anniversary on August 9 of this year. He was actually only nineteen years old when we met, and now he's been my husband half his life.

On his dresser sits a beloved picture that was taken outside of our college dining hall just a few months after we began dating.

In the photo, I have long, straight black hair with thick bangs. He has bushy, curly, blond hair. We are both in faded jeans and tennis shoes. I know exactly what we were wearing even without seeing the picture because I remember when the photo was shot. He and I were walking hand in hand, and when our friend with the camera yelled, "Smile!" Phil dropped my hand, put his arm around me, and grinned.

Now, almost twenty years later, Phil still holds my hand. Or, is it that I still hold his? Who is really holding whose? Hmmm.

When our youngest son Connor walks with me or his dad, he too reaches for a hand. He quickly places his small hand into our larger ones. He snuggles; we grasp. Even if Connor were to let go, he would still be held within our grasp. Again, who is holding whom?

To me, simple hand-holding is a lot like hope. It seems like we hold onto it, but really hope holds onto us. Since I first found faith in Christ, hope has held me and I have held onto the hope that holds me.

So if that's the case, what helps us hold on as we are being held? What keeps our little hand clinging within the larger hand of hope? According to Romans 15:4, it's two distinct things...perseverance and the encouragement of Scripture.

For whatever was written in earlier times was written for our instruction, so that through perseverance and the encouragement of the Scriptures we might have hope. (NASB)

Think for a moment how amazing this is. We have in our possession a book that is thousands of years old—and it is as relevant to life in the twenty-first century as this morning's newspaper or today's page in your date book. Why should an ancient book assembled by a diverse group of prophets, farmers, shepherds, kings, fishermen, and minor government officials offer any hope to men and women in the grip of contemporary problems, pressures, and heartaches?

Because God Himself put that Book together, that's why. It's a book that is not only relevant, it is *alive.*

> For the word of God is living and powerful, and sharper than any two-edged sword, piercing even to the division of soul and spirit, and of joints and marrow, and is a discerner of the thoughts and intents of the heart. (Hebrews 4:12, NKJV)

How can a book be alive? Because God spoke it, God continually works through it, and God's Spirit shines the light of understanding on its pages, for those who seek Him and His ways. The hope that touches the lives of those who read it, then, is not some shallow, surface-y, will-o'-the-wisp, wish-upon-a-star kind of hope, but a *living hope.* A hope that can reach anywhere, and to anyone. A hope that can overcome anything.

The words penned in Paul's day are the very source of encouragement and hope for us today. In fact, how fabulous that every lesson we learn in the Light leads us to greater perseverance and ultimate hope.

PERSEVERANCE

The New Living Translation phrases Romans 15:4 this way: "Such things were written in the Scriptures long ago to teach us. They give us hope and encouragement as we wait patiently for God's promises."

To "wait patiently" is to lay a steady, patient hand to the plow...even if the plow seems to be idle at the moment.

That's perseverance. It reminds me of the only kind of exercise I actually enjoy. It's called isometric contraction. You can do it while you wait in a long grocery line or while you're stuck in traffic. You can engage in it while you watch TV, or while you wash dishes.

Maybe you've tried it before. It's where you flex and firm your muscles even when you are supposedly still. It's actively participating in strengthening yourself even when you're not moving. It's a great picture of perseverance.

Moses set this example for us:

By faith Moses, when he had grown up, refused to be known as the son of Pharaoh's daughter. He chose to be mistreated along with the people of God rather than to enjoy the pleasures of sin for a short time. He regarded disgrace for the sake of Christ as of greater value than the treasures of Egypt, because he was looking ahead to his reward. By faith he left Egypt, not fearing the king's anger; he persevered because he saw him who is invisible. (Hebrews 11:24–27)

Perseverance is how we cling within the grasp of God. It's waiting, not pulling back prematurely; it's staying and standing even without visible results. That kind of trusting tenacity leads us to a hopeful expectation. Perseverance leads to hope in the same way quitting leads to feelings of hopelessness. When we give in or give up, we eventually give out.

The word *perseverance* in Romans 15:4 shows that the phrase "holding onto hope" is quite accurate: It is an unwavering unwillingness to let go and give up. As Tertullian said, "Hope is patience with the lamp lit." Is your lamp lit today, my friend?

Speaking of lamps, I have learned the tough lesson of perseverance from living with no physical light at all—the difficult, unrelenting teacher of blindness. There are times when I just want to quit. What is a small task to a sighted person can be an enormous feat for me. Walking to my mailbox, navigating unfamiliar restrooms in airports, negotiating different stages in different venues and cities every time I speak, and hundreds of other small and big challenges can really wear me out.

To be honest, my fatigue often exceeds my fortitude. It would be easier to just draw the lines a little closer to home, keep my world smaller, simpler. Venturing out of my "control zone" takes a lot of energy, and sometimes I have to give myself a pep talk to keep marching on.

But this I know—and I hope with all my heart I can explain it to you.

The hopelessness I feel when I give in to my blindness is far more debilitating than the fatigue I may feel from persevering through it.

Here's what I mean. There have been many a morning that I have gotten my boys off to school and husband off to work just to go straight back to my room and crawl right back into bed. Feeling overwhelmed, discouraged, I pull the covers over my head and try to disappear. When I give in to the temptation to give up like that, I find myself slipping toward the cliff edge of depression and despair. At least when I cry my way through hard days, at least when I forge on through my frustrations and keep on keeping on though I am discouraged and weary, my perseverance serves to strengthen my hope.

When I give up, I begin to relinquish hope. When I stop persevering, it's like I loosen my grip within the greater hand of hope. It's only when I keep clinging, grasping, and am unwilling to quit that I truly feel hope holding onto me.

We all feel the weight of hopelessness from time to time. I know you have felt it. Maybe you are feeling it right now. The Light offers constant pep talks that help us to persevere. In fact, the writer of Hebrews offered encouragement to the worn-out believers who were beginning to lose their grip on hope.

If you've ever felt yourself walking on that cliff edge of despair, sit yourself down and read the book of Hebrews. Read it in a modern translation or a paraphrase or whatever version you like—just open its pages and ask God's Spirit to stir you and speak to you in the deep places of your spirit. He will! That's precisely why the book of Hebrews was written. And God had *you* in mind even as it was being penned.

It was originally penned to a generation of believers who were experiencing the heat and pressure and heartbreak of unrelenting persecution. Some of them were on the verge of giving up, turning back to their old religion and their old ways. Knowing this, the writer poured out his heart, pleading with these discouraged men and women to remember those who had gone before them, and to keep their eyes on the greatest of all prizes, the Lord Jesus Himself.

Hope is strengthened by endurance and is eroded by quitting. So my friend, keep holding on, persevering, enduring. But don't forget the second thing Paul mentions that helps us hold onto hope...the encouragement of Scripture.

HOW SCRIPTURE ENCOURAGES

The Word of God can encourage you when you are discouraged. It can offer hope when you feel hopeless. It can shed light when your world is dark. God knows we need hope, and He provides the encouragement of His Word to remind us that we are held by an extraordinary hope.

Read His Word. Cling to it. Hold it so close to your own heart that you can hear the heartbeat of God in its pages. It will fill you with hope as it works in your heart.

And so, looking with you to the encouragement of Scripture, let me remind you of the hope which holds you.

Your hope is in God.

> Blessed is he whose help is the God of Jacob,
> whose hope is in the LORD his God....
> The LORD is good to those whose hope is in him,
> to the one who seeks him.
> (Psalm 146:5; Lamentations 3:25)

Your hope is not in yourself or in your ability to fix all of your problems. Your hope is not in your spouse or your romantic interest. Your hope is not found in your boss's reaction to your work or your children's acknowledgment of your worth. Your hope is not in church membership, religious rituals, or "keeping all the rules." Your hope is not in any other person, place, or institution in your life.

It is in God and God alone.

Hope in anything other than God Himself will always disappoint.

The psalmist understood these things very well. "Lord, where do I put my hope? My only hope is in you" (Psalm 39:7, NLT). When our hope is in God alone, not in what God can do for us, then we will not be shaken. Place your hope in Him and you will never be disappointed (Psalm 71:5).

Your hope is in the power and majesty of His Name.

> And his name will be the hope
> of all the world....
> I will praise you forever for what you have done;

in your name I will hope, for your name is good.
I will praise you in the presence of your saints.
(Matthew 12:21, NLT; Psalm 52:9)

Your hope is not in your own power and ability. Your hope is not in any influential relationships or associations you might have. Your hope is not in whom you know or who knows you. Your hope is not secured by or found in any authority except Christ. Your hope is profoundly and singularly in the powerful Name of Christ and in His majesty alone.

You can be joyful in hope.

Be joyful in hope, patient in affliction, faithful in prayer.
(Romans 12:12)

You can't always be joyful in your circumstances. You can't find joy in wishing, worrying, or wondering. But you *can* be joyful in hope, because it is a sure thing. It will never let you down. Hope never promotes sorrow or despair, and that's why you can be joyful.

Hope holds the seeds of faith and love.

We have heard of your faith in Christ Jesus and of the love you have for all the saints—the faith and love that spring from the hope that is stored up for you in heaven and that you have already heard about in the word of truth. (Colossians 1:4–5)

Hope does not promote lies or ill will. Hope will never deceive you or lead you into malice, ill will, or outright hatred. Hope is the incubator that nurtures your growing love and fortifies your belief in God's truth.

Hope is the foundation for faith and knowledge.

...a faith and knowledge resting on the hop.e of eternal life, which God, who does not lie, promised before the beginning of time. (Titus 1:2)

Hope is a sure bedrock upon which you can build your faith life. It is not a foundation of shifting sand; it is steady. It is not subject to cracks and compromise, so you can erect a fortress of truth and knowledge upon it with confidence. Hope will remain a secure rock even when all around you is shifting sand. It is a resting place for your trust and understanding.

Hope is your calling.

I pray also that the eyes of your heart may be enlightened in order that you may know the hope to which he has called you, the riches of his glorious inheritance in the saints, and his incomparably great power for us who believe. (Ephesians 1:18–19)

You are not called to despair, throw in the towel, and quit. You are called and equipped to choose hope. It is your invitation to a neverending party where water is turned into wine. You are called to and destined to believe, persevere, and thrive regardless of your situation. Despair is not your calling. Negativity is not your calling. Pessimism is not your calling. Hope is. Cling to your calling, and feel your calling cling to you.

Hope is a gift from God.

> "For I know the plans I have for you," declares the
> LORD, "plans to prosper you and not to harm you,
> plans to give you hope and a future." (Jeremiah 29:11)

You can't earn hope, like a salesperson racking up points for a company award. You can't manufacture hope through frenzied activities or dedication to some tried-and-true formula. You can't maneuver yourself into the path of hope, so that it somehow overtakes you because you're in the right place at the right time.

In fact, hope is a gift. A gift from God Himself. He gives us each hope, and it's up to you and me to unwrap the gift. Make hope your own. He gave it to you so you would use and enjoy it.

Hope will never disappoint you.

> And hope does not disappoint us, because God has
> poured out his love into our hearts by the Holy
> Spirit, whom he has given us. (Romans 5:5)

People will disappoint you. Loyalty fails, relationships change, friends drift away. Places where we have lived and loved and created happy memories change into places that feel strange and no longer like home. Someone cuts down the old trees or tears down the old, familiar buildings. Or blight sets in on a once lovely neighborhood, stealing its warmth and charm. Health disappoints us. We don't feel the way we'd love to feel, sleep the way we wish we could sleep, or heal from sickness and wounds the way we long to heal. Plans disappoint us. No matter how we dream and plan, things don't always turn out the way we expect. We can't control factors that can change everything in an instant. Sometimes all our strategizing crumbles before our eyes.

Disappointment is part of our fallen world, but hope will never disappoint us when our hope is from God and in God's Word. Say with the psalmist, "You are my refuge and my shield; I have put my hope in your word" (Psalm 119:114).

Hope is the anchor for your soul.

This hope we have as an anchor of the soul, a hope both sure and steadfast. (Hebrews 6:19, NASB)

Hope grounds you and ties you to that which is immovable. Instead of being tossed about by the winds of circumstance, you will become welded so that you can never be shifted, transplanted, or dislodged.

Hope will embolden you.

Since we have such a hope, we are very bold. (2 Corinthians 3:12, ESV)

Hope gives you guts. Boldness way beyond your own. It prompts you to act with the courage God has granted you. Despair cowers in the corner of disappointment, but hope makes you the brave believer God intended. Hope causes you to have the courage to claim God's promises and the bravery to believe revelation even when reason abandons you. Hope lets you shout optimism when others whisper dark words of cynicism and despair.

Hope is alive.

> Praise be to the God and Father of our Lord Jesus Christ! In his great mercy he has given us new birth into a living hope through the resurrection of Jesus Christ from the dead. (1 Peter 1:3)

Hope lives on, even if all your dreams blow away on the wind. When the widow of Zarephath made her last meal and then prepared to die, hope's cupboard was still full.

When Hannah cried out of her own barrenness, hope was ready and waiting to conceive.

When the lame man was lying beside the pool of Bethesda, hope was preparing his walking shoes.

When Naaman's flesh was being consumed by leprosy, the river of hope was able to cleanse.

When Gideon was afraid, hope was posturing for victory.

When Paul was thrown in prison for preaching, hope refused to be silent and spoke truth to the guards.

When the prophet Jeremiah cried tears of sorrow and disappointment, hope was his only comfort.

When Elisha's servant felt alone against the enemy, hope was the army that protected the prophet he served.

When David felt vulnerable, hope gave him security and refuge.

When Jesus' body lay lifeless in the tomb, hope was resurrection waiting to happen.

Hope is Jesus Himself.

Paul, an apostle of Christ Jesus according to the commandment of God our Savior, and of Christ Jesus, who is our hope... (1 Timothy 1:1, NASB)

Hope is not a philosophy or a theory. Hope is not a personality trait or a quirk. Hope is not a concept or a dream. Hope is a person. Hope is Jesus. And the most amazing part is that hope is Christ in you (Colossians 1:27). Other men see only a hopeless end, but the Christian rejoices in an endless hope.

Wow—what a hope. Hold onto it as it holds onto you. Don't fix your hope on earthly things like financial security, unruffled relationships, or restored health. The temporary things can never be a true source of hope. Instead, fix your hope on God and His eternal Word.

A week from now...a year from now...a million ages from now...you will not be disappointed.

CHAPTER TEN

Be God Conscious

A few years ago I was invited to a special dinner sponsored by a publishing house. As a rookie author, I was excited beyond measure. The evening held such a promise of joy that I began early that afternoon to get ready for the big night—trying on several dresses, and working harder than usual on my hair.

When I was fully groomed, I couldn't decide which earrings would provide the nicest finishing touch, so I placed a lovely and very dramatic silver earring in my left ear and then secured a graceful, more modest hoop in my right. I figured when Phil returned to the hotel he could help me decide which looked best.

But when Phil arrived, it was obvious he was *not* as excited as me about the dinner. Instead of preparing hours in advance, he burst into our hotel room five minutes before we were to leave. Trousers flew, shirts whisked straight from the suitcase onto his body, cologne splattered, and his hair was given a quick once-over.

Then he breathlessly announced, "We're gonna be late!"

Caught up in this chaos, I grabbed his tie and raced to the door, completely forgetting about my own appearance.

Despite Hurricane Phil, the Category Four who had just blown through my tranquil world, I was still excited. Nothing was going to ruin my evening. Brimming with anticipation, I entered the restaurant on my husband's arm, and we were shown to our seats.

To my delight, I found myself seated between a notable editor and a well-known chef. Our conversation was lively and captivating. I laughed, listened, learned, and loved every minute of it. I was conscious of nothing but the nuances of the moment. This was pure joy, and I allowed myself to simply be caught up in the wonder of the experience.

After descending from my cloud and floating back into our hotel room, Phil warily inquired, "Um, Jennifer, did you *mean* to wear two different earrings?"

"Oh, nooo!" I shrieked. "How *embarrassing!*"

I quickly became self-conscious, imagining how foolish I must have looked with my wildly mismatched earrings. I wondered what the folks at dinner must have thought of my fashion faux pas. They probably stared. Or snickered. Or at least did a double take.

Frankly, the thought began to ruin my evening...in retrospect. I hadn't been self-conscious for a moment during dinner. I was too swept along in the joy and pleasure of the occasion, the engaging people I had met, and the goodness of my God to even think much about myself.

But now...the more I recalled the experience, the more painfully self-aware and humiliated I felt. My great joy simply evaporated.

That's what self-consciousness does. It steals our joy. It deprives us of the prospect of living beyond ourselves. It places the magnifying glass of excessive scrutiny on us, enlarging our little mistakes and shortcomings completely beyond measure.

By contrast, God-consciousness continually preserves joy, keeping us fueled and focused on our faith journey.

When our awareness of God exceeds our self-awareness, we are positioned to thrive—even when things in our lives (like my earrings) don't match up.

THE NEVERENDING DANCE

It's a hard balance to strike...a healthy self-awareness and self-love coupled with a greater God-awareness and love for God.

You know what I mean. That tension between thinking about God and thinking about yourself is a constant struggle. But it shouldn't be a wrestling match or race to see which one wins.

Think of it more like a dance.

Think of it as a cooperative, step-by-step interplay

between us and God. He leads, we follow. We move to the rhythm of grace and truth that helps us to strike the perfect balance.

Here's how we can do it so our joy will really be complete. Think of yourself as a dwelling place—the place where the glory of God dwells. Here's the way Paul put it:

> Do you not know that you are a temple of God and that the Spirit of God dwells in you?... Or do you not know that your body is a temple of the Holy Spirit who is in you, whom you have from God, and that you are not your own? (1 Corinthians 3:16; 6:19, NASB)

God intended for us to have an awareness that He dwells in and with us. But because God dwells in the temple of our bodies and our personalities, we must also maintain a healthy self-awareness.

Self-consciousness is appropriate, as it directs us to good stewardship and management of our personal temple. The temple itself isn't the object of worship; it is the One housed in that temple who deserves our devotion and attention.

Stick with me for a moment while I take this thought just a step further. Paul told the Thessalonians there would come a day when the "man of lawlessness" or the "anti-Christ" would set himself up to receive the attention and worship that only Jesus deserves.

Paul describes the enemy of Christ as he "who opposes and exalts himself above every so-called god or object of worship, so that he takes his seat in the temple of God, displaying himself as being God" (2 Thessalonians 2:4, NASB).

Even though it's a radical picture, it reminds me of what I do in my own spirit of selfishness. In the temple God has given me, the place where He is to be enthroned, I set up my own throne, built brick by brick with the glue and mortar of self-awareness, self-consciousness, self-preservation, self-protection, and even self-promotion.

There is one temple, and only One in the temple worthy of worship.

And it's not me.

Imagine for a moment that your job was keeper of the Temple in ancient Israel. Every morning you wake before dawn to enter the Temple courts with your broom and your mop. All throughout the day—and until the last worshiper departs, rejoicing through the front doors at night—you occupy yourself with dusting, arranging, cleaning, oiling hinges, and polishing wood.

Now that's a good occupation, and pleasing to the Lord—if you are doing it just for Him and out of love of Him. But what if you say in your heart, "I don't need to be a part of any of the worship services. I don't need to sing the psalms or raise my hands to God or participate in the offerings. I'll just spend that extra time patching cracks in the plaster or sweeping along the baseboards"?

So as God's people weep and worship and repent before Him, bringing offerings of their best and pouring out their hearts in praise, you're back in one of the storerooms on hands and knees retouching the paint behind the door.

Is God pleased with you? Wouldn't He say to you, "I am pleased you honor My Temple, but the Temple is only a vehicle for approaching Me and connecting with Me. You have turned your back on the main thing—on life itself—to busy yourself with needless minutiae"?

When I am fully self-conscious, not God-conscious, I worship myself, not God. Self-exaltation never leads to joy. It only leads to further self-scrutiny—and then more painful self-awareness.

The Temple was erected to be a dwelling place for the presence of God. So is the temple of our lives. As David wrote, "In Your presence is fullness of joy" (Psalm 16:11, NKJV). Joy is a result of God-consciousness, not self-consciousness.

MIRROR, MIRROR, OFF THE WALL

To have that kind of view of myself, I must look in the one true mirror. I must pray like the psalmist, "Turn my heart toward your statutes and not toward selfish gain" (Psalm 119:36). Yes, to be more God-conscious than self-conscious, we must recognize that we are the temple dwelling of God, but we must also look into the mirror of God's Word.

Dwight L. Moody once said, "We ought to see the face of God every morning before we see the face of man."

The first face you see each day will greatly influence who occupies your thoughts throughout the day. When you look into your bathroom mirror, you see your face. But to see the face of God, you must look into the mirror of His Word.

In fact, the apostle James compares God's Word to a

mirror. He tells us that looking into God's mirror and applying what we see brings blessing. "But one who looks intently at the perfect law, the law of liberty, and abides by it, not having become a forgetful hearer but an effectual doer, this man will be blessed in what he does" (James 1:25, NASB).

If you've heard me speak before, you've probably heard me tell stories about mixing up my makeup. Yes, I have on occasion mixed up my eye liner and lip liners because I couldn't see into a mirror to behold the strange distortion I was creating.

Because the story of my makeup mishap is familiar to so many, I completely blew off the constructive criticism that Lucy Swindoll offered me one evening right before I went onstage at a Women Of Faith conference.

"Your eyes don't match," she said flatly.

"Very funny," I retorted. I was sure she was trying to capitalize on my story—or maybe just trying to keep me relaxed before I spoke.

But Lucy was serious. "No," she insisted, "really, one is black, and one is brown."

"That's impossible!" I replied. That funny and mischievous Lucy was not going to get the best of me on this one.

"Jennifer, I am *serious*," she said with as much maternal authority as possible. "Ask Nicole."

So I turned to Nicole Johnson, the talented dramatist on the Women of Faith team. But before I could ask, she gasped, "She's right. One is black and one is brown."

I opened my makeup bag and sure enough, I had two different eyeliner pencils. One black, one brown. (Note to the visually impaired reader: Never carry two different shades of eyeliner in the same makeup bag.)

It is true: I have not been able to see into a mirror since I was fifteen and lost the majority of my sight. Of course, even though I joke about my many mishaps, I still wish I could see myself. I would love to be able to look into a mirror to see what I look like. I would much prefer to choose my own hairstyle or blush color. And yes, eyeliner. What woman wouldn't?

But even though that reality is frustrating, it causes my eyes to gravitate to a mirror that I *can* see. In fact, the mirror I look into now shows me exactly what I look like, exactly who I am.

It is the mirror of God's Word.

My blind eyes can see 20/20 as I gaze into its light. I may not see my physical image in the bathroom mirror, but in God's mirror, I can see that I am created in God's image. I know from Ephesians 2:10 that I am the very workmanship of Creator God.

The mirror of God's Word helps us see ourselves and our God in a way that promotes a healthy balance between our God-consciousness and our self-awareness. Have you looked in that mirror lately? Gaining God's perspective on who we are allows us to find a healthy balance. It keeps us from an inflated or deflated view of ourselves and allows us to assess ourselves in the light of God-consciousness.

The mirror in your bathrooms—even clear of steam—doesn't reflect truth. It is at the mercy of your perspective and your interpretation. We know very well there are some attractive people out there who look into a mirror and see only ugliness. What is happening in that instance? They are looking, but they are not *seeing*.

Physical mirrors can't reflect truth; they only offer optical illusion. Only the mirror of God's Word reflects truth, because it *is* truth. It grants you a right perspective of yourself as it reveals a true view of your Father.

But don't just look at the mirror; look *into* it. Gaze long and hard, the way you do when you are applying eye shadow or fixing your hair. The way a man does when he is shaving around those small creases and tiny lines.

"The Bible is like a telescope," Philip Brooks wrote. "If a man looks *through* his telescope, then he sees the worlds beyond; but if he looks *at* his telescope, then he does not see anything but that. The Bible is a thing to be looked through, to see that which is beyond; but most people only look at it; and so they see only the dead letter."

He's right. How much we miss if we only give the Word a passing glance. Look into it, gaze, and feed on it like Jeremiah, and you will experience the same joy he wrote about. "When your words came, I ate them; they were my joy and my heart's delight, for I bear your name, O Lord God Almighty" (Jeremiah 15:16).

"OPEN THE EYES
OF MY HEART, LORD"

Our gaze into the mirror of God's Word is intended ultimately to reveal God, to allow us to see Him, and therefore heighten our awareness of Him. It is incredibly powerful. Powerful enough to actually alter what we see, and change our perspectives. No matter what we are experiencing, no matter which page we set our gaze upon, the Light is able to reveal realities we weren't even aware of.

My friend Marcey recently sent me an e-mail that reminded me of the sheer power of God's Word to shape our thoughts and perspective. Just for a moment, take a peek into my e-mail Inbox for an excerpt of her letter.

Dear Jennifer,

I just realized today how we (or maybe it's just me) have become such "topical" Christians. For instance, if I'm going through "divers temptations," there is an instantaneous feeling that I need to be spending all of my time in James. But right now, Scott and I are completing this 6-week study in Genesis on Abraham; I am working through a 28-day book on prayer and also preparing a Sunday school lesson each week. (Let alone sneaking peeks at the Strong-Willed Child book.) Who has time to expand to James and take care of three children, a husband, and a house?

My point being, after completing the prayer study and the study on Abraham during Neeley's morning nap, guess what I found? Peace! Order to my chaos! Absolute joy! Have we, as Christians, slowly slipped into a pattern of thinking that says, "In order to benefit from God's Word, we must find the Scripture that speaks specifically to our current circumstances or 'topic'"?

Wow, did I underestimate the power of God's
Word or what? Obviously, you can learn anything
from God's Word at any time, anywhere in the
test. But over the past two days of studying
Abraham, I have learned that He is *El Roi*, the God
Who Sees; He is *El Shaddai*, the All-Sufficient One;
He is *Adonai*, Lord and Master. And the understatement of the year is that I have grown and I
have been blessed!

    Your friend,

    Marcey

Marcey's right. The Light is incredibly powerful to open
our eyes, tenderize our view, focus us, and allow us to really
see. If you are struggling with a level of self-consciousness
that debilitates you and blinds you to really seeing your
Father, then keep looking into the mirror.

I have experienced firsthand the power of God's Word
to open eyes. I never cease to be overwhelmed at the comments I receive after I speak. Women will recite detailed
accounts of how God spoke to them through His Word
while I taught.

The amazing thing is that more often than not, what
they heard is not what I said. God's Word speaks for itself
and is always personal, applicable, and precise.

And it will always lead to unspeakable joy.

Do you want your joy to be full? I sure do. Learn this
lesson shown to us in the Light. Remember that the source

of joy is not found in us but in God. When you allow yourself to be full of God instead of full of yourself, you will be satisfied by the sweet fruit of joy.

Joy is from God (Psalm 16:11).
Joy is a promise (Psalm 30:5).
Joy is a mindset (James 1:2–3).
Joy is your strength (Nehemiah 8:10).
Joy is your inheritance (Isaiah 61:7).

Look into His mirror, my friend, and you will see who you are and who He is. As you see yourself, recognize that you are a temple, the place where almighty God chooses to make His dwelling.

Does He wear you well?

CHAPTER ELEVEN

Enjoy the Fishbowl

I was a typical new parent when my son Clayton made his entrance into the world. Everything our little guy did was duly noted and recorded in the pages of his baby book—and discussed in happy detail with all my friends who were new moms. Phil and I could go on and on talking about what a bright and delightful little man the Lord had given us.

So you can imagine the excitement in our apartment on the day Clayton spoke his first discernible word.

"Ball."

Yes, that was it.

Soon after that great verbal breakthrough, other words followed. Within days he added words like "up" and "juice" and "Dada." I was growing in anticipation with each new word, especially when "Dada" was added to Clayton's growing vocabulary.

The addition of "Dada" surely meant that the much coveted "Mama" was on the horizon, and I couldn't wait to hear it. After all, it seemed as though I had been pregnant for years...and I now had stretch marks in places I didn't even know were stretchable. I felt like it was only right that I should be rewarded for giving this little boy life by hearing his sweet voice lift up a tender "Mama."

But it didn't come.

Oh, he continued to add words, but "Mama" wasn't one of them. Frankly, I was growing jealous. It just didn't seem fair. Clayton constantly uttered his Daddy's name. "Dada, juice," he would say. Or he would beckon from his crib, "Dada, up." I don't think I was completely unreasonable in feeling slighted. It was his "Mama," not his "Dada," who had gone through labor. Shouldn't there be some reward?

It's not like Phil held it over me, either (he's too wise for that). Still, I couldn't help but think he sounded just a little bit smug when Clayton went on with his "Dada this" and "Dada that."

Well, I could either get upset over being unacknowledged by the apple of my eye, or I could just relax, stop stewing about it, and enjoy being a new mom.

I decided on the latter course. And as my jealousy cleared, so did my judgment. In fact, I began to notice an interesting pattern emerging in Clayton's vocabulary. *He was calling me a name.* It wasn't the name I was expecting to hear, so it took some time for me to notice. No, he wasn't calling me "Mama."

He was calling me *"God."*

I kid you not. If Clayton wanted juice from his daddy, he would call out, "Dada, juice peas!" But if he wanted me to get his juice, he would call out, *"God,* juice peas!"

Somewhere in the forming of his verbal repertoire, he inserted the name he chose to call his mother, and it was none other than God. (Now it was my turn to refrain from being smug.)

As a first-time mom, I, of course, called the pediatrician to make sure this was not a problem. He counseled that it was just probably easier for Clayton to say God than Mama, and I was not to worry. Besides, I could be called a lot worse. It's just that Phil and I couldn't figure out how Clayton had come to this conclusion. Phil, though he treated me with love and respect, certainly didn't refer to me as deity.

After contemplating the matter, the only reason I could come up with was this. Clayton would see me in the kitchen, preparing food for dinner, then we would sit at the dinner table and pray, "Thank You, God, for our food."

I guess Clayton just assumed that since I was the one who made the food, and we thanked God for the food...I must be God.

Whew! That's a lot of pressure—and I didn't want to start getting used to the title. I was grateful when, at thirteen months old, Clayton started calling me "Mommy."

Have you ever heard anyone call you God? Probably not, but that doesn't mean that others aren't thinking it.

There are people in your world who look at your life and

wonder, "Who is God, anyway?" If they know that you walk in the Light, they will undoubtedly look to you to discern what God is like.

They might not even do so consciously or deliberately. You may never be aware that you're being observed. But if you are known to believe in and belong to God, there will be those who are watching, wondering. *Is God patient? Is He kind? Is He consistent? Does He really care?* Recognizing that others watch our lives as a billboard advertisement for what God is like helps us take seriously all the lessons we learn in the Light.

Some of us like the challenge of such a predicament, but others of us might feel a tinge of pressure. It's like living in a fishbowl.

A PLACE TO SHINE

Sometimes I feel like I live in a fishbowl. My life is on display, every move noticed, every choice laid open for analysis. Let's face it. You don't have to be in public ministry to struggle with "fishbowl" feelings and issues. Your faith life puts you on display. The light within you shines in the darkness of this world, and people notice it.

But don't worry. Your fishbowl is not a place of pressure. It's a place of privilege.

A fishbowl is an opportunity for others to see God in you. It need not be perceived as a burden, but rather a blessing. A place to shine.

Fishbowls come in all shapes and sizes. They're not just pulpits and brightly lit stages. No, they can be kitchen sinks, carpool lanes, office cubicles, backyard fences, dinner tables, grocery store lines or shopping malls. In fact, a fishbowl is anyplace where your life is observed by others.

And if in fact you do find yourself in a position where you are noticed and observed, don't imagine that you climbed up to that place of prominence and visibility on your own. God lovingly placed you there so that you will reflect Him.

My son Clayton gave me a special gift many years ago, purchased out of his tender seven-year-old heart and his meager budget. It's a small ceramic turtle. It may or may not be artistic—that doesn't matter to me. The little turtle's worth doesn't lie in its aesthetic qualities. It was a spontaneous gift of love from my boy, and it is very precious to me.

The turtle rests within the ring section of my jewelry box. I don't leave it there because I want to hide it; I intentionally placed it there so that every morning when I feel for my rings, I will feel the little turtle.

Clayton chose the turtle for me because he remembered the story I once told him about the "turtle on the fence post." Have you heard of him? He sits proudly upon a tall fence post. He is in a place of prominence where everyone can see and admire him. The interesting thing, however, is that he didn't get there by himself. Someone had to place him there.

I'm like that turtle on a fence post...and so are you.

It's kind of like a fish swimming contentedly in a bowl. How did he get there? He didn't swim upstream to get there. He didn't arrive there by escaping the talons of an eagle. Chances are he wasn't born there.

A fish lives in a bowl because someone put him there. And once the bowl becomes his whole world, he is dependent on the person who placed him there.

Whatever you have "achieved" in life is precisely what you have *received* in life. So... "Don't hide your light under a basket! Instead, put it on a stand and let it shine for all. In the same way, let your good deeds shine out for all to see, so that everyone will praise your heavenly Father" (Matthew 5:15–16, NLT).

The transparent walls within which you swim are a place for you to shine, a place for you to reflect the One who placed you there. There is one problem, however. You won't show who God is if you are distracted by the three perils of fishbowl living.

Peril #1: Pride

Sometimes our fishbowls get cloudy. The pH (pride/humility) balance isn't quite right.

That's what happened to Shebna, the royal treasurer and manager of King Hezekiah's house (Isaiah 22:15). Shebna must have had boundless ambition and great skill to hold two such powerful and important kingdom posts. And though he may have been a capable man, neglect and corruption characterized his work ethic. He was more concerned with pomp, profit, and self-promotion than he was with the wealth of the palace or the welfare of the people.

Shebna's personal pride was no secret among the citizens—nor did it go unnoticed by God. How could it have, since Shebna erected a tomb as large as his pride and as ornate and pompous as his opinion of himself?

Here was a man who was determined to remain the center of attention, visible to all even after his death. God told the prophet Isaiah to confront Shebna. Here's the way Eugene Peterson paraphrases the Scripture:

The Master, GOD-of-the-Angel-Armies, spoke: "Come. Go to this steward, Shebna, who is in charge of all the king's affairs, and tell him: What's going on here? You're an outsider here and yet you act like you own the place, make a big, fancy tomb for yourself where everyone can see it, making sure everyone will think you're important." (Isaiah 22:15–16, *The Message*)

Shebna set up a fishbowl that was beyond compare. It wasn't enough for him to ride about the city in a magnificent chariot pulled by a prancing stallion. No, Shebna was concerned about his posterity. It bothered him to think that he might be forgotten or overlooked after he departed life. Would history remember his greatness and glory?

With that question burning in his mind, he set out to build a suitable monument to himself. He set it up on high so all could see and marvel. Matthew Henry had it right when he wrote: "Those that make stately monuments for their pride forget that, how beautiful soever they appear outwardly, within *they are full of dead men's bones.*"

High places, for all their view and prominence, are extremely slippery places to stand. The writer of Proverbs rightly warns that pride comes before a fall (Proverbs 16:18). And that's just what happened to this haughty, self-absorbed royal official. Isaiah tells the end of the story.

> "Yes, I will drive you out of office," says the LORD. "I will pull you down from your high position. And then I will call my servant Eliakim son of Hilkiah to replace you. He will have your royal robes, your title, and your authority. And he will be a father to the people of Jerusalem and Judah. I will give him the key to the house of David—the highest position in the royal court. He will open doors, and no one will be able to shut them; he will close doors, and no one will be able to open them." (Isaiah 22:19–22, NLT)

Shebna was displaced, disgraced, utterly debased, and eventually replaced. Perhaps the Assyrians captured him and took him away, or maybe King Hezekiah finally got wise to his steward's pride and treachery, and banished him. We don't know for sure. But what we do know is that God caused him to spend his remaining days in obscurity. I think it's a safe bet to assume that Shebna was buried in an unmarked grave. And if his name is remembered at all these days, he is remembered as a fool.

Pride is a legitimate risk of fishbowl living, but it is avoidable. Shebna was accused of being a "disgrace to [his] master's house" because he sought to gain glory from the position he held, stealing honor from the king himself.

And so it is with us. Our great King, the King of kings,

has placed you where you are, and your life should reflect His good character and bring Him glory. Remember that you are a steward, not the owner. Set your aspirations high by taking a low position. Serve the King and serve others with joy and a sincere heart. Don't let your fishbowl become a tomb. Instead, let it be a wellspring of life.

Peril #2: Performance

Because fishbowls have invisible walls, we can become distracted by curious onlookers. We might be intimidated by the audience and feel the need to perform. The praise of man becomes stimulating and we find that we enjoy the limelight.

But limelight is sour when you get a mouthful.

I'll bet that's how King Sennacherib felt.

He lived in a colossal fishbowl of his own making. As ruler of western Asia, he had celebrity status—more infamous than famous (which suited him just fine). Soon after rising to the throne of Assyria, he built a new royal residence in the capital city of Nineveh and called it "the palace without rival." Through all of his building schemes and military conquests, Sennacherib created an empire which served as a stage upon which he performed. He developed quite the public image as "the king without rival."

Subjugating one powerful nation after another and crushing coalitions of enemy kings, Sennacherib began to believe his own press clippings. Who could oppose him? Who could stop him? It reminds me of the classic line from the old science fiction movies: "Resistance is futile."

And then the great Assyrian juggernaut rolled into Judah,

ruled by godly King Hezekiah. The final act of Sennacherib's drama began as he sent a letter threatening the annihilation of Jerusalem, the city the God of Israel had chosen for His dwelling place:

> "Say to Hezekiah king of Judah: Do not let the god you depend on deceive you when he says, 'Jerusalem will not be handed over to the king of Assyria.' Surely you have heard what the kings of Assyria have done to all the countries, destroying them completely. And will you be delivered? Did the gods of the nations that were destroyed by my forefathers deliver them?" (2 Kings 19:10–12)

This is a classic case of overreaching. Question King Hezekiah's leadership? Fine. Insult King Hezekiah's military strategy? Fair game. But mock King Hezekiah's God? Insult God Most High? Watch out.

As protagonist in his own play, Sennacherib supposed his image to be superior to the Lord's. God responded by sending "the angel of the LORD...[who] put to death a hundred and eighty-five thousand men in the Assyrian camp" (2 Kings 19:35).

One angel. One night. One flick of God's little finger.

Death blew through the Assyrian camp like a cold wind sweeping across the plains of Kansas. And just that quickly, the great Sennacherib removed himself from the world stage. What was left of his army withdrew—*fast*. And a short time later, the final curtain fell when he was slain by his own sons.

In his personal chronicles, Sennacherib bragged that he had shut Hezekiah up in Jerusalem "like a bird in a cage." But the puffed-up performer left out a few important facts...like the utter, overnight devastation of his proud army. I guess those minor details don't quite make bestselling autobiographies or get you on the cover of *Time* as Man of the Year. They certainly didn't line up with his image of superiority and invincibility. Sennacherib thought his great performance would always be remembered, but today we consider him (*if* we consider him) as a has-been—little more than an asterisk in history.

Elvis Presley knew about the hollow life that grows from a performance mentality. In a 1972 press conference prior to his record-breaking Madison Square Garden shows in New York City, he told reporters, "The image is one thing and the human being is another.... It's very hard to live up to an image."

Not only is it hard to live up to an image, it's impossible.

An image is a mere snapshot. It can't possibly capture a genuine persona, and is really nothing more than a facade. It's like veneer. It peels and cracks when the temperature changes, revealing what lies beneath.

Living up to an image is an "outside-in" sort of life that majors on externals. How different from the way our God views life. When even a godly man like the prophet Samuel got caught up in the image game, God stepped in to correct him: "Do not consider his appearance or his height, for I have rejected him. The LORD does not look at the things man looks at. Man looks at the outward appearance, but the LORD looks at the heart" (1 Samuel 16:7).

Performance that comes from a true and devoted heart brings glory to God. Mere external performance that doesn't correspond to the man or woman on the inside is simply playacting...and will eventually be exposed as such.

Peril #3: Problems

When the fishbowl gets jostled, waves ensue. The difficulties of life can make it hard to desire staying so visible. Sometimes we just want to hide, nurse our wounds, or even escape the pressure.

I am so glad that David didn't jump out of the fishbowl and go into hiding after the whole Bathsheba tragedy. Think what you and I would have missed: his repentance and forgiveness...his broken, humbled spirit...his sweet psalms of restoration.

Psalm 32 would never have made it into the Book...

> Blessed is he whose transgressions are forgiven,
> whose sins are covered.
> Blessed is the man
> whose sin the LORD does not count against him
> and in whose spirit is no deceit. (vv. 1–2)

Psalm 51 would have never comforted us...

> Cleanse me with hyssop and I will be clean;
> wash me, and I will be whiter than snow. (v. 7)

Psalm 25 would have never helped us turn back to God...

For the sake of your name, O LORD,
forgive my iniquity, though it is great. (v. 11)

David knew what it meant to sin deeply and to experience deep forgiveness and overwhelming grace. And what he experienced has become a bright light to our pathway in the darkest of times.

Or what about Paul? What if every time he went on a missionary journey he was haunted by his past as a persecutor of Christians? What if he had never been able to let go of the images of innocent people condemned, becoming racked with guilt and paralyzed by regret? Would we still have the book of Romans—or any of the other epistles that reveal God's great plan and mysteries hidden for generations? How could he have ministered to anyone? He would have drowned in a sea of guilt and condemnation rather than sailing above the tumult of his past.

Instead of hiding, however, Paul humbly accepted the gracious call of God, declaring, "Forgetting what is behind and straining toward what is ahead, I press on toward the goal to win the prize for which God has called me heavenward in Christ Jesus" (Philippians 3:13–14).

Yes, when you're living in the fishbowl, people watch while you try to keep your head above water. It doesn't matter whether you're dealing with a shady past, a shaky present, or a clouded future; pressing trials and traumas and worries should alert us to our own brokenness and draw us to wholeness in God.

I have peered into two prominent fishbowls recently, and that is exactly what I saw...God's wholeness.

As a guest speaker for the national Women of Faith conferences, I am usually seated on the front row next to the other guests. In my first year at the huge conference, I was most often coupled with Sandi Patti and Chonda Pierce. During a conference in Minneapolis, Sandi, Chonda, and I sat in our usual seats.

Chonda is a bestselling author and hilarious comedienne who has saved my husband thousands of dollars in therapy bills—because she makes me laugh all my troubles away. Though she is excruciatingly funny, she is also acquainted with deep pain, having overcome a difficult past and struggles with depression. When she arrived at the Minneapolis conference to do her presentation, it was obvious that a tough battle with her depression had transpired before she got to the arena. She was emotionally worn out when she took her seat next to Sandi.

You probably know Sandi Patti. She's a phenomenal singer who has won Grammy awards, Dove awards, and has tons of blockbuster recordings to her credit. Sandi's world came crashing down about ten years ago when she made some choices that resulted in the demise of her marriage. She, too, is acquainted with deep pain and profound forgiveness.

When we were first introduced, I was struck by their legendary status. But the more time I spent with these women, the more I became impressed by their authenticity. Each knew what it meant to be broken, and each knew what it meant to be restored—rebuilt by God's Spirit from the inside out.

The crowd gave Chonda a thunderous ovation when she took the stage. I prayed for her strength. Sandi cheered and laughed at every joke as if it were the first time she had heard Chonda's routine. Toward the end of her presentation, she transitioned into some serious words. She told the eighteen thousand women gathered in that arena that she understood what it was like to feel alone, to feel hopeless, and to be overwhelmed with problems. She also told them God understood. As she began a song, the crowd was hushed, with the exception of a few sniffles.

As she finished the first verse, a few bars of accompaniment led into the chorus. It was in that moment that I heard something that reminded me why we stay in the fishbowl even when we struggle with problems: Sandi, knowing the lyrics Chonda was about to sing, spoke out with conviction during the hush of the music, "Tell 'em, Chonda!" Just as Sandi spoke those words, Chonda belted out from the bottom of her soul, "God loves you..."

My eyes filled with tears. Sandi Patty wanted the thousands of women gathered in that arena to know what she has learned in her brokenness—that God loves her. Chonda, in her frailty, stood boldly on that stage and proclaimed the same message of hope, the truth that has held her life together when her world fell apart: God loves her.

Sandi and Chonda know the love of God from the bottom of their beings. Because they are willing to stay in the fishbowl, all the onlookers who observe their lives can hear and see the profound message. God loves you...and He makes you whole.

My friend, that's why we stay in the fishbowl even when the water heats up or becomes icy cold. It is in the midst of problems that we taste the refreshing living water. It restores us, cleanses us, and gives us a message to speak.

HOLY FISHBOWL

Did you know that your fishbowl is brimming with living water? That's what Jesus offered to the woman at the well in Sychar. He described this fountain as a "spring of water welling up to eternal life."[43] The Light uses the revitalizing character of water as a symbol to picture the great gift of salvation, leading to eternal life. Water also portrays the indwelling life of the Holy Spirit[44] and the life-giving truth of God's Word.[45]

So, then, life in the fishbowl is really a life spent swimming about in a refreshing spring, a fountain of life. It is from this cascading stream that we receive the cleansing, comfort, and refreshment of the fishbowl life. And we can sum up that life in just one word: holiness.

Holiness had never seemed like a blessing to me; in fact, I had come to think of it as a crushing burden. It seemed so unattainable. It reminded me of constant striving, like swimming upstream. For years when I thought of holiness, I conjured up a picture of a stern, tight-lipped, mean-spirited preachin' woman with her hair in a bun, no makeup, and a long, bony finger scolding the rest of us spiritual peons with "Thou shalt's" and "Thou shalt not's." Not a beautiful picture is it?

Part of the reason for my misguided opinion grew out of a basic misunderstanding of what God told His people in the book of Leviticus. "You shall be holy to me; for I the LORD am holy and have separated you from the peoples, that you should be mine" (Leviticus 20:26, RSV).

God told His chosen people to be holy; now, in Christ, the same command applies to us. Intimidating? To me it used to be. Since I thought I couldn't attain holiness on my own, I would often try to simply "perform" holiness as I swam along in my fishbowl, maintaining all the "do's and don'ts."

The result, I assure you, was forced, artificial, and not attractive at all. I just couldn't see holiness as something lovely and desirable.

But it is. God calls holiness *beautiful*. Scripture speaks of the "beauty of holiness."[46] To understand why God calls it beautiful, you have to look at the original language. The word we translate as holiness derives from the same root from which we get our English word "wholeness." In other words, holiness means "wholeness," or being complete.

Holiness is not intended to evoke images of peculiarity or strangeness. It's supposed to bring to mind a picture of completeness—the whole of God filling the whole of you. To be "whole" or "holy" is to be full of God's completeness rather than our own brokenness.

What our Father said to His people in Leviticus was essentially, "I want you to be whole as I am whole." That's what He's saying to you and me, too. He wants to fill our brokenness with His wholeness. He is complete, in harmony with Himself, and He wants to replace our emptiness with

His balanced and radiant fullness. Wow! Holiness *is* beautiful. I want it and I need it. Don't you?

We all know what it's like to be broken. We know how it feels to be aware of our incompleteness. But to be whole is to have God take all the pieces of our personalities and our passions and perfectly balance us.

Without holiness, I am not capable of handling my life. In my brokenness, I put up a big facade and try to bluff my way through. It is then that I am most susceptible to the perils of fishbowl living. I puff up with pride to cover my insecurities, I conjure up a performance mentality, or I become overwhelmed with my own problems and just want to bail. Those are symptoms of a lack of wholeness—a deficiency that hurts both myself and others.

WHOLENESS

Some time ago, I was scheduled to be the final speaker at a large women's convention. Prior to my presentation, Beth Moore dazzled and inspired the thousands of women gathered in the arena. The worship had been skillfully and tenderly led by Travis Cotrell. Everything about the weekend had gone beautifully, and God was present with us.

When I awoke on Saturday morning, however, I was nervous. It was my turn to speak, and I felt intimidated to follow someone like Beth Moore. I was anxious and painfully self-aware. I prayed and read the Word, but I really felt like a wad of emotions inside.

I went to breakfast that morning with Mandisa

Hundley, a talented and gracious singer and worship leader, who was to lead worship that morning before I spoke. She, like me, was far less well-known than Beth and Travis.

And so, with Jennifer being full of Jennifer instead of God, I opened my mouth and began to speak. It went something like this: "Mandisa, I sure hope they give you and me a good introduction, since no one knows who we are." I continued on with more unnerving and unnecessary comments. Believe me, I feel a wave of embarrassment even as I write about this. I did not say anything ugly or sinful. I just didn't say anything that built up Mandisa or the potential of our ministry together. I said nothing that promoted wholeness in Mandisa and everything that exposed my own brokenness and insecurity.

As I continued, Mandisa grew quiet. Her unresponsiveness was my first clue that the whole of God was not filling the whole of me. Instead, there was a giant hole in me, and I was filling it with junk.

Within moments Mandisa arose, muttered something about brushing her teeth, and quickly excused herself. I sat alone. Well, not totally alone. With me was a growing awareness that I was full of myself, rather than God.

It was in that painful moment that Travis called out, "Hey, Jennifer. Do you want me to walk you to the green room?" I tried to keep my composure as we walked, but inside I was crumbling. The empty hole that could have been filled with God was acting as a vacuum and sucking the life out of me.

When we finally got into the green room, there sat

Mandisa. Evidently, Travis could tell by her wet eyes and dripping mascara that she had been crying. Without even seeing her, I could tell, too. As soon as the door closed behind us, I also burst into tears.

Now, at this point, I wish I could have seen Travis. Two women sobbing, for no apparent reason...and there he was—standing in the green room amidst the emotion and estrogen. I'll bet his silent prayer at that very moment was, "God, remind me once again that You have called me to work with a bunch of women."

While Travis was praying and possibly pondering his future in ministry, I maneuvered my way to the couch where Mandisa sat and said, my voice frail from my own emptiness, "I'm so sorry. I was wrong and I'm so sorry." She consoled me and I consoled her. (I don't know if anyone was consoling poor, bewildered Travis.)

All three of us prayed, and by the time she went out on stage, Mandisa seemed intact. As she began to minister, her holiness was obvious. I sat backstage and prayed and cried. My lack of holiness had hurt Mandisa—and could have damaged her ability to minister.

It hurt me, too. And God. I fought the shame, compelling myself to stand on the promise that God had forgiven me and cleansed me by the washing of His Word.

And then it was my turn to step out under the lights.

At least I wasn't struggling with pride or a performance mentality as I stepped into that vulnerable fishbowl moment. In fact, I had difficulty simply maintaining my composure. Honestly, it was one of the hardest messages I've ever presented. All I really wanted to say to that eager crowd of women was, "God was gracious to me. Mandisa is my hero. And I am desperate for God. If He doesn't fill me, I will fill myself—and the result is ugly. I need the whole of God to fill the whole of me. (And, by the way, please pray for Travis. I'm afraid I scared him out of the ministry.)"

Holiness is neither complicated nor self-propelled. It's not the sum of all the thou-shalts and thou-shalt-nots. It's not merely the absence of sin.

It's the absence of self.

The Pharisees in Jesus' day may have had a lack of sin—at least from their own narrow reading of the Law. But they had no lack of self. Jesus said of them, "You hypocrites! Isaiah was right when he prophesied about you: 'These people honor me with their lips, but their hearts are far from me. They worship me in vain; their teachings are but rules taught by men'" (Matthew 15:7–9).

When we live a Spirit-filled life, leaning hard on our Father, immersed in living water within our fishbowl, then His holiness will find expression through our lives. A radiant, lovely wholeness will wrap itself around us like a living fragrance.

My beloved pastor, John Marshall, often reminds us that "holiness matters most." He's right. It does matter most. Without it, we can neither enjoy nor reflect our heavenly Father.

Oh, my friend, let the Light within you shine.

As you enjoy life in a fishbowl, I encourage you to draw life from the living water and let it sustain you, grow you, nurture you, and fill you. Your purpose in the fishbowl is not to perform, but rather to reflect the One who placed you there. He is the one who chose you, and He is the one who will feed you, care for you, and empower you to thrive.

If you find yourself wanting to complain about a fishbowl life constantly observed by others, just remember that if you're filled up with God, they won't see you anyway.

Looking right through your brokenness, they will see the Lord in all His wholeness, tranquillity, and radiant beauty.

And that's why He put you in the fishbowl to begin with.

CHAPTER TWELVE

Live Like an Alien

When I was a little girl, my parents were missionaries near San Jose, Costa Rica. Our house in San Pedro Sula had a tin roof—designed to lessen the effects of an earthquake. Our front door opened directly to the sidewalk, eliminating any chance for a front yard. The small backyard was surrounded by a wall topped with pieces of broken glass to discourage would-be robbers from scaling it. Small windows were located high off the ground, again to deter thieves.

The only vulnerable window was a small jalousie window that opened onto the carport. Although we didn't own a car, the Catholic priest in the barrio parked his car there, and we'd leave the light on at night to protect his vehicle.

Word must have gotten around that some rich gringos lived in the house across from the church. As missionaries, we really had very little, and the house had been furnished by another missionary family home on furlough. Our borrowed home, however, was one of the few that had a car in the carport. So it was assumed we were rolling in the dough.

One night, my dad got up during the wee hours to check on my little brother. The house was still and silent as he walked to Lawson's bedroom. But just as he returned to his own room, he heard a sound coming from the dining room. As he got closer, he realized that someone was removing the jalousie window panels, one by one, between the carport and the dining room.

Dad's mind raced. He was keenly aware that he was a noncitizen and had to be very careful how he proceeded. He knew he couldn't use a weapon, and yet—what if the intruders were armed? How was he to protect his family?

My dad prayed silently, and a plan came to mind. It had to work, he reasoned, because he didn't have time to come up with another one. Slipping back into Lawson's room, he grabbed a rubber Halloween mask. It was grotesque—putrid green with eerily oversized eyes and electrified hair. Crouching beneath the curtains, he slipped on the mask, counting until the thieves were on the last window panel. As they pulled it out, a dark hand reached through the curtains.

Just then my masked father shot up, jerked the curtains open, and screamed at the top of his lungs.

Two young Latino thugs leaped backward with such force

that they dented the priest's car and broke the glass panels stacked at their feet. One made the sign of the cross and shrieked, "*Dios mío! Dios mío!*"

After that, word must have gotten out that the gringos weren't to be messed with...because we never were again.

During those years, we were sojourners in a foreign country. We remained American citizens even though we lived in Costa Rica, and we were always mindful that this was not home.

But really...who could ever forget that fact?

The living conditions and food, not to mention the language, were all different from our native land. Our cultural dispositions always reminded us that we were resident aliens.

RESIDENT ALIENS

Have you ever felt like you were living with aliens...in your own home?

I couldn't help but wonder that after an encounter in my fourteen-year-old son's room one Wednesday night.

"Clayton," I said, "since your violin concert is tomorrow night, we need to clean and press your uniform." Clayton dutifully rose from his computer and removed his embroidered shirt from the closet.

"It's clean," he shrugged. "No wrinkles."

"Now, what about your black pants?"

"I don't have any."

"What do you mean you don't have any? You wore them two weeks ago."

"Well, yeah, but—they're way too small. The waist is too tight, and when I sit, they come all the way up to my knees."

"Son, you know you need to *tell* me when your pants don't fit. Now there's no time to buy new ones before the concert. You've known for two weeks that the concert was tomorrow. You'll just have to wear the small ones."

Suddenly, Clayton hit on a brainstorm. "I know what I'll do, Mom. I'll just wear Dad's pants."

Now, Clayton and his dad have probably worn the same size at one time in their lives—but never at the *same* time. I was certain that Phil's pants would be entirely too big.

Even so, we rifled through his dad's closet and grabbed some black pants. I insisted he try them on, and was a little surprised to note that the length was perfect. Unfortunately, that was all that was perfect. The waist was huge.

"Oh, Clayton," I said, "they're much too big."

"They look great, Mom. It'll be okay."

He hung the supersized pants with his shirt and went back to his computer. I, on the other hand, was confused and agitated. The battle of the britches had gone silent, but a quiet voice began to sound in my mind. *A daughter would never dream of putting on a pair of slacks three sizes too big for her. Why doesn't it bother Clayton? Should I buy him new pants? This is going to be embarrassing for him...for me...for the entire Dockers clothing brand. Oh well, learning responsibility is more important than wearing well-fitting pants.*

So when concert time arrived on Thursday night, my husband, Droopy Drawers, and I all headed to the middle school gym. It was teeming with sharply dressed young musicians and proud parents. Minuets and Christmas carols filled the room. Then the conductor announced that the orchestra would play a waltz by Strauss.

How lovely, I thought as I settled into my seat.

Instruments were raised and a sweet melody resonated through the gym. My husband, Phil, gently placed his hand on my back. I found myself relaxing and getting lost in the moment.

But as the bows gently caressed the strings, Phil began to rub my back—in rhythm with the waltz. In fact, as the beautiful piece continued, I noticed that each time the students plucked the strings of their instruments, Phil would poke my back right along with their plucking. An apparently frustrated musician, Phil was playing the *Blue Danube* across my back!

Rub-rub-rub-rub-rub, *poke-poke, poke-poke.*

Just like the night before, I was bewildered and frustrated. I thought, *He's not going to stop. He's going to rub and poke his way through the entire waltz!* As I turned toward him I heard him snicker.

"Phil," I huffed, "we're sitting in the front row!"

He pulled his hand away and chuckled.

That's when it hit me—I live with aliens. One is fourteen and the other is forty, but they cannot be from this planet. (Or maybe it's a women-are-from-Venus, men-are-from-Mars thing.) Both Phil and Clayton seemed unmoved and uninfluenced by cultural norms like well fitting pants and basic concert decorum.

So what's a girl to do? I live in a houseful of aliens—

three males and just one reasonable, sensible female...me.

When I think about it, though, I realize being an alien isn't so bad. Being queen of the manor can be pretty nice sometimes.

In a general sense, being an alien simply means you have no permanent ties to the place you live. And shouldn't that describe us as believers?

When my family lived in Costa Rica, we were not permanent inhabitants. As we live here on earth as believers, our residency is not permanent, either. It reminds me of Augustine's idea of the *civitas peregrina*. It's the thought that you and I are simply passing through. We are resident aliens here on earth. Our true home is what Augustine called the "City of God." But until we are actually home, we live in the "City of Man."

According to 1 Peter 2:11, while on earth we are called pilgrims, strangers (KJV), foreigners (NLT), sojourners (ESV), and aliens (NIV). Most world religions consider "alienation" part of their teachings, but the New Testament is unique in that it actively reminds us of our alien status. The Word encourages us to really understand what it means to be an alien here. In so doing, we discover the key to life in Christ. "To believe in heaven is not to run away from life; it is to run toward it."[47]

CULTURE SHOCK

When we lived in Costa Rica, I remember vividly that my mother warned us against eating certain dishes that were served after church, because many of our precious Latin brothers and sisters left their tamales sitting out in the hot sun during the worship service.

My mom, of course, was concerned that we would get food poisoning. I have no idea if those who partook every Sunday got sick, but I doubt it, because it seemed to be their habit, their custom. But it wasn't our custom to eat meat that sat out for hours, so we stuck close to rice and vegetables. Even though we lived there, we still maintained our habits, not theirs. That's how it is as believers. As aliens, we really aren't conformed to the ways of the world within which we live.

The apostle John writes: "Stop loving this evil world and all that it offers you, for when you love the world, you show that you do not have the love of the Father in you" (I John 2:15, NLT).

As sojourners, our customs are not those of this world; they're kingdom customs.

When the world tells us to keep a big chip on our shoulders and make our violators pay dearly, our custom is forgiveness.[48] What an alien idea. How odd that must seem to many people outside of Christ.

When the world tells us to "look out for number one" and that "charity begins at home," our custom is sacrificial compassion.[49]

When the world tells us to get all we can, buy now and pay later, and go for the gusto, our custom is wide-open generosity.[50]

When the world tells us to "just do it," our custom is self-discipline.[51]

When the world says you can "have it your way," our custom is altruism and humility.[52]

When the world claims that it is "the real thing," our custom is to fix our eyes on unseen realities.[53]

When the world tells us to say, "I'm worth it," our custom is to say, "He is worthy."[54]

As aliens, we speak our own language—the language of love spoken with words of wisdom.[55]

The world we're passing through has a lengthy list of cultural norms. But who has decided what those norms should be? The normal people? And who are they? The things we call normal are nothing more than the result of faulty measuring sticks used by faulty people. So you and I must be less influenced by the cultural norms of this world. And instead we should "not conform any longer to the pattern of this world, but be transformed by the renewing of [our] mind" (Romans 12:2).

To practice this kind of countercultural living is to conform to the culture of heaven, the country of our real citizenship. But our behavior, language, and cultural norms can make us unwelcome in the world at large, and we might feel the sting of isolation.

EXILED AND UNWELCOME

While in Costa Rica, my parents were students at the Spanish Language Institute in San Jose. Dad and three of his missionary buddies were invited by a Catholic priest in a small village to sell Bibles on a Sunday morning. Although my dad would have gladly given the Bibles away, the priest insisted that they sell them, so that the parishioners would view it as a paid for and therefore prized possession. The missionaries were thrilled to partner with the priest in promoting the Word.

The four of them left one Saturday to travel by train to the village, some four hours away from San Jose. Upon their arrival, they immediately sensed they were unwelcome. They made their way to the local Catholic church, but my dad later told me, "When the priest came to the door, he was extremely shaken that we Americans were in town. We introduced ourselves and told him why we had come. Indignant, he told us it was not by *his* invitation. He said that the priest who invited us was no longer at that parish." He proceeded to tell them that they were not to sell Bibles, and that they were not welcome in that village.

The disappointed men returned to the train station. Then, remembering that there wouldn't be another train until morning, they went to a small hotel—but were not allowed to register. They ventured out to a small café for some dinner, but again they were refused service and asked to leave.

The men realized that word had spread quickly—the Americans were not welcome. "We didn't know what we would do for the night," my dad confessed. But through the providence of God, a local man approached them. He was a Christian also. He told them that there were several other Christians in the village that met together for worship. Although none in this small group could house the four missionaries, they did offer a small, deserted railroad shack they used as a meeting place.

As darkness fell, my dad and his friends found themselves in a cramped and vacant shack furnished with only six wood plank benches that the local believers used for their meetings. Some local Christians had provided some candles, water, and a few pieces of bread for their breakfast.

In those days, of course, there were no cell phones, no e-mail. My dad had never felt so alienated and isolated. They truly were unwelcome foreigners with no access to home.

The missionaries found strength in their fellowship, but sleep did not come easily. "Finally," my dad recalled, "we decided to extinguish the candle and seek some sleep. Peace came as we felt that a God who never slept guarded and protected us. As I recall, the four of us did some singing in the dark. It was so very quiet.

"Within minutes, however, the quiet was broken. We knew something—or someone—was in the shack with us. We hurriedly lit the candle, and there, roaming across the rickety floorboards, were rats—five or six of them weighing four or five pounds each. Well, that was enough sleep!"

The men decided to take turns sleeping. It was a difficult night. They knew they were not welcome, and they feared what might happen to them. The reality of harm was there, not so much from the rats, but from the villagers who resented them as intruders. But as my father put it, their fear of man was replaced by their trust in the promise of their heavenly Guardian.

Through the long night, the men meditated on Scripture. Someone quoted from Psalm 139:

Where can I go from your Spirit? Where can I flee from your presence? If I go up to the heavens, you are there; if I make my bed in the depths, you are there. If I rise on the wings of the dawn, if I settle on the far side of the sea, even there your hand will guide me, your right hand will hold me fast. (Psalm 139:7–10)

These truths became the candle that radiated light into their darkness. A golden sunrise came at last, bringing with it the train that would carry them home. As it arrived, they gave thanks to the Eternal Watchman.

Even when we're away from home, our Father is with us in this foreign land. When we feel the sting of exclusion from the world in which we live, we are assured that we are not alone—that God is with us, just as He was with my dad and his friends in a tiny shack in some nameless village in Central America.

He is with you, and you are never alone. Your heart is His sovereign domain, even in your alienation. He is the local believer who feeds you, gives you lodging, and provides shelter and safety. In the dark, His Word is the candle that gives you light.

And there will come a morning, my friend, a bright and cloudless morning when you feel the earth rumble and hear the distant whistle of an approaching train. You are promised a ride home. You have a ticket. No matter your traveling fatigue, no matter your longing for home, remember that there's a train coming.

Part of the reason we can lose heart and run out of steam as we run our race is because we forget that we're just passing through. We begin to think of our earthbound assignment—

with its attendant fears and hurts and sorrows—as permanent. But it's not true. This world in which we live is not all there is. We are simply sojourners; our true home is our true destination.

"Why should my heart be fixed where my home is not?" someone once asked. "Heaven is my home; God in Christ is all my happiness; and where my treasure is, there my heart should be."[56] The writer of Hebrews reminds us that here we have no lasting city, but we seek the city to come.

Heaven is our home.

I've never been to heaven, but I have been to Starbucks.

Please don't be offended. I have no desire to trivialize the magnificence of heaven. But the Lord knows that the only way we earthbound people can think about eternal realities is through earthly comparisons, inadequate as they may be. The Bible compares the Holy Spirit to wind, the Word of God to a radiant light, and even His own presence to the sheltering wings of some great bird.

And Starbucks? Well, it's just the most blissful, relaxing, and thoroughly enjoyable place on the planet to me.

The Bible says that "eye has not seen and ear has not heard...all that God has prepared" (1 Corinthians 2:9, NASB). I just can't imagine how blissful, pleasurable, and magnificent heaven must be. But if I multiply the pleasure of Starbucks by infinity to the power of ten thousand million, then I think I am getting a little glimpse of what it must be like. Here's what I mean.

Heaven is a place of pleasure.

Few things in life are as pleasant to me as a piping hot cup of Starbucks coffee sipped slowly in one of their tiny cafes. In fact, I never really enjoyed coffee until I tasted theirs. I love the fragrance of coffee that permeates every molecule in the store. I love to breathe in its richness and warmth. Even the muted roar of the bean grinder makes me happy.

When I go to Starbucks, I am far removed from my daily reality. I get lost in the atmosphere and am transported to a relaxed place of pure delight. My love for the experience is so intense that I even burn a hazelnut coffee candle in my study when I'm writing, just so I can be reminded of that place I enjoy so much. That may seem silly or obsessive, but it's a little slice of heaven to me.

And little slices are all we're allowed this side of life.

Heaven is the place of ultimate pleasure for those who believe in Christ. It's the place where no tears fall, no sighs escape, and no burdens weigh down our shoulders. It's the place where all things are made new. The Bible tells us:

> "He will wipe every tear from their eyes. There will be no more death or mourning or crying or pain, for the old order of things has passed away." (Revelation 21:4)

Sometimes here on earth, we get a little glimpse that ignites our longing. Sometimes we breathe in a fragrance that wafts through our spirit...a reminder and shadow of what is to come. As C. S. Lewis says, "If I find in myself a desire which no experience in this world can satisfy, the most probable explanation is that I was made for another world." We were made for heaven, where ultimate pleasure is realized.

Heaven is a place of passion.

Did you know that Starbucks serves more than thirty blends of single-origin coffees? I know that little fact because Starbucks is one of my passions.

I also know that the first Starbucks opened in Seattle in 1971 at Pike Place Market, and that it got its name from the first mate in Herman Melville's *Moby-Dick*. Starbucks has coffee houses in thirty-four countries outside the United States, and in October 2004, the Starbucks gift card hit the $1 billion mark for total activations and reloads.

Have I convinced you yet that Starbucks is one of my passions?

When we're passionate about something, we learn about it, think about it, and even long for it. Heaven is one of my passions. It's my ultimate destination, and I want to know more about it, think about it, and long for it. Did you know that...

Heaven serves its fruit twelve times each year in abundance from the Tree of Life. And what's more, the leaves of the trees provide healing for the nations. Main Street is paved with transparent gold. Its high wall contains entrance gates made of single pearls, and the gates will always stand open. Jesus Himself will light the heavenly city, doing away with any need for sun or moon. The new heaven and new earth will be established when our sin-cursed planet passes away. The New Jerusalem will experience the peace that the old one never did, and King Jesus will reign forever on its throne. And when we hit the one-billion-year mark for time spent there, we'll not even take note—for time will be no more.

"We talk about heaven being so far away," said Dwight L. Moody. "It is within speaking distance to those who belong there."

Heaven is more real than all we taste, feel, hear, and see here on earth, and it should be an all-consuming passion. Since this world really isn't our home, there should be a healthy sense of alienation at the heart of all our experiences...even in the fragrant embrace of a Starbucks coffeehouse.

We reside here but we are restless.

We are foreigners with a faraway passion.

We are resident aliens with treasures in heaven.

Heaven is a place of purpose.

Every Friday that I'm not on the road, Karen and I go to Starbucks and work on my latest writing project. As you might expect, we begin by ordering a grande skinny mocha with whipped cream for me, and a grande hot chocolate for her. Then we settle in at a tiny table for a three-hour chat on the finer and deeper things of life. We grapple with all we don't understand, we consider truths, we wonder about apparent inconsistencies, and eventually we end up pondering the enormous love of God. We both marvel at the greatness and goodness of God. When we really try to fathom our amazing Savior, it's incomprehensible—all we can do is praise.

That's what heaven will be—a place of purpose. A place to eternally ponder and praise the goodness and greatness of our God. The most amazing thing is that we will "know" as we are "known" (1 Corinthians 13:12, NASB). That means that all that we ponder here, we will realize there. All that we grapple with here, we will grasp there.

Yet I don't think we ever really will get over the magnificence. As Robert Browning once said, "Things learned on earth, we shall practice in heaven." I believe that we will marvel at our Savior, ponder His great love for us, and praise. Praise quietly, praise loudly. Heaven will be the place in which we worship forever.

If heaven is a place of pleasure, passion, and pondering, then earth is the place of our pilgrimage and preparation. Living on earth is our time and place to:

- Look for our heavenly country.[57]
- Turn our faces toward Zion.[58]
- Keep our eyes on our promised dwelling.[59]
- Rejoice in God's Word as we travel.[60]
- Seek the light of God's direction for our journey.[61]
- Remember that we are not at home in this world.[62]
- Shine as lights in the world.[63]
- Gather our treasure in heaven.[64]

As sojourners, we do long for our pilgrimage to come to a close.

That's why we live with such good cheer. You won't see us drooping our heads or dragging our feet! Cramped conditions here don't get us down. They only remind us of the spacious living conditions ahead. It's what we trust in but don't yet see that keeps us going. Do you suppose a few ruts in the road or rocks in the path are going to stop us? When the time comes, we'll be plenty ready to exchange exile for homecoming. (2 Corinthians 5:6–8, *The Message*)

This earthly life God designed for us includes a holy discontent, a longing for our true home, a lingering awareness that we will never feel fully settled or at home here. As with the psalmist, we inwardly yearn, "Oh, that I had wings like a dove! I would fly away and be at rest" (Psalm 55:6, NASB).

Paul makes our citizenship clear by declaring that when "God raised us up with Christ," He also "seated us with him in the heavenly realms in Christ Jesus" (Ephesians 2:6). God has indeed extended an invitation to us to be with Him in eternity, and He welcomes us in and gives us a seat. And He does so at the same moment that He "raises us up with Christ." While your feet are still here on earth, you are seated in heavenly places.

So, my fellow sojourner, tread lightly on this sod. Let your heart keep longing for heaven. Live in this world, feel its pain, cry its tears, and breathe in its air. Let it ignite a sojourner's longing within you. As C. S. Lewis said, "Aim at heaven and you will get earth thrown in." Ephesians 2:19 echoes, "You are no longer foreigners and aliens, but fellow citizens with God's people and members of God's household."

So, come on in. Coffee's on.

Have a seat, and make yourself at home.

Lighting the Way Home

A friend of mine told me about a conversation he had years ago with a man in Portland, Oregon, who lived on a high hill called Rocky Butte.

At that time, there weren't very many houses on the butte, and at night it was a dark, bulky shadow on the horizon. The man traveled as part of his job and found himself away from home for a few days every week. He described how, when he drove south from Washington state into Oregon, he often crossed the Interstate bridge over the Columbia River at night. Looking off to his left, far in the distance, he would see a tiny pinpoint of yellow light twinkling from the dark bulk of Rocky Butte's northern slope.

His porch light.

And the sight of that tiny gleam in the darkness filled his heart with longing and joy...because it told him he was almost home, almost back in the embrace of his loving family.

That's what God's Word is like for His children on the way Home. This world can be a dark and sorrowful place at times, as we make our way toward heaven and our eternal home in God's presence. There are days (and nights) when the way seems long, and hope begins to die within us. That's when we open the pages of the Word of God, and catch a glimpse of Home...a tiny light twinkling in the darkness.

It reminds us that Jesus is coming soon.

"Behold, I am coming quickly, and My reward is with Me." (Revelation 22:12, NASB)

For in just a very little while, "He who is coming will come and will not delay." (Hebrews 10:37)

We who are still alive and are left will be caught up with together with them in the clouds to meet the Lord in the air. And so we will be with the Lord forever. (1 Thessalonians 4:17)

It reminds us that we have a place and a future in heaven.

...into an inheritance that can never perish, spoil or fade—kept in heaven for you. (1 Peter 1:4)

In my Father's house are many rooms...I am going there to prepare a place for you. (John 14:2)

"Father, I want those you have given me to be with me where I am, and to see my glory." (John 17:24)

Finally, it reminds us that while we still walk through this life, difficult as our path might be, He is with us every step of the way.

I will ask the Father, and he will give you another Counselor to be with you forever—the Spirit of truth. (John 14:16–17)

"Never will I leave you; never will I forsake you." (Hebrews 13:5)

"Surely I am with you always, to the very end of the age." (Matthew 28:20)

Don't lose sight of the Light, my friend.
We'll all be Home before we know it.

Let's Keep in Touch...

Thank you for spending your time learning lessons in the Light with me. I pray God has used these lessons to strengthen, encourage, and challenge you to keep running your race with perseverance.

It would be such a thrill for me to hear from you. Did you know I have a computer that reads my e-mail to me? I can't promise the digital voice will sound like yours, but it does allow me to hear how God is working in your life, and through this book. If you'd like to write me, send an e-mail to:

JR@JenniferRothschild.com

Or better, go to the "contact us" link at:

www.JenniferRothschild.com

While you're there, sign up for my Jennifer Rothschild Friends eNewsletter. It's a great way to keep in touch.

I would love to hear how God has illuminated your path through His Word.

And now, my friend...

Let's pray like the psalmist did:

O send out Your light and Your truth, let them lead me; let them bring me to Your holy hill and to Your dwelling places. (Psalm 43:3, NASB)

Blessings,
Jennifer

NOTES

1. Get more of the context of this amazing story in Genesis 12:1–9.
2. Read the full story in Exodus 2–3.
3. This is a tender, beautiful account worth reading all the way through in 1 Samuel 1.
4. 1 Samuel 17.
5. Hosea 1:2–3.
6. Matthew 4:20.
7. Philemon 12–16.
8. Philippians 2:6–8.
9. Galatians 5:16–18.
10. Malachi 3:10.
11. 2 Peter 1:3.
12. Leviticus 1–9.
13. Genesis 4:3–12; Hebrews 9:22.
14. 2 Samuel 6:3–7.
15. Exodus 33:20.
16. Galatians 3:13.
17. Hebrews 2:9.
18. 2 Corinthians 8:9.
19. Ephesians 2:12.
20. 2 Corinthians 12:9.
21. 1 Peter 1:12.
22. Exodus 34:6; Nehemiah 9:17.
23. John 1:14, 17.
24. Mark 5:15.
25. John 4:25–26.
26. John 8:9–11, 17, 26.
27. John 21:18.

28. Acts 9:5–6.

29. *The Quotable Christian*, Robert Chapman.

30. Romans 1:10; 15:30–31.

31. 2 Corinthians 1:10–11.

32. Ephesians 6:19-20.

33. Colossians 4:3–4.

34. 2 Thessalonians 3:1.

35. Hebrews 13:19.

36. 2 Corinthians 13:7, 9.

37. Ephesians 1:15; 3:16–18.

38. Philippians 1:3–19.

39. Colossians 1:3, 9–10.

40. 1Thessalonians 3:10; 2 Thessalonians 1:11–12.

41. Philemon 6.

42. Betsy Childs, "A Slice of Infinity: Does Prayer Work?" Ravi Zacharias International Ministries, September 27, 2005.

43. John 4:10, 14.

44. John 7:37–39.

45. Ephesians 5:26.

46. 1 Chronicles 16:29; 2 Chronicles 20:21; Psalm 29:2; 96:2.

47. Joseph Blinco.

48. Matthew 6:14; Luke 17:3–4.

49. Ephesians 4:32; Colossians 3:12.

50. Matthew 5:41–42.

51. 1 Peter 1:5–8.

52. Philippians 2:13.

53. 2 Corinthians 4:18.

54. Revelation 4:11; 1 Corinthians 6:20.

55. Ephesians 4:29; Colossians 4:6.

56. Margaret Charlton Baxter.

57. Hebrew 11:16.

58. Jeremiah 50:5.

59. Hebrews 11:13.

60. Psalm 119:54.

61. Psalm 43:3; Jeremiah 50:5.
62. Hebrews 11:9.
63. Philippians 2:15.
64. Matthew 6:19; Luke 12:33; Colossians 3:1–2.